Typesetting Documents

in

Scientific WorkPlace®

and

Scientific Word®

Third Edition

A Guide to Typesetting with Scientific WorkPlace
and Scientific Word

Typesetting Documents in Scientific WorkPlace[R] and Scientific Word[R]

Third Edition

A Guide to Typesetting with Scientific WorkPlace and Scientific Word

Susan Bagby
George Pearson
MacKichan Software, Inc.

Printed in the United States of America

10 9 8 7 6 5 4 3 2 1

Trademarks

Scientific WorkPlace, *Scientific Word*, *Scientific Notebook*, and EasyMath are registered trademarks of MacKichan Software, Inc. EasyMath is the sophisticated parsing and translating system included in *Scientific WorkPlace*, *Scientific Word*, and *Scientific Notebook* that allows the user to work in standard mathematical notation, request computations from the underlying computational system (MuPAD in this version) based on the implied commands embedded in the mathematical syntax or via menu, and receive the response in typeset standard notation or graphic form in the current document. MuPAD is a registered trademark of SciFace GmbH. Acrobat is the registered trademark of Adobe Systems, Inc. TEX is a trademark of the American Mathematical Society. TrueTEX is a registered trademark of Richard J. Kinch. PDFTEX is the copyright of Hàn Thế Thành and is available under the GNU public license. Windows is a registered trademark of Microsoft Corporation. MathType is a trademark of Design Science, Inc. ImageStream Graphics Filters and ImageStream are registered trademarks of Inso Kansas City Corporation:

ImageStream Graphic Filters
Copyright 1991-1999
Inso Kansas City Corporation
All Rights Reserved

All other brand and product names are trademarks of their respective companies. The spelling portion of this product utilizes the Proximity Linguistic Technology. Words are checked against one or more of the following Proximity Linguibase® products:

Linguibase Name	Publisher	Number of Words	Proximity Copyright
American English	Merriam-Webster, Inc.	144,000	1997
British English	William Collins Sons & Co. Ltd.	80,000	1997
Catalan	Lluis de Yzaguirre i Maura	484,000	1993
Danish	IDE a.s	169,000	1990
Dutch	Van Dale Lexicografie bv	223,000	1996
Finnish	IDE a.s	191,000	1991
French	Hachette	288,909	1997
French Canadian	Hachette	288,909	1997
German	Bertelsmann Lexikon Verlag	500,000	1999
German (Swiss)	Bertelsmann Lexikon Verlag	500,000	1999
Italian	William Collins Sons & Co. Ltd.	185,000	1997
Norwegian (Bokmal)	IDE a.s	150,000	1990
Norwegian (Nynorsk)	IDE a.s	145,000	1992
Polish	MorphoLogic, Inc.		1997
Portuguese (Brazilian)	William Collins Sons & Co. Ltd.	210,000	1990
Portuguese (Continental)	William Collins Sons & Co. Ltd.	218,000	1990
Russian	Russicon		1997
Spanish	William Collins Sons & Co. Ltd.	215,000	1997
Swedish	IDE a.s	900,000	1990

This document was produced with *Scientific WorkPlace*.

Authors: *Susan Bagby and George Pearson*
Editorial Assistant: *John MacKendrick*
Compositor: *MacKichan Software Inc.*
Printing and Binding: *Malloy Lithographing, Inc.*

Contents

What's New

Typesetting Documents is a response to the many users who have requested more information about LaTeX typesetting in *Scientific WorkPlace (SWP)* and *Scientific Word (SW)*. This revised edition contains expanded information about typesetting in Versions 3.5, 4, and 5 of *SWP* and *SW*. It presents many new techniques for achieving special typesetting effects and includes a new chapter containing extensive troubleshooting information.

About This Manual

Our purpose is threefold:

- to answer common questions and solve common problems related to typesetting in *SWP* and *SW;*

- to help you choose document shells appropriately;

- to explain when and how you can tailor typesetting specifications and document shells *from within the program* so that you can create documents that more precisely meet your typesetting needs.

To these ends, we begin the manual with what may be the only thing you need to read: the answers to the questions users ask most frequently about working with LaTeX typesetting in *SWP* and *SW*. Chapter 1 "Tailoring Typesetting to Your Needs" provides tips on modifying page layout, document elements, tables and figures, and mathematics in *SWP* and *SW* documents.

If you need more basic information, we suggest you start with Chapter 2 "Working with Typesetting Specifications and Document Shells." The chapter briefly discusses the structure of LaTeX documents. It explains how typesetting specifications work and addresses the most basic and perhaps most important document development task: how to choose a document shell—or template—that meets the typesetting requirements of you and your publisher. The chapter discusses how and to what extent you can tailor a document using available document class and LaTeX package options and, where necessary, TeX commands. Chapter 2 also explains how to create *SWP* and *SW* documents using typesetting specifications obtained from an outside source and how to work with LaTeX documents not created with *SWP* or *SW*.

The LaTeX packages provided with the program are the focus of Chapter 3 "Using LaTeX Packages." The discussion explains how the packages extend TeX typesetting capabilities and notes how each package interacts with and, occasionally, conflicts with other typesetting elements.

Chapter 4 "Troubleshooting" offers information to help you isolate and resolve common errors generated by *SWP* and *SW* and by LaTeX and PDFLaTeX. The information is related to problems that can occur at various stages of document preparation.

Accompanying this manual is another volume, *A Gallery of Document Shells for Scientific WorkPlace and Scientific Word,* available on your program CD as a PDF file. *A Gallery of Document Shells* explains the key characteristics of the shells provided with the program. It contains brief discussions and illustrations of typeset documents created with each shell except those created with *Scientific Notebook,* which were intended for direct printing instead of typesetting.

Please note that this manual doesn't apply to *Scientific Notebook* or *Scientific Viewer,* which don't support typesetting. The manual excludes any detailed discussion of the processes involved in producing a document without typesetting. Further, it excludes an in-depth discussion of working with document shells created with the Style Editor. Extensive Style Editor documentation is available online (see Online Help on page xv).

This manual assumes that you have successfully installed *SWP* or *SW* and that you have a working knowledge of the program. Although certain procedures are explained here, you will find fuller explanations in these accompanying manuals:

- *Getting Started with Scientific WorkPlace, Scientific Word, and Scientific Notebook*

- *Creating Documents with Scientific WorkPlace and Scientific Word*

- *Doing Mathematics with Scientific WorkPlace and Scientific Notebook*

The instructions in this manual occasionally differ for different versions of *SWP* and *SW.* When several sets of instructions are provided, be sure to follow the set of instructions corresponding to your version of the product.

This manual also assumes you're familiar with basic TEX, the extraordinary mathematics typesetting program and language designed by Donald Knuth, and with LATEX, the set of macros designed by Leslie Lamport to enhance TEX with document-structuring features such as tables of contents, chapters and sections, lists, and bibliographies. The Windows implementation of TEX and LATEX that is supplied with the program is TrueTEX, a product of TrueTEX Software. The TrueTEX software distributed with Version 5 of *SWP* and *SW* includes PDFTEX support.

The manual often includes detailed information about TEX and LATEX, document classes, LATEX packages, typesetting options, and document shells. While a good understanding of TEX and LATEX will help you better understand how these often complex elements interact, a thorough discussion of TEX and LATEX is beyond our scope here. If you need additional information, we suggest you refer to these excellent sources:

- *The TEXbook* by Donald E. Knuth.

- *LATEX, A Document Preparation System* by Leslie Lamport.

- *The LATEX Companion* by Michel Goossens, Frank Mittelbach, and Alexander Samarin.

- *A Guide to LATEX: Document Preparation for Beginners and Advanced Users* by Helmut Kopka and Patrick W. Daly.

- The TEX Users Group website at http://www.tug.org.

- The Usenet newsgroup news:comp.text.tex.

Typesetting Basics

With Version 3.0 and later of *SWP* and *SW*, you can produce your documents either with or without LaTeX typesetting. Our focus here is on typesetting. Even if you have a basic understanding of the program, it's important to review how typesetting works and why the appearance of your printed document differs so noticeably when you typeset compared to when you don't. You can find basic information in more detail in the online Help and in *Creating Documents with Scientific WorkPlace and Scientific Word.*

With Version 5.0, we introduced an important new feature: creating typeset Portable Document Format (PDF) files with PDFTeX, which provides all the beauty and features of LaTeX typesetting in PDF form. Now you can use *SWP* and *SW* to typeset files for viewing across platforms with PDF viewers.

In our documentation, we refer to the processes that you use to typeset your documents with LaTeX as *typeset compile, typeset preview,* and *typeset print.* We refer to the processes that you use to typeset your documents with PDF as *typeset compile PDF, typeset preview PDF,* and *typeset print PDF.* All these processes are available only as commands on the Typeset menu or as buttons on the Typeset toolbar. In general, we use the term *typesetting* to refer to either set of processes. Where necessary, we distinguish between them. We refer to the processes that don't involve typesetting as *preview* and *print.* These commands are available on the File menu and the Standard toolbar.

Producing Documents with Typesetting

When you process your document with LaTeX, the program compiles it with LaTeX to create a *device independent*—or *DVI—file,* which is a finely typeset version of your document. The DVI file may contain automatically generated document elements such as cross-references, tables of contents, and numbers for equations. The program then sends the DVI file to the typeset previewer or to the printer.

Typesetting with PDFTeX in Version 5 is just like typesetting with LaTeX, except that you produce a PDF file. Like the DVI file, the PDF file is a finely typeset version of your document. It contains the same automatically generated document elements and, if you have added the *hyperref* package to your document, live hypertext links, bookmarks, and thumbnails. The PDF file also contains embedded fonts and, if you have specified PDF output settings, graphics converted to formats appropriate for PDF viewers. The program sends the PDF file to the screen or the printer using your PDF software.

The appearance of the PDF and DVI files is almost identical. However, a typeset document has a noticeably different appearance from what you see as you work in the document window or when you produce your document without typesetting.

The typeset appearance of your document depends on typesetting specifications from three different sources, all set initially by the shell you use to create your document:

- The *typesetting specifications*, a collection of TeX and LaTeX instructions related to typesetting document elements, including those represented by the tags on the Tag toolbar in the program window.

- Any LaTeX *packages* or *options* specified for the document or the shell.

- Any additional LaTeX *commands* that appear in the document preamble or in the body of the document.

These specifications don't affect the appearance of your document if you don't typeset.

The chapters that follow explain how to modify some of these specifications from within *SWP* and *SW*. However, we advise against attempts at extensive modification of the specifications if you aren't extremely familiar with TEX and LATEX.

▶ **To typeset a document**

1. If you have Version 5, select an output option for typesetting:

   a. From the Typeset menu, choose Output Choice.

   b. Select the option you want. DVI Output is the default.

   c. If you're creating a PDF file,

      i Check Convert .tex link targets to .pdf to convert any .tex extensions in hypertext link addresses to .pdf extensions.

      ii Choose PDF Graphics Settings to specify the file type and location of graphics and plots exported during the typesetting process, and then choose OK.

   d. Choose OK.

2. On the Typeset toolbar, click the button for the typesetting command you want or, from the Typeset menu, choose the command (commands for typesetting with PDFLATEX appear only in Version 5):

Menu	Command	Button	Menu	Command	Button
Typeset	Compile		Typeset	Compile PDF	
Typeset	Preview		Typeset	Preview PDF	
Typeset	Print		Typeset	Print PDF	

3. If you choose a Compile command, select the options you want and choose OK.

   Note that the Compile dialog box indicates the name and location of the typeset file to be created.

4. If you choose a Preview or Print command, set the number of LATEX passes.

   The program compiles your document if necessary, saving a transcript of the process in a .log file. When the compilation is complete, the program either displays your typeset document in the TrueTEX Previewer or prints it on the printer you indicate. If you chose to create a typeset PDF file, the program opens your PDF viewer to display the typeset file or print your document.

You can also print your document from the TrueTEX Previewer or your PDF viewer.

Producing Documents without Typesetting

When you produce your document without typesetting it, the program sends the document directly to a non-LATEX previewer or to the printer using many of the same routines with which it displays the document in the document window. Consequently, what you see in the preview window or in print is similar to what you see as you work on your document in the document window. (The program doesn't reflect the page setup specifications or the print options in the document window.)

When you don't typeset, the appearance of your document depends on three sets of specifications; like the typesetting specifications, they are all set initially by the document shell:

1. The *style,* a collection of the specifications for the appearance of each tag in the document window and in print.

2. The *page setup specifications.*

3. The *print options.*

The online Help and *Creating Documents with Scientific WorkPlace and Scientific Word* provide information about modifying these specifications and about previewing and printing without typesetting. These three sets of specifications don't affect the typeset appearance of your document in any way, although the style determines how the document appears on the screen when you're working on it.

Understanding the Differences in the Final Product

Each time you produce your document in *SWP* or *SW,* you can choose whether or not to typeset it. The results differ noticeably.

If you typeset, the program compiles the document and generates any specified automatic elements such as front matter items (tables of contents or lists of figures and tables), cross-references, footnotes and margin notes, numbered equations, indexes, and bibliographies. LaTeX and PDFLaTeX also provide hyphenation, kerning, ligatures, sophisticated paragraph and line breaking, and other automatic formatting features.

If you don't typeset, the program produces the document using many of the same routines it uses to display the document in the document window. No document elements are automatically generated, and the printed results are similar to what you see as you work on the document.

Conventions

Understanding the notation and the terms used in our documentation will help you understand the instructions. We assume you're familiar with basic Windows procedures and terminology. If necessary, review your Windows documentation. In our manuals, we use the notation and terms listed below.

General Notation

- Text like this indicates the name of a menu, program command, or dialog box.
- TEXT LIKE THIS indicates the name of a keyboard key.
- **Text like this** indicates information you should type exactly as it is shown.
- *Text like this* is a placeholder for a information that you must supply.

- `Text like this` indicates the name of a file or directory, a LATEX command, or other code.

- *Text like this* indicates a term that has special meaning in the program.

- *Typeset your file* means to process your document with LATEX or, if you have Version 5, PDFLATEX.

- *Choose* means to designate a command for the program to carry out. As with all Windows applications, you can choose a command with the keyboard or the mouse. Commands may be listed on a menu or shown on a button in a dialog box. For example, the instruction "From the File menu, choose Open" means you should first choose the File menu and then from that menu, choose the Open command.

- *Select* means to highlight the part of the document that you want your next action to affect or to highlight a specific option in a dialog box or list.

- *Check* means to turn on an option in a dialog box.

Keyboard Conventions

We also use standard Windows conventions to give keyboard instructions.

- The names of keys in the instructions match the names shown on most keyboards. They appear like this: ENTER, F4, SHIFT.

- A plus sign (+) between the names of two keys indicates that you must press the first key and hold it down while you press the second key. For example, CTRL+G means that you press and hold down the CTRL key, press G, and then release both keys.

- The notation CTRL+**word** means that you must hold down the CTRL key, type the word that appears in bold type after the +, then release the CTRL key. Note that if a letter appears capitalized in the instructions, you should type that letter as a capital.

Mouse Conventions

The program uses these mouse pointers:

Pointer	Indication
I	The pointer is over text
	The pointer is over mathematics
	A selection is being dragged
	A selection is being copied
	A selection is being copied or dragged with the right mouse button
	A graphic is being panned
+	A graphic is being resized
	The pointer is over a hypertext link

Additionally, the program displays a pointer for the computational engine when a computation is in progress.

In this manual we give mouse instructions using standard Windows conventions. The instructions assume you have not changed the mouse button defaults.

- *Point* means to move the mouse pointer to a specific position.

- *Click* means to position the mouse pointer, then press and immediately release the left or right mouse button without moving the mouse.

- *Double-click* means to position the mouse pointer, then click the left mouse button twice in rapid succession without moving the mouse.

- *Drag* means to position the mouse pointer, press the left mouse button and hold it down while you move the mouse to a new location, then release the button.

As in most Windows applications, you can use the right mouse button to display a Context menu for the current selection or the item under the mouse pointer. Pressing the Application key 🗈 also displays the menu.

Getting Help

In addition to the information available in the manuals supplied with the program, you can get information about *SWP* and *SW* from the online Help system, the library of reference materials about mathematics and science, and, if you have an Internet connection, the MacKichan Software website. If these resources don't contain the information you need, technical support is available. We also regularly make additional information available on our unmoderated discussion forum and email list. You can find an errata sheet for this book at this URL: **http://www.mackichan.com/techtalk/errata.html**.

Online Help

Without leaving *SWP* and *SW,* you can search the online Help system to find information about all program commands and operations, including those related to numeric, symbolic, and graphic computations. Also, you can find additional material regarding TEX, LATEX, LATEX packages, and other related topics. In addition, two associated programs—the Style Editor and the Document Manager—have their own online Help systems.

▶ **To get help from the** Help **menu**

Choose	To
Contents	See a list of online information
Search...	Find a Help topic
Index	Access the online index to Computing Techniques, General Information, or the Reference Library
MacKichan Software Website	Open the link to the MacKichan Software, Inc. website
Register...	Register your software and obtain a license
System Features...	See a list of available features; change the serial number for your installation
License Information	Obtain information about registering your system
About...	Obtain information about your installation

▶ **To go directly to the Help Contents, press** F1.

Supplemental Technical Documents

We urge you to explore the supplemental technical documents supplied with the program. You can use *SWP* or *SW* to open, view, and print the documents. In particular, we urge you to read the following documents:

- In the `Help\general` directory, the document `techrefv5.tex`, which contains technical information on the features in Version 5.

- In the `Play` directory, the sample documents, which demonstrate the use of computation in *SWP*.

- In the `SWSamples` directory,

  - The sample documents, which illustrate the use of various LaTeX packages in *SWP* and *SW*.

  - The file `OptionsPackagesLaTeX.tex`, which describes and contains links to information about the options, packages, and other TeX-related items provided with the program.

  - The file `BibTeXBibliographyStyles.tex`, which lists and describes the BibTeX style (`.bst`) files installed with the program.

Obtaining Technical Support

If you can't find the answer to your questions in the manuals or the online Help, you can obtain technical support from our website at

http://www.mackichan.com/techtalk/knowledgebase.html

or from our Web-based Technical Support forum at

http://www.mackichan.com/techtalk/UserForums.htm

You can also contact our Technical Support staff by email, telephone, or fax. We urge you to submit questions by email whenever possible in case our technical staff needs to obtain your file to diagnose and solve the problem.

When you contact us by email or fax, please provide complete information about the problem you're trying to solve. We must be able to reproduce the problem exactly from your instructions. When you contact us by telephone, you should be sitting at your computer with the program running.

Please provide the following information any time you contact Technical Support:

- The MacKichan Software product you have installed.

- The version and build number of your installation (see Help / About...).

- The serial number of your installation (see Help / System Features...).

- The version of the Windows system you're using.

- The type of hardware you're using, including printer and network hardware.

- A description of what happened and what you were doing when the problem occurred.

- The exact wording of any messages that appeared on your computer screen.

▶ **To contact Technical Support**

- Contact Technical Support by email, fax, or telephone between 8 AM and 5 PM Pacific Time:

Internet email address: support@mackichan.com
Fax number: 360-394-6039
Telephone number: 360-394-6033
Toll-free telephone: 877-SCI-WORD (877-724-9673)

Additional Information

You can learn more about *SWP* and *SW* on our website, which we update regularly to provide the latest technical information about the program. The site also houses links to other TEX and LATEX resources. We maintain an unmoderated discussion forum and an unmoderated email list so our users can share information, discuss common problems, and contribute technical tips and solutions. You can link to these valuable resources from our home page at **http://www.mackichan.com**.

1 Tailoring Typesetting to Your Needs

The typeset appearance of your *SWP* or *SW* document depends on typesetting specifications, all set initially by the shell you use to create the document. Starting a new document with a carefully chosen shell is important; it minimizes the typesetting modifications you may have to make. If the document shell adheres closely to your typesetting requirements, you may then be able to create the perfect typeset appearance for your document just by making one or two small changes from within the program. Once you've tailored your document to your typesetting requirements, you can export it as a shell so that you can use it repeatedly. See Chapter 2 "Working with Typesetting Specifications and Document Shells" for a more detailed explanation of basic LaTeX document structure and for information about choosing an appropriate shell and creating your own shells.

The information in this chapter answers the typesetting questions we receive most often from users. The questions involve page layout, front and back matter, tables and graphics, and mathematics. The table near the end of the chapter refers you to additional information about other typesetting tasks. If you have a basic knowledge of TeX and LaTeX and are familiar with *SWP* or *SW,* this chapter may be all you need to adapt an existing document shell to your requirements.

You can find more information in the online Help system, in links from the file `OptionsPackagesLaTeX.tex` in the `SWSamples` directory of your installation, and in the TeX and LaTeX references noted on page x.

Note The instructions for the basic processes to which we refer in this chapter appear in Chapter 2.

Cautions

The techniques we suggest for modifying the typeset appearance of your document involve working from within *SWP* or *SW* rather than using an ASCII editor to work directly with the TeX and LaTeX code. The techniques involve modifying the document class options (see page 63), adding and modifying LaTeX packages (see page 71), and inserting TeX commands in your document (see page 76). The techniques should work successfully for typesetting both device independent (DVI) files and, in Version 5, Portable Document Format (PDF) files.

The suggested techniques are general. They work with many, *but not all,* document shells. The techniques are most likely to be successful with document shells based on standard LaTeX typesetting specifications. They are less likely to be successful if you have added an unusual combination of packages to your document, because they may cause LaTeX conflicts. If your document uses a Style Editor shell, you may find that using the Style Editor to make the changes you need is easier and more successful than working from within the document. The suggestions in this chapter may not work with Style Editor documents.

We are unable to predict the effect of these modifications on documents created with LaTeX typesetting specifications that you have added to the program. In other words, we can't guarantee results. Please note that we do not support documents created with typesetting specifications not provided with our program. Note too that some LaTeX packages are distributed with the program only as a convenience or for compatibility and may not necessarily work with *SWP* or *SW* or with other packages.

Some of the suggestions involve bypassing the way LaTeX naturally works, an approach that can sometimes have unpredictable results. Other suggestions involve placing LaTeX code in the document preamble and otherwise sending commands directly to LaTeX. Any time you add TeX fields or raw TeX code to your document, you run the risk of damaging it.

Important   Even seemingly small coding errors can have large and unwelcome effects. Errors may prevent compilation, or they may damage or truncate your document irrevocably. *Save a copy of your document* before you attempt any of the modifications suggested here.

Most importantly, we urge you not to attempt extensive modifications of the typesetting specifications unless you're very familiar with TeX and LaTeX.

Tailoring the Page Layout

Making small changes to the page layout may yield the perfect typeset appearance for your document. Often, the most straightforward way to affect the page layout is by modifying one or more of the class options in effect for your document, and most of the techniques presented in this section take advantage of that capability. The class options control many fundamental aspects of page layout and document design, such as paper size, body text point size, title and author information, page orientation, or columns. See LaTeX Class Options on page 63 for more information.

Remember   Save a copy of your document before you attempt to modify it.

Changing the Margins

Your document has two sets of margins, one for producing your document without typesetting and one for producing your document with typesetting. If you don't intend to typeset your document, you can change the margins using the page setup specifications. Access this set of specifications with the Page Setup command on the File menu. Remember that the changes you make to the margins using the page setup specifications have no effect on the typeset appearance of your document.

Margins for typesetting are generally set in the document class specifications (.cls) file; see page 61. The .cls file usually contains different margin defaults for each paper size, so changing the paper size default automatically changes the margin defaults. The LaTeX article class defines margins of about $1\frac{7}{8}$ inches on all sides when $8\frac{1}{2}$x11 inch paper is specified, but those margins change subtly when A4 paper is specified. Regardless of the paper size, you can modify the margin settings for most but not all shells by adding the *geometry* package (see page 125). See Changing the Headers and Footers on page 5 for additional information.

Fitting More Text on a Page

Without any other modifications, adding the *geometry* package to a document enlarges the margins. This happens because LaTeX gives precedence to the *geometry* package margin settings, which usually differ from those of the document class. When you add *geometry* to your standard LaTeX article class document, the package specifies a $1\frac{5}{16}$-inch margin on the right, left, and top and a 2-inch margin on the bottom.

Changing the Margin Settings

You can use the default margins for the *geometry* package or specify the margins you want by adding a command to the preamble of your document.

▶ **To change the margins of a document**

1. Add the *geometry* package to your document.

2. From the Typeset menu, choose Preamble.

3. Click the mouse in the entry area.

4. On a new line at the end of the entries, type

   \geometry{left=win,right=xin,top=yin,bottom=zin}

   where *w* and *x* are the measurements for the left and right margins, *y* is the measurement for the top margin, and *z* is the measurement for the bottom margin. The syntax shown in this instruction uses inches as the measurement unit, but you can use any of the usual TeX measurement units in the command:

Unit	Value
sp	Scaled point (65536 sp = 1 pt)
pt	Point ($\frac{1}{72.27}$ in)
bp	Big point ($\frac{1}{72}$ in)
dd	Didôt point (0.376 mm)
mm	Millimeter
pc	Pica (12 pt)
cc	Cicero (12 dd)
cm	Centimeter
in	Inch

5. Choose OK.

Changing the Line Spacing

SWP and *SW* support multiple-line spacing in typeset documents. The typesetting specifications for each document shell initially determine the line spacing of documents created with the shell. Some specifications have class options that change the line spacing, but others don't. Although line-spacing specifications are sometimes presented as *draft* or *manuscript* (double spacing) or as *final* or *camera-ready* (single spacing), print quality options don't necessarily imply line-spacing changes. See LaTeX Class Options on page 65 for more information about examining and changing class options.

When class options for line spacing aren't available, you can use the LaTeX *setspace* package (see page 156) to change line spacing. With the package, you can select single, one-and-one-half, or double spacing for the document as a whole or for parts of the document. If you find a shell that otherwise meets your typesetting requirements, add the *setspace* package and then change the spacing as needed.

Some shells and some documents created with older versions of *SWP* and *SW* may require the *doublespace* package, now superseded by *setspace.* The *doublespace* package is provided with the program only for compatibility. We recommend you use the *setspace* package instead. Note that if your document was created with a Style Editor shell, these packages probably won't work. Use the Style Editor to make any necessary line spacing changes.

▶ **To change the line spacing of the entire document**

1. Add the *setspace* package to your document.

2. If you're using Version 4.0 or later,

   a. On the Typeset toolbar, click the Options and Packages button ⊞ or, from the Typeset menu, choose Options and Packages.
   b. Choose the Package Options tab.
   c. From the Packages in Use box, select setspace and choose Modify.
   d. In the Category box, select Line Spacing.
   e. In the Options box, select the spacing you want.
   f. Choose OK twice to return to your document.

   or

   If you're using an earlier version of the program,

   a. From the Typeset menu, choose Preamble and click the mouse in the entry area.
   b. On a new line at the end of the entries, type the command that corresponds to the spacing you want: **\singlespacing, \onehalfspacing,** or **\doublespacing.**
   c. Choose OK.

▶ **To change the line spacing for a portion of a document**

1. Add the *setspace* package to your document.

2. Place the insertion point at the start of the first paragraph whose spacing you want to change.

3. Enter a TEX field.

4. In the entry area,

- Type **\singlespacing**, **\onehalfspacing**, or **\doublespacing**, depending on the spacing you want.

or

- Type **\setstretch{*x*}** where *x* is a number indicating the spacing you want. For example, the command `\setstretch{3}` produces triple spacing.

5. Choose OK.

6. Place the insertion point where you want to return to the original spacing.

7. Repeat steps 3–5.

Changing the Font Size of Body Text

Most document classes have a default setting for the font size used for body text. You can change the setting by modifying the document class options. Note that the body text font size is used as the basis for determining many other typesetting specifications, such as script size. Note also that some typesetting specifications override the font size class options.

▶ **To change the body text font size with the class options**

1. On the Typeset toolbar, click the Options and Packages button [image] or, from the Typeset menu, choose Options and Packages.

2. Choose the Class Options tab and choose Modify.

3. In the Category box, select Body text point size.

4. In the Options box, select the font size you want.

5. Choose OK.

6. Choose OK to return to your document.

Changing the Headers and Footers

Most typesetting specifications automatically generate page headers and footers using information from various LATEX counters to generate header and footer content, such as page numbers or chapter and section headings. You may need to modify the content or format of the headers and footers or even suppress it on certain pages. Two packages—*fancyhdr* and *geometry* (see pages 120 and 125)—can simplify many of these changes. TEX commands accomplish the rest.

Specifying Header and Footer Information

LaTeX automatically creates headers and footers from the information in the typesetting specifications and the section headings in your document. You can override the automatic headers and footers by adding the *fancyhdr* package and making some changes to the preamble or to the body of your document. Occasionally, the typesetting specifications override the page style for certain pages, especially *exceptional pages* such as the title page or the first page of a chapter or section. Instead of specifying the headers and footers for the entire document, you can specify them for a particular page by placing TeX commands in the body of the document instead of the preamble. Also, you may want to suppress header and footer information on certain pages; see page 7 for instructions.

The instructions below explain how to specify a header that has the title of the work on the right and a footer that has the author's name on the left and the page number on the right. Use the commands in step 4 as models for creating the headers and footers you want.

▶ **To specify header and footer information for the entire document**

1. Add the *fancyhdr* package to your document.

2. From the Typeset menu, choose **Preamble**.

3. Click the mouse in the entry area.

4. At the end of the entry area, add new lines to specify the content of the right, center, and left areas of the header and footer (any information that follows a % is a comment and is not necessary):

   \pagestyle{fancy}

   \lhead{} %Leave the left of the header empty

   \chead{} %Leave the center of the header empty

   \rhead{Title of This Document} %Display this text on the right of the header

   \lfoot{By Author} %Display this text on the left of the footer

   \cfoot{} %Leave the center of the footer empty

   \rfoot{Page:\ \thepage} %Print the page number in the right footer

   \renewcommand{\headrulewidth}{0pt} %Do not print a rule below the header

   \renewcommand{\footrulewidth}{0pt} %Do not print a rule above the footer

5. Choose OK.

▶ **To specify header and footer information for selected pages**

1. Add the *fancyhdr* package to your document.

2. Place the insertion point on the page for which you want to specify header or footer information.

3. Enter an encapsulated TEX field containing the lines that follow to specify the content of the right, center, and left areas of the header and footer.

   Modify the commands as necessary (any information that follows a % is a comment and is not necessary):

   \thispagestyle{fancy}

   \lhead{} %Leave the left of the header empty

   \chead{} %Leave the center of the header empty

   \rhead{Title of This Document} %Display this text on the right of the header

   \lfoot{By Author} %Display this text on the left of the footer

   \cfoot{} %Leave the center of the footer empty

   \rfoot{Page:\ \thepage} %Print the page number in the right footer

   \renewcommand{\headrulewidth}{0pt} %Do not print a rule below the header

   \renewcommand{\footrulewidth}{0pt} %Do not print a rule above the footer

4. Choose OK.

Suppressing Headers and Footers

On individual pages of your document, you can suppress the header and footer or you can take a more extreme approach and entirely eliminate the space allotted for them, as described on page 8. See page 66 for illustrations of standard LATEX page layouts.

▶ **To suppress the header and footer on an individual page**

1. Place the insertion point on the page for which you want no header or footer.

   If the page has a section heading, place the insertion point after the heading.

2. Enter an encapsulated TEX field.

3. In the entry area, type **\thispagestyle{empty}** and choose OK.

   When you typeset preview your document, you may find that the typesetting specifications for the first page of a part or chapter have been defined differently from the rest of the document and have not been affected by your change. In this case, you must suppress the header and footer information on the individual pages.

   If you create special headers and footers with the *fancyhdr* package, as described on page 6, you may want to suppress headers and footers on certain pages. In particular, you may not want a page number on the first page of a chapter or section. You can override the *fancyhdr* package to suppress the information.

▶ **To suppress headers and footers created with *fancyhdr***

1. Place the insertion point on the page for which you want to suppress headers and footers, and enter an encapsulated TEX field.

2. In the entry area, type **\thispagestyle{plain}** and choose OK.

Changing the Format of the Header and Footer Space

If you want to expand the amount of information you can get on a page, you can eliminate headers and footers entirely and expand the text area into the space they ordinarily occupy. Use the *geometry* package with some TeX commands to accomplish the change. On the other hand, you may find that the space allotted for headers and footers is inadequate. You can increase the space easily. Also, you can separate the headers from the text by adding a line, or *rule,* under the header; use the *fancyhdr* package and a few TeX commands in the document preamble.

▶ **To eliminate the header and footer space throughout the document**

1. From the Typeset menu, choose Preamble and click the mouse in the entry area.

2. On a new line at the end of the entries, type **\pagestyle{empty}** and choose OK.

3. On the Typeset toolbar, click the Options and Packages button ▦ or, from the Typeset menu, choose Options and Packages.

4. Choose the Package Options tab.

5. Add the *geometry* package to your document.

6. In the Packages in Use box, select geometry and choose Modify.

7. In the Category box, select Header/footer space.

8. In the Options box, select No header space, No footer space, or No header or footer space.

9. Choose OK twice to return to your document.

▶ **To increase the space available for headers and footers**

1. From the Typeset menu, choose Preamble and click the mouse in the entry area.

2. Change the header space:

   a. Add a new line at the end of the preamble entries.
   b. Type **\setlength{\headheight}{x}** where x is the height of the header you want. You can use any TeX measurement unit.

3. On a new line, type **\setlength{\textheight}{x}** where x is the desired text height.

   The text height should reflect the original text height set for the document less the amount you added to the header.

4. On a new line, type **\setlength{\footskip}{x}** where x is the distance from the bottom of the text to the bottom of the footer.

5. Choose OK.

▶ **To add a rule under the header**

1. Add the *fancyhdr* package to your document.

2. Enter an encapsulated TEX field on the first page of the body of the document.

3. In the entry area, type these two commands:

   \pagestyle{fancy}

   \renewcommand{\headrulewidth}{*x*pt}

   where *x* is the point size of the rule you want.

   For reference, this is a 1-point rule ——————— and this is a 5-point rule ▬▬▬▬.
   If you want to remove a rule under a header, set the headrulewidth to zero.

4. Choose OK.

Fitting Headings into Headers

If you find that a heading is too long to fit in the header, you can define a short heading to use in its place. The short title will appear in the page header and also in the table of contents of your document (see page 18). This technique works for standard LATEX typesetting specifications, but may not work for other typesetting specifications.

▶ **To define a short heading for a section**

1. Place the insertion point at the beginning of the section heading.

2. Type the short heading enclosed in square brackets.

   The heading might then look something like this:

   [New Shorter Heading]A Much Longer Heading to Announce This Section of My Document

Changing the Page Numbering

Page numbering is produced automatically by the typesetting specifications for your document and in particular by the document class for the shell. However, you may require subtle changes in the page numbering scheme, perhaps to reset the numbering at some point in your document, to use lowercase roman numerals instead of arabic numbers in the front matter, to move the page number elsewhere on the page, or to remove it altogether. You can change the page numbering in your document by using packages and, in some cases, by inserting TEX commands in the body of your document.

You may find additional information is helpful when you try to modify the page numbering. See the TEX and LATEX resources noted on page x and the information available about the *fancyhdr* package on page 120.

Resetting the Page Number

Page numbering sometimes requires subtle changes. You may need to set an arbitrary page number at some point in your document.

▶ **To set an arbitrary page number**

1. Place the insertion point where you want the page number to be reset.

2. Enter an encapsulated TEX field.

3. In the entry area, type **setcounter{page}{x}** where *x* is the number from which you want page numbering to begin at this point.

4. Choose OK.

Changing the Page Numbering Style

You may need to use a different style for the page numbers in one part of your document. With a LATEX command, you can change the page numbering style to upper- or lowercase roman numerals, upper- or lowercase letters, or arabic numbers. When you change the page numbering style, LATEX resets the page number to 1, so you may want to reset the page number after you change the style.

▶ **To change the style of the page numbering**

1. Place the insertion point on the page whose page numbering style you want to change.

2. Enter an encapsulated TEX field.

3. In the entry area, type the command corresponding to the page numbering style you want:

Command	Page numbering style
pagenumbering{roman}	lowercase roman numerals: i, ii, iii, ...
pagenumbering{Roman}	uppercase roman numerals: I, II, III, ...
pagenumbering{arabic}	arabic numbers: 1, 2, 3, ...
pagenumbering{alph}	lowercase letters: a, b, c, ...
pagenumbering{Alph}	uppercase letters: A, B, C, ...

4. Choose OK.

Shells based on the standard LATEX book document class (see page 63) use lowercase roman numerals for the page numbers in the front matter of the document but arabic numbers for page numbers throughout the rest of the document. If the shell you've chosen has a different document class and therefore a different page numbering scheme, you can change the numbering by placing LATEX commands in your document.

▶ **To use roman numerals in the front matter only**

1. From the Typeset menu, choose Preamble.

2. Click the mouse in the entry area.

3. Create a new line at the end of the preamble entries.

4. Type **pagenumbering{roman}** and choose OK.

5. Place the insertion point at the beginning of the first paragraph of body text in your document.

6. Enter an encapsulated TEX field.

7. In the entry area, type **pagenumbering{arabic}** and choose OK.

   Remember that LATEX will reset the page number to 1; reset the page number if necessary.

Moving the Page Number

If your document style places the page number in a less than ideal spot, you can move it with the *fancyhdr* package. The package defines the content of the right, center, and left sections of the header and footer. You can place the page number in one of these areas. For more information about the *fancyhdr* package, see the online Help system and the information on pages 5 and 120.

Because your document shell may already define the content of some header and footer areas, you may need to redefine them before your changes will work correctly. For example, if you want to remove the page number from the bottom center of the page, you must redefine the area as blank so the number doesn't appear there. The instructions below explain how to move a page number from the center bottom of the page to the top right. Use them as a guideline for moving page numbers to any part of the header or footer.

▶ **To move the page number from the bottom center to the top right of the page**

1. Add the *fancyhdr* package to your document.

2. Move the page number:

   a. In the body of the document, enter an encapsulated TEX field.
   b. In the entry area, type **pagestyle{fancy}** to establish a new page style.
   c. On the next line, type **fancyhf{}** to clear the header and footer.
   d. On the next line, type **rhead{\\thepage}** to force the page number to the top right of the page.
   e. If you want to remove the automatically created rule under the header, type the command **renewcommand{\\headrulewidth}{0pt}** on the next line.
   f. If you want to remove the automatically created rule above the footer, type the command **renewcommand{\\footrulewidth}{0pt}** on the next line.
   g. Choose OK.

or

    a. From the Typeset menu, choose Preamble, and click the mouse in the entry area.

    b. Start a new line at the end of the preamble entries.

    c. Type the commands specified in steps 2b–f, above, then choose OK.

Removing the Page Number

If the typesetting instructions for your document specify that a page number occurs on a page where you prefer not to have a number, you can suppress page numbering on the page by inserting a LaTeX command in the body of your document. Page numbering will continue as before on the next page of the document.

▶ **To suppress the page number on a page**

1. Place the insertion point on the page for which you want no page number.

2. Enter an encapsulated TeX field.

3. In the entry area, type **\thispagestyle{empty}** and choose OK.

Creating Multiple Columns

Most *SWP* and *SW* documents can be typeset in multiple columns. The typesetting specifications for each document shell determine the number of columns initially created with the shell, but you can modify the setting. Although most shells default to a single column, some default to double columns; skim through *A Gallery of Document Shells* to identify the double-column shells.

Creating double-column output for your document may require little more than changing the document class options. If you specify the double-column option, LaTeX typesets the entire body of the document in two columns. The option doesn't necessarily apply to all parts of the document front matter.

If you want finer control over which document elements are and are not typeset in multiple columns, you can use the *multicol* package to create as many as 10 columns of text, and to combine single and multiple columns on the same page. For more information, see page 138.

▶ **To create double columns**

1. On the Typeset toolbar, click the Options and Packages button ▣ or, from the Typeset menu, choose Options and Packages.

2. Choose the Class Options tab and then choose Modify.

3. In the Category box, select Columns.

4. In the Options box, select Two columns and choose OK.

5. Choose OK to return to your document.

► **To create multiple columns**

1. Add the *multicol* package to your document.

2. Define the start of the multicolumn environment:

   a. Place the insertion point where you want multiple columns to begin.
   b. Enter an encapsulated TₑX field.
   c. In the entry area, type **\begin{multicols}{*x*}** where *x* is the number of columns you want.
   d. Choose OK.

3. Define the end of the multicolumn environment:

   a. Place the insertion point where you want multiple columns to end.
   b. Enter an encapsulated TₑX field.
   c. In the entry area, type **\end{multicols}**.
   d. Choose OK.

Changing the Page Orientation

You can typeset most documents using portrait or landscape orientation for all or part of the document. You can change the orientation of your entire document by changing the options for the document class or by adding the *geometry* package to the document and then modifying the package options. Because the document class and package options you specify can conflict, you must be careful not to use contradictory orientation settings. The printed output depends on your printer's capabilities and settings.

► **To change the orientation of the entire document**

- Use the class options:

  a. On the Typeset toolbar, click the Options and Packages button or, from the Typeset menu, choose Options and Packages.
  b. Choose the Class Options tab and choose Modify.
  c. In the Category box, select Orientation.
  d. In the Options box, select the orientation you want, and then choose OK.
  e. Choose OK to return to your document.

  or

- Use the *geometry* package:

  a. On the Typeset toolbar, click the Options and Packages button or, from the Typeset menu, choose Options and Packages.
  b. Choose the Package Options tab.
  c. Add the *geometry* package to your document.
  d. From the Packages in Use box, select geometry and choose Modify.

e. In the Category box, select Orientation.

f. In the Options box, select the orientation you want.

g. Choose OK twice to return to your document.

If you need to create a section of your document in a different orientation, we suggest that you use the *portland* package (see page 147). You can also use packages that provide text rotation, such as *lscape* (page 133) or *rotating* (page 151), to orient pages differently. However, packages that use rotation aren't compatible with the TrueTEX Previewer provided with *SWP* and *SW*. Note that PDF viewers do support rotation, so you can successfully use the packages to rotate text in typeset PDF files.

▶ **To change the orientation of a single page**

1. Add the *portland* package to your document.

2. Place the insertion point where you want the orientation change to occur.

3. Enter a TEX field.

4. In the entry area, type **landscape** or **portrait**, depending on the orientation you want, and choose OK.

5. Place the insertion point where you want to return to the original orientation.

6. Enter a TEX field.

7. In the entry area, type **portrait** or **landscape**, whichever is appropriate.

8. Choose OK.

Remember that you may need to change the orientation settings for your printer so that your document prints properly. Instructions differ for each printer, but most changes originate from a Setup tab. The instructions below are guidelines only.

If you have a single page with an orientation different from that of the rest of the document, you may need to print it separately after changing the printer settings accordingly.

▶ **To change the printer settings for a different orientation**

1. If you're printing from the document window, choose Print or Print PDF from the Typeset menu.

   or

   If you're printing from a previewer, choose Print or Print Setup from the File menu.

   Note that menu commands may differ depending on your print driver and previewer.

2. Look for a Setup or Properties tab or button and choose it.

3. Select the orientation you want.

4. Choose OK to return to your document or to the previewer.

Note that you may want to change the orientation of the TrueTEX display in order to properly preview documents with landscape orientation.

▶ **To change the orientation of the TrueTEX Previewer display**

1. On the Typeset toolbar, click the Typeset DVI Preview button ⊞ or, from the Typeset menu, choose Preview.

2. From the Options menu in the TrueTEX Previewer, choose Preferences.

3. Choose Page Orientation and select the orientation you want.

The TrueTEX Previewer remembers the page orientation most recently set and uses it the next time you preview a document.

Changing to a Different Paper Size

The program can typeset most documents for a variety of paper sizes. You can specify the paper size by changing the class options or by adding the *geometry* package. (The package works with most but not all shells; for more details about the *geometry* package, see page 125.) Because the document class and package options you specify can conflict, you must be careful not to use contradictory paper size settings. Printing the document successfully involves changing the settings for your printer and, of course, using the correct paper in the printer.

▶ **To change the paper size**

- Modify the class options:

  a. On the Typeset toolbar, click the Options and Packages button ⊞ or, from the Typeset menu, choose Options and Packages.
  b. Choose the Class Options tab and choose Modify.
  c. In the Category box, select Paper size.
  d. In the Options box, select the paper size you want, and then choose OK.
  e. Choose OK to return to your document.

  or

- Use the *geometry* package:

  a. On the Typeset toolbar, click the Options and Packages button ⊞ or, from the Typeset menu, choose Options and Packages.
  b. Choose the Package Options tab.
  c. Add the *geometry* package to your document.
  d. From the Packages in Use box, select geometry and choose Modify.
  e. In the Category box, select Paper size.
  f. In the Options box, select the paper size you want.
  g. Choose OK twice to return to your document.

▶ **To change the TrueTₑX Previewer settings for paper of a different size**

1. On the Typeset toolbar, click the Typeset DVI Preview button 🔳 or, from the Typeset menu, choose Preview.

2. From the Options menu in the TrueTeX DVI Previewer window, choose Preferences and then choose Page Size.

3. Select the paper size you want and choose OK.

The TrueTₑX Previewer remembers and uses the page size selected most recently the next time you preview a document.

▶ **To change the printer settings for a different paper size**

1. From the Typeset menu, choose Print or Print PDF.

2. In the Page Setup tab, scroll the list of sizes in the Paper Size box to select the size you want.

Commands and their menu location may differ depending on your print driver.

3. Choose OK to close the succession of dialog boxes and begin printing.

Tailoring the Front and Back Matter

The typesetting specifications determine the appearance of elements in the front and back matter of your document. The front matter is the information that appears before the body of your document, including elements such as a title area, table of contents, list of figures, and abstract. The back matter is the information that follows the body of the document, perhaps including an appendix, bibliography, and index. The appearance of the front and back matter may require modification to adhere to your requirements. You can make many of these changes from within *SWP* and *SW*.

Changing the Title Page

The typesetting specifications determine which elements appear on the title page of your document. If you need different information on the title page of your book, report, or thesis, you can discard the automatically generated front matter and place the information you want in a titlepage environment and a series of TₑX fields in the body of your document. You must provide all required formatting for the information on the new page. Also, because the titlepage environment resets the page number of the following page to 1, you may need to reset the page numbering scheme; see page 9.

▶ **To create a customized title page**

1. At the beginning of the body of your document, enter an encapsulated TₑX field.

2. In the entry area, type **\begin{titlepage}** and choose OK.

3. Enter the information for the title page, using tags and spacing commands to format the information according to your requirements.

4. At the end of the information, enter an encapsulated TEX field.

5. In the entry area, type **\end{titlepage}** and choose OK.

6. If you want to insert a table of contents or another front matter element such as a list of figures, or list of tables, enter an encapsulated TEX field.

7. In the entry area, type the TEX command for the element.

   These commands include **\tableofcontents**, **\listoffigures**, and **\listoftables**.

8. Choose OK.

9. On the Typeset toolbar, click the Front Matter button 🗎 or, from the Typeset menu, choose Front Matter.

10. Delete everything and choose OK.

11. Save and preview the document, setting the number of LATEX passes to 3 if your document has a table of contents.

Some journals require that information about the author be included in an unnumbered footnote, with the footnote marker appearing as an asterisk next to the author's name in the title area and the footnote itself appearing with an asterisk at the bottom of the title page or first page.

▶ **To add an unnumbered footnote to the title page**

1. From the Typeset menu, choose Front Matter.

2. Place the insertion point at the end of the author's name in the Author field.

3. On the Field toolbar, click the Note button 🗎 or, from the Insert menu, choose Note.

4. Enter the text of the footnote.

5. In the Type of Note area, select footnote.

6. Choose OK.

When you typeset the document, the footnote appears with an asterisk at the bottom of the first page. Footnotes in the body of the document are numbered beginning with 1. Results can differ if the class options for the document include a title page option and that option is selected, as explained on page 65. We suggest you experiment using the style you have selected for your document.

Changing the Table of Contents

The typesetting specifications define the way each division of your document is presented in the table of contents. They determine which division headings appear in the contents, whether unnumbered headings are included, and how certain heading are listed. Changing these specifications from within the program is straightforward.

Changing the Division Levels Displayed in the Table of Contents

The `tocdepth` counter setting in the typesetting specifications determines which division headings are included in the table of contents. LATEX uses *section* as level 1, regardless of the document class. For information about which division headings carry numbers, both in the table of contents and the text, see page 27.

▶ **To modify the level of division headings reflected in the table of contents**

1. From the Typeset menu, choose Preamble and click the mouse in the entry area.

2. On a new line at the end of the entries, type **setcounter{tocdepth}{***x***}** where *x* is the deepest heading level you want to display.

3. Choose OK.

Creating Page Breaks in the Table of Contents

LATEX generates the entries in a typeset table of contents from the division headings in your document. You can force a table of contents entry to move from the bottom of one page to the top of the next, or vice versa. Use LATEX commands in the body of your document to lengthen pages and create page breaks in the table of contents.

▶ **To force an entry to the next page of the table of contents**

1. Compile your document to generate a table of contents.

2. Determine the table of contents entry you want to force to the next page.

3. In the body of your document, find the corresponding division heading.

4. Place the insertion point immediately above the heading.

5. Enter a TEX field.

6. In the entry area, type **addtocontents{toc}{\protect\pagebreak}**.

7. Choose OK.

When you compile your document to create a new table of contents, LATEX places a page break before the table of contents entry for the division heading, and forces the entry to the next page of the table of contents. The body of your document remains unchanged.

▶ **To force an entry to the previous page of the table of contents**

1. Compile your document to generate a table of contents.

2. Determine the table of contents entry you want to force to the previous page.

3. In the body of your document, find the corresponding division heading.

4. Place the insertion point immediately above the heading and enter a TEX field.

5. In the entry area, type **\addtocontents{toc}{\protect\enlargethispage*{1000pt}}** where the actual point value depends on how much information you're trying to fit on the page.

6. Choose **OK**.

7. Place the insertion point in the paragraph following the heading and enter a TEX field.

8. In the entry area, type **\addtocontents{toc}{\protect\pagebreak}** and choose **OK**.

   When you compile your document to create a new table of contents, LATEX forces the entry for the division heading to the previous page of the table of contents and places a page break after the entry. The body of your document remains unchanged.

Creating Short Table of Contents Entries

If a division heading in your document is long, you can define a short heading for use in the table of contents. The short heading is also used for the page header, as described on page 9.

▶ **To define a short heading for a division**

1. Place the insertion point at the beginning of the division heading.

2. Type the short heading enclosed in square brackets.

   The heading might then look something like this:

   [Short Heading]A Long Heading to Announce This Section of My Document

Listing Unnumbered Divisions

Generally, the specifications exclude unnumbered divisions, such as the introduction or acknowledgments, from the table of contents. You can force LATEX to include them.

▶ **To include an unnumbered division in the table of contents**

1. Place the insertion point just after the unnumbered heading.

2. Enter an encapsulated TEX field.

3. In the entry area, type **\addcontentsline{toc}{*sectionlevel*}{*Name*}** where ***section-level*** is the level of the heading you want to include, such as chapter or section, and ***Name*** is the text you want to appear in the table of contents.

4. Choose **OK**.

Listing the Bibliography and Index

The headings for two divisions—the bibliography and the index—are both unnumbered and automatically generated. They typically appear in the body of the document but not in the table of contents. You can create a contents entry for both.

▶ **To add the bibliography or index to the table of contents**

1. Create the bibliography list or index entries.

2. Typeset compile the document to generate the index and, if you're using BIBTEX, the bibliography.

3. Create the table of contents entry:
   - If you have Version 4.0 or later, add the *tocbibind* package to your document. The package automatically includes the bibliography and the index in the table of contents.

     or
   - If you have an earlier version,

     i Place the insertion point just before the index or the gray box for the BIBTEX bibliography.

     ii Enter an encapsulated TEX field.

     iii In the entry area, type **clearpage** if you're working in an article or report shell or **cleardoublepage** if you're working in a book shell.

     iv Press ENTER.

     v Type **addcontentsline{toc}**{*divisionlevel*}{*Name*} where *divisionlevel* is the level of the heading you want to include, such as chapter or section, and *Name* is the text you want to appear in the table of contents.

     vi Choose OK.

Listing the Appendices

Typesetting specifications can automatically format certain table of contents entries. For example, some specifications create contents entries for each appendix using the appendix number only; others precede the number with the word *Appendix*. If your document shell uses only the appendix number in the table of contents, you can modify the entry by adding the word *Appendix*.

▶ **To force the word *Appendix* to appear in the table of contents**

1. Place the insertion point where you want the appendix title to appear in the document.

2. Enter an encapsulated TEX field.

3. In the entry area,
   - If you're using an article shell, type
     section*{Appendix *x. The Title of the Appendix*}
     where *x. The Title of the Appendix* indicates the number and title of the appendix.

or

- If you're using a book shell, type
  \chapter*{*Appendix x. The Title of the Appendix*}.

This command removes the automatic generation of the appendix number and changes the appearance of the title in the text to what you have entered inside the curly braces.

4. Type a second command to add the now unnumbered section to the table of contents:

   \addcontentsline{toc}{section}{*Appendix x. The Title of the Appendix*}.

   If you're using a book or report shell, substitute the word *chapter* for the word *section.*

5. Choose OK.

Changing the List of Figures

If the captions for the floating graphics in your document are too long to appear in a list of figures, you can shorten the way they appear in the list of figures but keep the full text of the caption in the body of your document.

▶ **To define a short caption for a floating graphic**

1. Select the graphic.

2. Choose Properties.

3. Choose the Labeling tab.

4. Choose the position of the caption in the body of the document (Above or Below).

5. In the Caption text area, type the caption as you want it to appear in the body of your document.

6. Check the box marked Short form.

7. In the Caption text area, type the caption as you want it to appear in the list of figures.

8. Choose OK.

Creating an Unnumbered Manual Bibliography

At times, you may want to customize the typeset appearance of items in a manual bibliography and the citations that refer to them. For example, you may want to remove the numbers from the bibliography item list, alphabetize the items themselves, or create citations with certain content, such as the author's name and year of publication. See page 34 for additional information about formatting citations.

▶ **To create an unnumbered manual bibliography**

1. Create your document using one of the standard LaTeX shells.

2. From the Typeset menu, choose Bibliography Choice, check Manual Entry, and choose OK.

3. Remove the typesetting of the labels from the bibliography item list:

   a. From the Typeset menu, choose Preamble.
   b. Click the mouse in the entry area and add these lines to the end of the preamble:
      \makeatletter
      \def\@biblabel#1{\hspace*{-\labelsep}}
      \makeatother
   c. Choose OK.

4. Create the bibliography item list, giving a label to each item:

   a. Place the insertion point where you want the bibliography item list to begin.
   b. Apply the Bibliography Item tag.
   c. In the Key box, type a key for the item.
   d. In the Label box, type the citation information as you want it to appear in the text. The typesetting specifications define the appearance of the label, adding brackets automatically as necessary.
   e. Choose OK.
   f. Type the bibliography item as you want it to appear in the list and press ENTER.
   g. Repeat steps c–f for each item in the list, and then press F2 to exit the list.

5. Manually alphabetize the bibliography items.

6. Create citations in the text:

   a. Place the insertion point where you want a citation to appear.
   b. On the Typeset Objects toolbar, click the Citation button ⬛ or, from the Insert menu, choose Typeset Object and then choose Citation.
   c. In the Citation dialog box, enter the key of the item you want to cite and choose OK.

7. Typeset your document.

   LaTeX places the label for the bibliography item in the citation but omits it from the bibliography list.

Creating an Appendix for Each Chapter

Creating a single appendix for your document requires no special procedures, but creating an appendix for each chapter of a book or report or for each section of an article requires the addition of the *appendix* package (see page 99). The package implements a subappendices environment to contain the appendix.

▶ **To create subappendices**

1. Add the *appendix* package to your document.

2. Begin the subappendices environment:

   a. Place the insertion point where you want the appendix to appear.
   b. Enter an encapsulated TEX field.
   c. In the entry area, type **begin{subappendices}** and choose OK.

3. Type the title of the appendix and apply the section tag (for appendices within chapters of a book or report) or the subsection tag (for appendices within sections of an article).

4. Type the content of the appendix.

5. If you want additional subappendices, repeat steps 3 and 4.

6. End the subappendices environment:

   a. Place the insertion point where you want the appendix to end.
   b. Enter an encapsulated TEX field.
   c. In the entry area, type **end{subappendices}** and choose OK.

The subappendices you create are numbered with the chapter or section number and an uppercase alphabetic letter, as in 2.A, 2.B, and so on. You can modify the numbering scheme to remove the chapter or section number.

▶ **To remove the number from a subappendix**

1. From the Typeset menu, choose Preamble and click the mouse in the entry area.

2. On a new line at the end of the preamble entries,

   - For books and reports, type
     renewcommand{\\setthesection}{\\Alph{section}}
     or
   - For articles, type
     renewcommand{\\setthesubsection}{\\Alph{subsection}}

3. Choose OK.

Creating Two Separate Indices

Some publications require that you include both a subject index and an author index in your document. You can generate a double index if you use both the *makeidx* and *nomencl* packages in your document (see pages 135 and 141). The *makeidx* package generates a standard subject index. You can use the features of the *nomencl* package, along with the MakeIndex program provided with *SWP* and *SW,* to create the author index.

▶ **To generate two indices**

1. Add the *makeidx* and *nomencl* packages to your document.

2. Modify the options for the nomencl package:

   a. From the Typeset menu, choose Options and Packages and choose the Package Options tab.
   b. In the Packages in Use box, select nomencl and choose Modify.
   c. In the Category box, choose Add page references.
   d. Select the Yes option.
   e. Choose OK to close the dialog boxes and return to your document.

3. Create standard index entries for the subject index throughout your document.

4. Create each entry for the author index:

   a. Place the insertion point to the right of the name you want to index.
   b. Enter an encapsulated TeX field.
   c. In the entry area, type **\nomenclature{*name*}{\hspace{-1ex}}** where *name* is the author name you want to appear in the list, shown as you want it to appear, and the second parameter is some negative horizontal space that offsets a blank space added by the package before the page number.
      The word *page* is added automatically.
   d. Choose OK.

5. Modify the document preamble:

   a. From the Typeset menu, choose Preamble and click the mouse in the entry area.
   b. If you're using the Portable LATEX filter, skip to step 5d.
   c. If the highest division level in your document is section (that is, the chapter division isn't used):

      i Save, close, and reopen the document.
      ii From the Typeset menu, choose Preamble.
      iii Click the mouse in the entry area and scroll to the bottom.
      iv After the line \input{tcilatex}, add a new line and type
         \let\chapter\undefined
   d. At the end of the preamble entries, add these new lines:
      \makeglossary
      \makeindex
      \renewcommand{\nomname}{Author Index}
      \renewcommand{\indexname}{Subject Index}
   e. Choose OK.

6. Include both indices in your document:

   a. Place the insertion point at the end of your document.
   b. Enter an encapsulated TeX field.

   c. In the entry area, type
      \printglossary
      \printindex
   The order of these commands determines the order in which the indices are printed.
   The `\printglossary` command indicates the author index; the `\printindex`
   command indicates the subject index. Change the order as necessary.

   d. Choose **OK**.

7. Compile your document to create the subject index:

   a. Save the document.

   b. On the Typeset toolbar, click the Typeset DVI Compile button   or, from the
     Typeset menu, choose **Compile**.

   c. Check **Generate an Index** and choose **OK**.
     Make sure the number of LaTeX passes is set to 2.

8. Run the MakeIndex program to create the author index:

   a. From the Windows **Start** menu, choose **Run**.

   b. Enter the command appropriate for your version of *SWP* or *SW* in the Open box,
     changing the name of the program directory as necessary. Where line breaks occur
     in these instructions, enter a space.

      • With Version 5.5, enter this command on a single line:
        c:\swp55\TCITeX\web2c\makeindex -o
        c:\swp55\docs*filename*.gls -s
        c:\swp55\TCITeX\TeX\LaTeX\contrib\nomencl\nomencl.ist
        c:\swp55\docs*filename*.glo

      • With Version 4.x or 5.0, enter this command on a single line:
        c:\swp50\TCITeX\web2c\makeindex -o
        c:\swp50\docs*filename*.gls -s
        c:\swp50\TCITeX\TeX\LaTeX\contrib\supported\nomencl\nomencl.ist
        c:\swp50\docs*filename*.glo

        • With an earlier version of the program, enter this command on a single line:
          c:\swp35\TCITeX\SWTools\bin\makeindx -o
          c:\swp35\docs*filename*.gls -s
          c:\swp35\TCITeX\TeX\LaTeX\contrib\supported\nomencl\nomencl.ist
          c:\swp35\docs*filename*.glo

   c. Choose **OK**.

9. Typeset compile the document file from outside the program.

   Note   If you compile using *SWP* or *SW,* the compiler won't find the .gls file
   and won't include the author list in the typeset document.

   a. From the *SWP* or *SW* submenu in the Windows **Programs** list, choose the
     TrueTeX Formatter.

   b. Select the file and choose **OK**.
     If your document contains a table of contents or cross-references, you many need
     to compile it two or three times.

Tailoring the Body of the Document

The typesetting specifications determine the appearance of division headings, text, lists, footnotes and other generated elements, and other parts of the body of your document. Using LaTeX packages and TeX commands, you can modify the typeset appearance of these various elements.

Changing the Appearance of Division Headings

The typesetting specifications for your document determine how the program treats the headings and numbers for chapters, sections, and other divisions. You may need to modify the specifications for all division headings or just for a few occurrences of a given division to achieve a different placement, numbering scheme, or naming scheme.

Repositioning Headings

The designers of most document shells carefully consider the placement of chapter, section, and other division headings. Nevertheless, you may need to change some or all of the heading placement specifications. With the commands available through the *sectsty* package (see page 154), you can change the location of a category of division headings, such as all chapter headings or all subsection headings. Note, however, that this process also removes the division number and therefore excludes the division from the table of contents. (See page 19 for information about adding the unnumbered division to the table of contents.) If your document was created with a Style Editor shell, use the Style Editor to reposition the headings.

▶ **To relocate all headings for a given division level**

1. Add the *sectsty* package to your document.

2. From the Typeset menu, choose **Preamble** and click the mouse in the entry area.

3. On a new line at the end of the preamble entries, type this command for each division heading level you want to move: ***divisionfont{x}**

   where ***divisionfont** reflects the heading you want to move (such as \\partfont, \\allsectionsfont, \\chapterfont, or \\sectionfont) and *x* is the command for the new heading location:

Command	Effect
centering	Centered heading
raggedleft	Set flush right with a ragged left margin
raggedright	Set flush left with a ragged right margin

4. Choose OK.

If you need to relocate only one heading instead of an entire category of headings, you can replace the heading with a TeX command. The process maintains the division number and includes the division in the table of contents. We don't recommend this process for shells with numbered chapter headings preceded by the word *Chapter.*

▶ **To relocate a single division heading**

1. Place the insertion point where you want the heading to appear and enter an encapsulated TₑX field.

2. In the entry area, type **{*location**division*{*Name*}}** where ***location*** is the location you want, ***division*** is the division level you want to move, and ***Name*** is the name of the heading as you want it to appear. Use **\centering**, **\raggedleft**, or **\raggedright** to define the location, as described above.

3. Choose OK.

4. Delete the original heading.

Adding and Removing Division Numbering

Occasionally, you may need to extend numbering to deeper levels of division headings than the document shell specifies. On the other hand, you may need to remove the number from all headings below a certain level or from an individual heading. (See page 19 for instructions about adding the unnumbered division to the table of contents.)

▶ **To extend or remove division numbering**

1. From the Typeset menu, choose Preamble and click the mouse in the entry area.

2. On a new line at the end of the preamble entries, type **\setcounter{secnumdepth}{*x*}** where *x* is the deepest heading level you want to number.

x	If division numbers are to extend only to
-1	Parts
0	Chapters
1	Sections
2	Subsections
3	Subsubsections
4	Subsubsubsections
5	Subsubsubsubsections

Remember that LATₑX uses *section* as level 1, regardless of the document class.

3. Choose OK.

▶ **To remove the number from an individual division heading**

- If you're using Version 4.0 or later,

  a. Place the insertion point at the beginning of the heading and choose Properties.
  b. In the Section Properties dialog box, check Unnumbered.

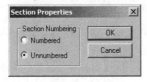

  c. Choose OK.

or

- If you're using an earlier version,

   a. Place the insertion point where you want the heading to appear.
   b. Enter an encapsulated TeX field.
   c. In the entry area, type *division**{*Name*} where *division* is the level of the heading and *Name* is the name of the division as you want it to appear.
   d. Choose OK.
   e. Delete the original heading.

Note that LaTeX ignores unnumbered divisions when it creates page headers. Thus, if you create an unnumbered appendix, the page headers on the appendix pages reflect the name of the previous division heading rather than the appendix.

Changing the Division Numbering Scheme

You may need to change the style of the numbers used to designate a certain division level. For example, you may want chapters to have uppercase roman numerals, sections to have capitalized alphabetic characters, and subsections to have arabic numbers. You can insert TeX commands in the preamble of your document so that your headings are numbered according to a particular scheme.

▶ **To change the numbering scheme for division headings**

1. From the Typeset menu, choose Preamble and click the mouse in the entry area.

2. At the end of the preamble entries, type **renewcommand**{*level*}{*scheme*{*counter*}} where *level* is the division level you want to renumber, such as thechapter or thesubsection; *scheme* is the numbering scheme, such as Roman or arabic (see page 10 for a list of numbering schemes); and *counter* is the counter for the division level, such as part or chapter.

3. Choose OK to return to your document.

To produce chapters with uppercase roman numerals, sections with capitalized alphabetic characters, and subsections with arabic numbers, use these commands:
renewcommand{**thesection**}{**Alph**{**section**}}
renewcommand{**thechapter**}{**Roman**{**chapter**}}
renewcommand{**thesubsection**}{**arabic**{**subsection**}}

Changing Automatic Division Numbering

You can begin division numbering in your document with a number other than 1 by adding a command to the document preamble.

▶ **To create division numbering that doesn't begin with 1**

1. From the Typeset menu, choose Preamble and click the mouse in the entry area.

2. On a new line at the end of the preamble entries, type **setcounter**{*name*}{*x*} where *name* is the division for which you want to modify the numbering, as shown in the following table, and *x* is one less than the starting number you want.

Division	*name*
Part	**part**
Chapter	**chapter**
Section	**section**
Subsection	**subsection**
Subsubsection	**subsubsection**
Subsubsubsection	**paragraph**
Subsubsubsubsection	**subparagraph**

3. Choose OK.

The command increments the division counter before it is first used by the document. As an illustration, if you want the first section in the document to carry the number 2, use the command \setcounter{section}{1} in the preamble.

Changing Automatic Division Names

Some typesetting specifications automatically give names, such as *Chapter* or *References,* to certain heading levels. If necessary, you can change the automatic names from, for example, *Chapter* to *Lesson* or from *References* to *Bibliography.* Making changes to the headings specifications can have wide-ranging effects, particularly if your document has a table of contents.

▶ **To change an automatically generated division name**

1. From the Typeset menu, choose Preamble and click the mouse in the entry area.

2. At the end of the preamble entries, add a new line and type

    \renewcommand{*name*}{*Newname*}

    where ***name*** is the title of the part of the document you want to change (see the list below) and ***Newname*** is the title you want.

3. Choose OK.

Document part	*name*	Document part	*name*
Preface	**prefacename**	Table	**tablename**
References	**refname**	Part	**partname**
Abstract	**abstractname**	encl	**enclname**
Bibliography	**bibname**	cc	**ccname**
Chapter	**chaptername**	To	**headtoname**
Appendix	**appendixname**	Page	**pagename**
Contents	**contentsname**	see	**seename**
List of Figures	**listfigurename**	see also	**alsoname**
List of Tables	**listtablename**	Proof	**proofname**
Index	**indexname**	Glossary	**glossaryname**
Figure	**figurename**		

Thus, you can use the command `\renewcommand{\contentsname}{Table of Contents}` to change the title *Contents* to *Table of Contents*. Similarly, to change *Chapter* to *Lesson*, use `\renewcommand{\chaptername}{Lesson}`; to change *References* to *Bibliography*, use `\renewcommand{\refname}{Bibliography}`. Other titles work the same way. Note that the *babel* package works successfully with redefined titles. If you're using *babel*, the commands must be placed in the body of the document inside a TEX field.

Each document class treats the bibliography title differently. To save work, you can use the *chbibref* package (see page 108) to change the title for three LATEX document classes: article, book, and report.

▶ **To change the title of the bibliography for all document classes**

1. If you're using Version 3.51 or lower, obtain and install the *chbibref* package.

   The package is distributed with Versions 4.0 and later.

2. Add the *chbibref* package to your document.

3. From the Typeset menu, choose Preamble and click the mouse in the entry area.

4. At the end of the preamble, add a new line and type **\setbibref{*name*}** where ***name*** is the bibliography title you want.

   Note   If you're using *babel*, place the command in the body of the document inside a TEX field.

5. Choose OK.

Changing the Appearance of Paragraphs

In documents based on standard LATEX typesetting specifications, the paragraphs that immediately follow section headings are not indented, but subsequent paragraphs are indented, as in this manual.

You can remove indention for all paragraphs in your document by modifying the document preamble. However, because the beginning of unindented paragraphs is somewhat harder to see, you may also want to increase the spacing between paragraphs.

Removing Indention from Paragraphs
LATEX determines the paragraph indention by the length `\parindent`. You can set this length to zero in the document preamble.

▶ **To remove indention for all paragraphs in the document**

1. From the Typeset menu, choose Preamble and click the mouse in the entry area.

2. At the end of the preamble, add a new line and type **\setlength{\parindent}{0in}**.

3. Choose OK.

4. Typeset preview the document to make sure the indention is correct.

Changing Paragraph Justification

Although most LaTeX typesetting specifications default to full justification for text in paragraphs, you can create text that isn't fully justified for all or part of the body of your document.

You can change the justification of the entire body of your document with declarations in the document preamble. Three declarations correspond to alternate justification settings: \centering, \raggedright, and \raggedleft. Most typesetting specifications typeset the entire body of the document as flush left if you add the \raggedright declaration to the preamble and, similarly, typeset the entire body of the document as flush right if you add the \raggedleft declaration.

▶ **To modify the paragraph justification for the entire body of a document**

1. From the Typeset menu, choose Preamble and click the mouse in the entry area.

2. On a new line, type the justification declaration you need: **centering**, **raggedright**, or **raggedleft**.

3. Choose OK to return to your document.

You can change the justification of a portion of the document with LaTeX environments in encapsulated TeX fields in the body of your document. Three environments correspond to alternate justification settings: center, flushleft, and flushright. The center environment is available with the Centered tag, available from the Section/Body Tag popup list; apply the tag to the paragraph you want to center. With Version 5.0 Build 2606 and later, you can turn on the Flush Left and Flush Right tags from the Tag Appearance dialog box, if they don't already appear in the Section/Body Tag list for your document.

▶ **To modify paragraph justification for a portion of a document**

1. Place the insertion point at the beginning of the text for which you want to change the justification, and enter an encapsulated TeX field.

2. In the entry area, enter **begin{flushleft}** or **begin{flushright}** and choose OK.

3. Place the insertion point at the end of the text for which you want to change the justification, and enter an encapsulated TeX field.

4. In the entry area, enter **end{flushleft}** or **end{flushright}** and choose OK.

   Note   With Version 5.0 Build 2606 and later, don't encapsulate these TeX fields. The screen appearance will be appropriate the next time you open your document.

Changing the Spacing Between Paragraphs

LaTeX defines the space between paragraphs by the length \parskip. The default space is 0pt plus 1pt, which means the spacing between lines can increase by as much as 1pt, depending on how LaTeX fits the text vertically on the page. The increase translates to about $\frac{1}{10}$ to $\frac{1}{12}$ of the height of a line of text, depending on the base font point size.

If you have removed paragraph indention, a reasonable space between paragraphs is about the height of a line of text, with additional stretch or shrinkage to allow LATEX to fit text on a page the best way possible. Therefore, if the base font size is 10pt, you might use a \parskip value of 10pt plus 1pt minus 1pt.

▶ **To modify spacing between paragraphs**

1. From the Typeset menu, choose Preamble.

2. Click the mouse in the entry area and place the insertion point on a new line at the end of the entries.

3. Type **\setlength{\parskip}{*10*pt plus *1*pt minus *1*pt}**, adjusting the values according to your needs.

4. Choose OK.

5. Typeset preview the document to make sure the spacing is correct.

Changing the Appearance of Numbered Lists

The program can accept a wide variety of numbering schemes for all four levels of list items, which are designated in TEX as *theenumi* through *theenumiv.* You can change the default scheme for your entire document by entering TEX commands in the preamble or change the scheme for a portion of the document by entering TEX commands in the body of the document. You can also use the *points* or *newpnts* package (see page 146) to begin the list at a number other than one.

▶ **To change the list numbering scheme for the entire document**

1. From the Typeset menu, choose Preamble and click the mouse in the entry area.

2. On a new line at the end of the entries, type this command for each list level you want to renumber: **\renewcommand{*level*}{*style*{*level_counter*}}**

   where **level** is the numbered list level you want to renumber (theenumi, theenumii, theenumiii, or theenumiv), **style** is the numbering style you want (Roman, roman, Alph, alph, or arabic), and **level_counter** is the counter for the list level (enumi, enumii, enumiii, or enumiv).

3. Choose OK.

   For example, many people want list levels numbered as a standard outline: I, A, 1, a. You can achieve an outline numbering scheme by entering these commands:

   \renewcommand{\theenumi}{\Roman{enumi}}
   \renewcommand{\theenumii}{\Alph{enumii}}
   \renewcommand{\theenumiii}{\arabic{enumiii}}
   \renewcommand{\theenumiv}{\alph{enumiv}}

▶ **To change the list numbering scheme for a portion of the document**

1. Begin the new numbering scheme:

   a. Place the insertion point where you want the numbering scheme to begin.

   b. Enter an encapsulated TEX field.

   c. In the entry area, type this command for each list level you want to renumber:
      \renewcommand{*level*}{*style*{*level_counter*}}
      where *level* is the numbered list level you want to renumber (theenumi, theenumii, theenumiii, or theenumiv), *style* is the numbering style you want (Roman, roman, Alph, alph, or arabic), and *level_counter* is the counter for the list level (enumi, enumii, enumiii, or enumiv).

   d. Choose OK.

2. Revert to the original numbering scheme:

   a. Place the insertion point where you want the numbering scheme to revert to the default.

   b. Enter an encapsulated TEX field.

   c. In the entry area, type this command for each list level you renumbered:
      \renewcommand{*level*}{*style*{*level_counter*}}
      and designate the original style of the counter.

   d. Choose OK.

▶ **To create a numbered list that doesn't begin with 1**

1. Add the *points* or *newpnts* package to your document.

2. Place the insertion point where you want the numbered list to begin.

3. Enter an encapsulated TEX field.

4. In the entry area, type **\setcounter{enumi}{*x*}\RESUME**

   where *x* is a value one less than the starting number you want.

   In other words, if you want your list to begin at 10, use the command

   \setcounter{enumi}{9}\RESUME. Note that the command is case-sensitive.

5. Choose OK.

You can also use the *points* or *newpnts* package to create a numbered list interrupted by an unnumbered paragraph.

▶ **To create an interrupted numbered list**

1. Add the *points* or *newpnts* package to your document.

2. Place the insertion point where you want the numbered list to begin.

3. Enter an encapsulated TEX field.

4. In the entry area, type **\setcounter{enumi}{*x*}\RESUME** where *x* is a value one less than the starting number you want.

   The command is case sensitive. If you want your list to begin at 1, use the command **\setcounter{enumi}{0}\RESUME**.

5. Choose OK.

6. Begin entering the numbered list.

7. Enter the unnumbered paragraph that interrupts the list.

8. At the end of the unnumbered paragraph, enter an encapsulated TeX field.

9. In the entry area, type **\RESUME** and choose OK.

10. Complete the list.

Customizing the Appearance of Citations

By default, standard LaTeX shells place square brackets around citations. You may want to remove the brackets, especially if you add labels for items in a manual bibliography, so that the label appears as a natural part of your text. Suppose the citation in this sentence

As shown by cite: key, the methodology was inadequate to....

refers to a bibliography item for which the label is *Pearson 2004*, and you want the typeset text to read

As shown by Pearson 2004, the methodology was inadequate to....

When you typeset the document, the label appears as the citation, but inside square brackets:

As shown by [Pearson 2004], the methodology was inadequate to....

You can remove the brackets by modifying the typesetting specifications or by using the *cite* package (see page 110).

▶ **To omit brackets around all inline citations**

1. Create your document using a standard LaTeX shell.

2. Remove the brackets from the typesetting specification for citations:

   a. From the Typeset menu, choose Preamble and click the mouse in the entry area.
   b. Add these lines to the preamble:

      \makeatletter
      \renewcommand{\@cite}[1]{#1}
      \makeatother

   c. Choose OK.

3. Create a manual bibliography with labels for each item and create the citations in the text.

4. Typeset your document.

▶ **To use the cite package to omit brackets around inline citations**

1. Add the *cite* package to your document.

2. From the Typeset menu, choose Preamble and click the mouse in the entry area.

3. On a new line at the end of the preamble, type **\let\cite=\citen** and choose OK.

4. Create a manual bibliography with labels for each item and create the citations in the text.

5. Typeset your document.

Underlining and Striking Through Content

Although the program has no underlining command in the usual sense, you can add emphasis to your content with simple underlines if you use the *ulem* package. The package temporarily changes the behavior of the \em and \emph commands to support single and double underlining, wavy underlining, a single line drawn through text, and text marked over with slashes, as shown on page 171.

▶ **To add simple underlines**

1. Add the *ulem* package to your document.

2. Select the information you want to underline and apply the Emphasize tag to it.

▶ **To add varied underlines and strikethroughs**

1. Add the *ulem* package to your document.

2. Place the insertion point where you want the underline or strikethrough to begin.

3. Enter an encapsulated TEX field.

4. In the entry area, type **\command{text}** where **command** is one of the following:

Command	Effect
\uline	Single underline
\uuline	Double underline
\uwave	Wavy underline
\sout	Line through text
\xout	Text marked over with slashes

and **text** is the information you want emphasized.

5. Choose OK.

Stopping Hyphenation

By default, the typesetting specifications for most shells specify hyphenation. With the *hyphenat* package (see page 130), you can suppress all hyphenation.

▶ **To suppress hyphenation in a document**

1. Add the *hyphenat* package to your document.

2. On the Typeset toolbar, click the Options and Packages button ▦ or, from the Typeset menu, choose Options and Packages.

3. Choose the Package Options tab.

4. In the Packages in Use box, select hyphenat and then choose Modify.

5. In the Category box, choose Hyphenation.

6. In the Options box, select None.

7. Choose OK twice to return to your document.

Note that because the *None* option prevents all hyphenation, you may get LATEX messages about bad line breaks and overfull boxes when you typeset compile your document. See Chapter 4 "Troubleshooting."

Working with Footnotes

Although numbered footnotes are usually the default, the program can designate footnotes with symbols and can typeset both footnotes and endnotes for most documents.

Using Symbols to Designate Footnotes

You can use standard footnote symbols instead of numbers to designate footnotes by modifying the preamble and then indicating the symbol you want when you enter the footnote.

▶ **To designate footnotes with symbols**

1. Open your document.

2. Modify the preamble:

   a. From the Typeset menu, choose Preamble and click the mouse in the entry area.
   b. Type **\renewcommand{\thefootnote}{\fnsymbol{footnote}}**.
   c. Choose OK.

3. Insert the footnote:

   a. Place the insertion point where you want the footnote.
   b. From the Insert menu, choose Note.
   c. In the Type of Note box, select footnote.
   d. Type the text of your footnote.

4. Specify the symbol you want:

    a. Choose Options.

    b. Check Override Automatic Number.

    c. In the Footnote Number box, enter the number for the symbol you want:

Number	Symbol
1	asterisk *
2	dagger †
3	double dagger ‡
4	section symbol §
5	paragraph ¶
6	parallel lines ‖
7	two asterisks **
8	two daggers ††
9	two double daggers ‡‡

    d. Choose OK twice to return to your document.

Changing Footnotes to Endnotes

You can gather footnotes in a list at the end of your document by adding the *endnotes* package (see page 117). Instead of replacing the list of footnotes generated by LaTeX, the package stores the endnote list in a separate file with the extension .ent and deletes the list after you typeset your document.

▶ **To typeset existing footnotes as endnotes**

1. Add the *endnotes* package to your document.

2. From the Typeset menu, choose Preamble and click the mouse in the entry area.

3. At the end of the preamble entries, add a new line and type
   \renewcommand{\footnote}{\endnote}

4. Choose OK.

5. Place the endnotes list in your document:

    a. Place the insertion point at the end of your document.

    b. Enter an encapsulated TeX field.

    c. If you want the endnotes to begin on a new page, type **\newpage** and press ENTER.

    d. Type **\begingroup** and press ENTER.

    e. If you want the endnotes to be set in a normal size font instead of a smaller font, type **\renewcommand{\enotesize}{\normalsize}** and press ENTER.

    f. If you want to list the endnotes in the table of contents, type the command **\addcontentsline{toc}{section}{Notes}** and press ENTER.

    g. Type **\theendnotes** and press ENTER.

    h. Type **\endgroup** and choose OK.

Tailoring Mathematics

Together with LaTeX, *SWP* and *SW* provide for detailed formatting of mathematics. The document shells provided with the program have been designed to produce typeset mathematics that meet the formatting requirements of many different publishers. Nevertheless, your document may require some modifications.

Changing Theorem Numbering

Theorems and theorem-like statements may be numbered consecutively throughout your document (Theorem 1, Corollary 2, Lemma 3, Theorem 4, ...) or they may be numbered independently (Theorem 1, Corollary 1, Lemma 1, Theorem 2, ...). Usually, the numbering scheme is established with \newtheorem statements. The basic syntax for the \newtheorem command has two forms. The first is

$$\text{\textbackslash newtheorem\{\textbf{\textit{counter}}\} [\textbf{\textit{counter\_basis}}] \{\textbf{\textit{counter\_title}}\}}$$

where ***counter*** is the environment to be counted (such as theorem, lemma, or corollary), ***counter_basis*** is the source of the count, and ***counter_title*** is the label for the environment. The second form is

$$\text{\textbackslash newtheorem\{\textbf{\textit{counter}}\}\{\textbf{\textit{counter\_title}}\}[\textbf{\textit{numbered\_within}}]}$$

where ***counter*** is the environment to be counted (such as theorem, corollary, or lemma), ***counter_title*** is the label for the environment, and ***numbered_within*** is the name of an already defined counter, usually some divisional unit, such as part, chapter, or section. The use of this form is described on page 39.

In most documents with theorem-like environments, the environments are numbered on the basis of the theorem environment. Therefore, in the preamble of the document, you might see a series of statements similar to these, which use the first syntax explained above:

```
\newtheorem{theorem}{Theorem}
\newtheorem{algorithm}[theorem]{Algorithm}
\newtheorem{axiom}[theorem]{Axiom}
\newtheorem{condition}[theorem]{Condition}
\newtheorem{conjecture}[theorem]{Conjecture}
\newtheorem{corollary}[theorem]{Corollary}
    ⋮
```

The first statement establishes independent numbering for theorems, then numbers all other theorem-like environments on the basis of the theorem counter. Thus, these statements produce a single numbering sequence for all types of theorem environments and might yield a numbering sequence such as this: Theorem 1, Theorem 2, Conjecture 3, Theorem 4, Conjecture 5, ...

Usually, the \newtheorem statements appear in the document preamble. If so, you can modify the preamble to change the numbering scheme as necessary. However, sometimes the \newtheorem statements are included in the typesetting specifications for the shell. In this case, don't attempt to change the specifications. If you need a different numbering scheme for theorem environments, choose a different shell for your document. The instructions that follow pertain only to those documents for which theorem numbering schemes are defined in \newtheorem statements in the document preamble.

Creating Independent Numbering for Theorem Environments

If you have a single numbering sequence for all types of theorem environments but you need to number them independently, you can change the numbering sequence by modifying \newtheorem commands in the document preamble. By eliminating or varying the *counter_basis* argument in the command, you can create a large variety of numbering schemes for theorem environments.

▶ **To number a theorem environment independently**

1. From the Typeset menu, choose Preamble and click the mouse in the entry area.

2. Scroll through the commands to find the \newtheorem statement for the environment whose numbering you want to change.

3. Remove the [counter_basis] argument from the command.

4. Choose OK.

Thus, these preamble statements, from which the [counter_basis] argument has been removed:

```
\newtheorem{theorem}{Theorem}
\newtheorem{algorithm}{Algorithm}
\newtheorem{axiom}{Axiom}
\newtheorem{condition}{Condition}
\newtheorem{conjecture}{Conjecture}
\newtheorem{corollary}{Corollary}
```

$$\vdots$$

cause the theorem-like environments to be numbered independently. Your document might contain a series like this: Theorem 1, Theorem 2, Conjecture 1, Theorem 3, Conjecture 2, ...

Resetting Theorem Numbering For New Divisions

Instead of numbering theorem-like statements consecutively throughout your document, you may want to reset the numbering to 1 for each new document division. You can achieve this effect with an alternate form of the \newtheorem command that bases the numbering on a division counter instead of a theorem environment counter. The command syntax is

$$\newtheorem\{\textit{counter}\}\{\textit{counter\_title}\}[\textit{numbered\_within}]$$

where *counter* is the environment to be counted (such as theorem, corollary, or lemma), *counter_title* is the label for the environment, and *numbered_within* is the name of an already defined counter, usually some divisional unit, such as part, chapter, or section. The *numbered_within* argument determines when the counter is reset to 1 for this particular theorem environment. For example, the command

```
\newtheorem{conjecture}{Conjecture}[chapter]
```

causes each new conjecture in your document to be labeled *Conjecture* and to be numbered in sequence by chapter. You might see numbers such as Conjecture 1.1, Conjecture 1.2, Conjecture 2.1, ..., in which the first digit is the chapter number and the second digit is the number of the conjecture within the chapter.

▶ **To reset the counter for a theorem environment**

1. From the Typeset menu, choose Preamble and click the mouse in the entry area.

2. Scroll through the commands to find the \newtheorem statement for the environment whose numbering you want to reset.

3. Remove the *[counter_basis]* argument from the command.

4. Add the *[numbered_within]* argument to the end of the command.

5. Choose OK.

Thus, if you want to reset the numbering for theorem-like environments at the beginning of every chapter, your preamble might contain these lines:

```
\newtheorem{theorem}{Theorem}[chapter]
\newtheorem{algorithm}{Algorithm}[chapter]
\newtheorem{axiom}{Axiom}[chapter]
\newtheorem{condition}{Condition}[chapter]
\newtheorem{conjecture}{Conjecture}[chapter]
\newtheorem{corollary}{Corollary}[chapter]
        ⋮
```

and you might see a numbering series like this: Theorem 1.1, Theorem 1.2, Conjecture 1.1, Theorem 2.1, Conjecture 2.1, Theorem 2.2, ...

Changing Theorem Formatting

Many typesetting specifications set the content of theorem environments in italics, but you can override the specifications and use upright fonts for theorems instead.

▶ **To set theorems in upright fonts**

1. Add the *theorem* package to your document.

2. From the Typeset menu, choose Preamble and click the mouse in the entry area.

3. Place the insertion point on a new line at the beginning of the preamble, before any \newtheorem statements.

4. If you want to change the font that LaTeX uses for the header of the theorem environment, type **\theoremheaderfont{*font*}** where *font* is the font family you want LaTeX to use. Because \theoremheaderfont is a global setting, it changes the header

font for all theorem-like environments in the document. The command should be used only once. Values for *font* can be combined. Possible values for *font* are:

font	Effect	*font*	Effect
\mdseries	Medium Series	\upshape	Upright Shape
\bfseries	Boldface Series	\itshape	Italic Shape
\rmfamily	Roman Family	\slshape	Slanted Shape
\sffamily	Sans Serif Family	\scshape	Small Caps Shape
\ttfamily	Typewriter Family	\normalfont	Normal (document main text font)

Not all combinations make sense and LaTeX compensates by placing a warning in the `.log` file and substituting a similar font.

5. If you want to change the font that LaTeX uses for the body of the theorem environment, type **\theorembodyfont{*font*}** where *font* is the font family you want LaTeX to use.

   Use the command **\theorembodyfont{\upshape}** to use upright text in the body of a theorem.

   The font used for the body of a theorem-like environment can be restricted to a single environment or a group of environments by using curly braces to enclose the environments.

6. Choose OK.

Note   These instructions pertain only to those documents for which theorem numbering schemes are defined in the document preamble.

Formatting Mathematical Expressions

Occasionally, long mathematical expressions create line-breaking problems. Instead of surrounding an expression with a pair of expanding brackets, you may be able to create more pleasing line breaks by placing TeX brackets at either end of the expression. The brackets exist as independent objects; therefore, the program doesn't consider the entire expression to be a single unbreakable unit as it does when you use expanding brackets.

You enter the brackets with bracket commands in TeX fields at each end of the expression. The command has this syntax:

$$\backslash SizeLocationSymbol\backslash$$

The *Size* element determines the height of the brackets. The choices are

- **ordinary**—the size of the ordinary bracket that you get when you press the bracket key on the keyboard.
- **big**—just enough taller than ordinary so that the difference can be perceived.
- **Big**—50% taller than big.

- **bigg**—twice as tall as big.

- **Bigg**—2.5 times as tall as big.

Since the brackets do not expand automatically, be sure to select a size that adequately contains the entire expression.

The *Location* element determines how TEX handles the spacing before and after the brackets. Telling the program whether the bracket occurs at the left or right end of an expression is important. The available choices are

- **l**—left bracket.

- **r**—right bracket.

The *Symbol* element define the kind of bracket you want. They must all be entered as TEX macros

Symbol	Name	Symbol	Name
(	left parenthesis	\rangle	right angle bracket
)	right parenthesis	/	slash
[or \lbrack	left bracket	\backslash	reverse slash
] or \rbrack	right bracket	| or \vert	vertical bar
\{ or \lbrace	left curly brace	\\| or \Vert	double vertical bar
\} or \rbrace	right curly brace	\uparrow	upward arrow
\lfloor	left floor bracket	\Uparrow	double upward arrow
\rfloor	right floor bracket	\downarrow	downward arrow
\lceil	left ceiling bracket	\Downarrow	double downward arrow
\rceil	right ceiling bracket	\updownarrow	up-and-down arrow
\langle	left angle bracket	\Updownarrow	double up-and-down arrow

You don't have to use a left bracket symbol at the left end of the expression or a right bracket symbol at the right end.

Thus, the command `\Bigl(` yields $\Big($, and the command `\Biggr]` creates $\Bigg]$, a bracket over twice the size of the] symbol on the keyboard.

▶ **To use TEX brackets around an expression**

1. Remove the expanding brackets from around the expression.

2. Place the insertion point at the beginning of the expression with the insertion point in mathematics.

3. Enter a TEX field.

4. In the entry area, enter the command for the left bracket and choose **OK**.

5. Place the insertion point at the end of the expression with the insertion point in mathematics.

6. Enter a TEX field.

7. In the entry area, enter the command for the right bracket and choose **OK**.

8. Typeset your document and examine the line breaks.

Tailoring Graphics and Tables

The layout of graphics and tables depends on the typesetting specifications for your document. By using LaTeX packages and commands in your document, you may be able to format captions, vary the layout, wrap text around graphics and tables, resolve problems with certain kinds of graphics, and manage objects that are too wide for the page. Graphics and tables that float sometimes require special attention, particularly if they seem to prevent LaTeX from compiling your document. TeX commands in the body of your document can force LaTeX to process all floating objects so the document can compile successfully.

Formatting Captions

If your document contains graphics and tables, you may want special formatting for the captions or titles, especially if they contain mathematics. With the *caption* package (see page 107), you can change the font attributes of the caption text for floating objects. If you let the graphics and tables float, you can also use the *caption* package to center a multiline caption or title. (Captions and titles contained on a single line are automatically centered.) You can insert a caption for multiple figures with the *subfig* package, as explained on page 161, or using a floating frame.

LaTeX defines the space above and below the captions of floating objects (both graphics and tables) with the macros \abovecaptionskip and \belowcaptionskip. Many typesetting specifications use these macros, including sebase.cls, which defines each value as 10 pt. Although the Style Editor doesn't provide a method for changing these values, you can alter the space between floating objects and their captions by adding an external macro that is associated with the typesetting specifications for your document. Alternatively, you can change the spacing for all floating objects in a document by modifying the document preamble, and you can change the spacing for an individual floating object by placing TeX commands before and after the object.

To avoid typesetting difficulties, you must use correct LaTeX commands to enter any mathematics appearing in the caption for a floating object, such as this:

Table 1: According to the identity $\sin^2\theta + \cos^2\theta = 1$

θ	$\sin^2\theta$	$\cos^2\theta$
0	0	1
$\frac{\pi}{4}$	$\frac{1}{2}$	$\frac{1}{2}$
$\frac{\pi}{3}$	$\frac{3}{4}$	$\frac{1}{4}$

The mathematics in the caption appears correctly because it is surrounded with LaTeX \protect statements. You can adapt the process described in the instructions that follow to include mathematics in any TeX field.

▶ **To include mathematics in the caption for a floating table**

1. Create the table:

   a. Place the insertion point where you want the table to appear and enter the Table - (4x3, floating) fragment, which looks like this in your document:

Head	Head	Head
entry	entry	entry
entry	entry	entry
entry	entry	entry

   [B] ... caption marker: TableKey [E]

   b. Edit the number of rows and columns as necessary and replace the predefined cell contents with the information you want.

   c. Save your document.

2. Create the caption:

   a. Open a new document using the Blank - Standard LaTeX Article shell.

   b. In a new paragraph, enter the text of the table caption.

   c. Apply the Section tag to the paragraph.

   d. Save the document using the same file type as for the document containing the table.

   e. Using an ASCII editor, open the new document and scroll to the caption.
   The caption will begin with \section, as in this example:

   ```
   \section{According to the rule $\sin ^{2}\protect\theta
       +\cos ^{2}\protect\theta =1$}
   ```

   f. Change the word *section* to **caption**.

   g. Select both lines of the caption and copy them to the clipboard.

3. Place the caption in the table:

   a. Return to the document containing the table.

   b. Place the insertion point to the right of the Caption gray box and choose **Properties**.

   c. Select the entire contents of the field.

   d. Paste the contents of the clipboard into the field, and choose **OK**.

4. Save and typeset your document.

▶ **To change the caption font attributes for a floating object**

1. Add the *caption* package to your document.

2. On the Typeset toolbar, click the Options and Packages button ⊞ or, from the Typeset menu, choose **Options and Packages**.

3. Choose the Package Options tab.

4. In the Packages in Use box, select caption, and then choose Modify.

5. If you're using Version 5.5,

a. In the Category box, choose the font attribute category you want to change:

Category	Controls font attributes for
Caption and label font attributes	Both caption and label of floating object
Caption font attributes	Caption of floating object
Label font attributes	Label of floating object

b. In the Options box, select the font size you want and choose OK.

or

If you're using an earlier version,

a. In the Category box, choose Caption font size.
b. In the Options box, select the font size you want.
c. In the Category box, choose Caption label attribute.
d. In the Options box, choose the font attribute you want.
e. Choose OK to close the dialog boxes and return to your document.

▶ **To center a multiline caption for a floating object**

1. Add the *caption* package to your document.

2. On the Typeset toolbar, click the Options and Packages button ▦ or, from the Typeset menu, choose Options and Packages.

3. Choose the Package Options tab.

4. In the Packages in Use box, select caption and then choose Modify.

5. In the Category box, choose Caption justification.

If you're using Version 3.5, choose Alignment.

6. In the Options box, choose Centered.

7. Choose OK to close the dialog boxes and return to your document.

▶ **To apply a single caption to multiple figures**

1. Enter a floating frame:

a. Place the insertion point where you want the figures to appear.
b. Insert the Table - (4x3, floating) fragment.
c. Replace the table in the fragment with a new table that contains a cell for each figure to which you want to apply the caption.

2. Insert the figures:

   a. Place a figure in each cell of the new table.

   b. For each figure:

      i Select the figure and choose **Properties**.

      ii Select the **Layout** tab.

      iii In the **Placement** section, choose **In Line**.

      iv Choose **OK**.

3. Create the caption:

   a. Select the gray box marked **caption**.

   b. In **TeX Field** dialog box, replace the words `Table Caption` with the caption you want all the figures to share.

   c. Choose **OK**.

4. If you want the figures to be labeled as *Figure x* instead of *Table x,*

   a. Select the gray button labeled B and choose **Properties**.

   b. Change the contents of the TₑX field from `\begin{table}[tbp] \centering` to **\begin{figure}[tbp] \centering**.

   c. Choose **OK**.

   d. Select the gray button labeled E and choose **Properties**.

   e. Change the contents of the TₑX field from `\end{table}` to **\end{figure}**.

   f. Choose **OK**.

5. If you want individual captions in addition to the single caption created in step 3, for each figure,

   a. Select the figure and choose **Properties** and select the **Labeling** tab.

   b. In the **Caption Text** box, enter the caption for the selected figure.

   c. Choose **OK**.

You may need to add space or additional table cells before or after the caption to achieve the typeset appearance you want.

▶ **To change the caption spacing for all floating objects in a document**

1. Open your document.

2. From the **Typeset** menu, choose **Preamble** and click the mouse in the entry area.

3. Enter these lines:

\setlength{\abovecaptionskip}{0pt}

\setlength{\belowcaptionskip}{0pt}

4. Choose **OK**.

You may need to experiment with the values in the commands to achieve the spacing you want.

▶ **To change the caption spacing for an individual floating object**

1. Place the insertion point at the end of the line before the floating object and press ENTER.

2. Enter a TEX field.

3. In the entry area, type

   \setlength{\abovecaptionskip}{0pt}

   \setlength{\belowcaptionskip}{0pt}

4. Choose OK.

   You may need to experiment with the values in the commands to achieve the spacing you want.

5. To restore the default values, place the insertion point on the line after the floating object and press ENTER.

6. Enter a TEX field.

7. In the entry area, type

   \setlength{\abovecaptionskip}{10pt}

   \setlength{\belowcaptionskip}{10pt}

8. Choose OK.

Wrapping Text Around Graphics and Tables

Wrapping text around graphics and tables adds interest to the appearance of a document. You can wrap text around objects at the side of the page with the *wrapfig* package. The package creates an artificial floating environment, so the graphics and tables can carry captions that appear in the text and the list of

Pi

graphics. Suppose you want to wrap text around a graphic with a caption, as we do here. We have placed the graphic on the inside edge of the page, with no overhang into the margin. We've wrapped four lines of text around the graphic, allowing room for both the graphic and the caption. To create this effect, we followed the instructions on the next page, using this command in an encapsulated TEX field to define the placement: `\begin{wrapfigure}[4]{i}[0pt]{0pt}`.

In this paragraph, we've again used the *wrapfig* package to place a small table on the outside edge of the page, this time with an overhang of about half an inch into the margin. We've wrapped five lines around the table and have omitted both a table title and the

Choose	To
Typeset/Print	Print with LATEX
File/Print	Print without LATEX

space for one. We used this command in an encapsulated TEX field to define the placement: `\begin{wraptable}[5]{o}[35pt]{0pt}`.

Another package, *picins* (see page 144), provides precise control over the placement of inline graphics, but doesn't support inline tables.

▶ **To wrap text around a floating object**

1. Add the *wrapfig* package to your document.

2. Place the insertion point where you want to insert the floating object.

3. Begin the wrapfigure or wraptable environment:

   a. Enter an encapsulated TeX field and in the entry area, type
   \begin{wrapfigure}[*w*]{*x*}[*y*]{*z*} or **\begin{wraptable}**[*w*]{*x*}[*y*]{*z*}
   where

   > *w* is the number of vertical lines to be narrowed to accommodate the graphic or table (optional).

   > *x* is the placement of the graphic or table (required). Uppercase indicates *float;* lowercase indicates *exactly here*:

Position	Effect
r or R	Right side of text
l or L	Left side of text
i or I	Inside edge, near the binding (two-sided documents)
o or O	Outside edge, away from the binding (two-sided documents)

   > *y* is the amount of overhang—the distance the graphic or table should extend into the margin (optional).

   > *z* is the width of the graphic or table (required). If you specify a width of zero (0pt), the package uses the actual width of the graphic or table to determine the wrapping width.

   b. Choose OK.

4. Insert the inline object.

5. If you want the object to have a caption or title,

   a. Enter an encapsulated TeX field.
   b. In the entry area, type **\caption{***text***}** where ***text*** is the caption or title you want, and choose OK.

6. End the wrapfigure or wraptable environment:

   a. Enter an encapsulated TeX field.
   b. In the entry area, type **\end{wrapfigure}** or **\end{wraptable}**, and choose OK.

If your document combines both objects wrapped around text and objects that float, LaTeX may not sequence both kinds of objects correctly, although the graphic or table numbers will be correct. You may be able to correct the situation by adding the *float* package and revising each regular floating object—but not the wrapfigure or wraptable objects—to specify the Here placement option. See page 123 for more information about the *float* package.

Managing EPS Graphics in DVI Files

Documents containing Encapsulated PostScript (EPS) graphics can appear incorrectly typeset in DVI files because the PostScript filter supplied with the program occasionally misrenders the graphics. Letters that appear in the graphics may be displaced, or the appearance of the graphic may be incorrect. You can bypass the problem using the *graphicx* package. This problem doesn't occur with typeset PDF files.

The *graphicx* package (see page 126) has options for several different typeset output drivers. When the driver option is unchanged, LaTeX typesets your document using the default driver for the current LaTeX installation. For *SWP* and *SW* installations, the default driver is tcidvi, which uses the supplied graphics filter. Thus, the graphics can be misrendered. However, if you actively choose the dvips driver option, which is the default driver for typical LaTeX installations, LaTeX uses the native PostScript capabilities for the current display device. Thus, when you typeset, the graphic appears on the TrueTEX Previewer screen as a box containing the path name of the EPS file, but it appears in print correctly using the PostScript interpreter in the printer.

▶ **To bypass difficulties with EPS graphics in DVI files**

1. Add the *graphicx* package to your document.

2. Save the document as a Portable LaTeX file.

3. On the Typeset toolbar, click ▣ or, from the **Typeset** menu, choose **Options and Packages**.

4. Choose the **Package Options** tab.

5. In the **Packages in Use** box, select **graphicx**, and then choose **Modify**.

6. In the **Options** box, select **dvips**.

7. Choose **OK** to close the dialog boxes and return to your document.

If your document is a Style Editor document or a LaTeX 2.09 document, it can't be saved as a Portable LaTeX file. However, you can import the contents of your document into a new document, modified as described above, and successfully bypass the EPS difficulty.

Formatting Tables

Although the typesetting specifications automatically create space between the rows of tables in your documents, you can change the distance between rows for a single table, a group of tables, or all tables in the document.

▶ **To change the distance between rows for a single table**

1. Place the insertion point immediately before the table.

2. Insert a TEX field.

3. In the TeX Field window, enter **\renewcommand{\arraystretch}{*x*}** where *x* is the factor by which you want to multiply the default distance between the rows.

   For example, the command `\renewcommand{\arraystretch}{1.5}` will increase the distance between the rows by 50%.

4. Choose OK.

5. Place the insertion point immediately after the table and insert another TEX field.

6. In the TeX Field window, enter **\renewcommand{\arraystretch}{1}** to return to the default.

7. Choose OK.

You can apply the spacing factor to several subsequent tables by placing the first TEX field before the first table in the series and the second one after the last table in the series.

▶ **To change the distance between table rows for the entire document**

1. From the Typeset menu, choose Preamble and click the mouse in the entry area.

2. In the entry area, enter **\renewcommand{\arraystretch}{*x*}** where *x* is the factor by which you want to multiply the default distance between the rows for all tables in the document.

3. Choose OK.

Creating Landscaped Objects

If a table is too wide for portrait orientation, you can place it on a landscaped page using the *portland* package as described on page 14. Remember that you may need to change the printer settings to print landscape pages properly. You may also need to print any landscaped pages in a separate printing run.

Alternatively, you can orient pages differently with one of the packages, such as *lscape* (page 133) or *rotating* (page 151), that rotate text. Note that packages that use rotation aren't compatible with the TrueTEX Previewer provided with *SWP* and *SW*. Therefore, to produce a DVI file that uses one of these packages, you must use a DVI previewer and print driver that also support text rotation. PDF viewers do support rotation, so you can successfully use the packages to rotate text in typeset PDF files.

The *rotating* package implements several environments within which you can rotate graphics or tables by an arbitrary number of degrees. You enter the environments as commands in encapsulated TEX fields, one to begin and another to end the environment. The graphic or table to be rotated sits between the two.

▶ **To rotate an inline graphic or table**

1. Add the *rotating* package to your document.

2. Place the insertion point where you want the rotation to begin and begin the rotation environment:

a. Enter an encapsulated TₑX field.

b. In the entry area, type **begin**{*environment*}{*x*}) where *environment* is one of these commands:

environment	**Effect**
sideways	Turn the contents of the environment 90 degrees
turn	Turn the contents of the environment an arbitrary number of degrees
rotate	Turn the contents of the environment an arbitrary number of degrees (space for the results may not be created)

and *x* is the number of degrees to be rotated. When *x* is positive, the rotation is counterclockwise; when negative, clockwise. The `sideways` command doesn't require the degree argument.

c. Choose OK.

3. Enter the graphic or table to be rotated.

4. End the rotation environment:

a. Enter an encapsulated TₑX field.

b. In the entry area, type **end**{*environment*} where *environment* is the rotation environment.

c. Choose OK.

▶ **To rotate a floating graphic or table**

1. Add the *rotating* package to your document.

2. Place the insertion point where you want the rotation to begin and begin the rotation environment:

a. Enter an encapsulated TₑX field.

b. Type **begin**{**sidewaysfigure**}**centering** or **begin**{**sidewaystable**}**centering**.

c. Choose OK.

3. Enter an inline graphic or table.

4. If you want a caption,

a. Enter an encapsulated TₑX field and in the entry area, type **caption**{*text*} where *text* is the caption for the graphic or table.

b. Choose OK.

5. If you want to add cross-references to the object, enter a marker.

6. End the rotation environment:

a. Enter an encapsulated TₑX field.

b. Type **end**{**sidewaysfigure**} or **end**{**sidewaystable**}.

c. Choose OK.

Managing Floating Objects

Documents that contain many floating objects may occasionally encounter LATEX process-ing problems. When you typeset your document, LATEX tries to process floating objects as it encounters them, anchoring them throughout the document. However, if it can't place an object because of its size or if float placement options don't fit, LATEX will hold the floating object, and all following floating objects, until the end of the document and then generate the error "Too many unprocessed floats." You can force LATEX to process floating objects with a TEX command in the body of your document. Also, if you're not creating a Portable LATEX or PDF file, you can use the *float* package (see page 123) to manage the placement of floating objects. Finally, you can add the *placeins* package (see page 7) to create barriers in your document beyond which floating objects can't be typeset.

▶ **To force the output of floating objects**

1. Place the insertion point in an appropriate location in your document, such as the end of a chapter or section.

   Because forcing the output will end the page, you may have to experiment to find the best location for the TEX command. See page 92 for information about using the *afterpage* package, which offers more flexibility in the placement of the TEX field.

2. Enter a TEX field.

3. In the entry area, type **clearpage** and choose OK.

   When LATEX encounters this command as it typesets your document, it outputs any floating objects that occur in the document before the command.

   If you add the *float* package to a document and select only the *here* placement option for a floating graphic, the program automatically uses the H placement option. (This option isn't available if you are using the Portable LATEX filter.)

▶ **To manage the output of floating objects**

1. Add the *float* package to your document.

2. Revise the properties of all floating graphics to select only the *here* option.

3. Revise the properties of all tables that float:

   Remember that a table that floats is implemented with the fragment Table - (4x3, floating), which has this structure:

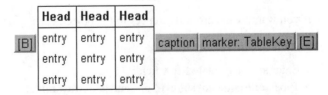

a. Select the TEX field named [B] and choose **Properties**.
The program opens the field, which contains the string
`\begin{table}[tbp]\centering`.

b. Change `[tbp]` to **[H]**.

c. Choose **OK**.

▶ **To prevent floating objects from appearing in the next section**

1. Add the *placeins* package to your document.

2. On the Typeset toolbar, click the Options and Packages button 🔳 or, from the Typeset menu, choose **Options and Packages** and then choose the **Package Options** tab.

3. Select the *placeins* package from the **Packages in Use** list and choose **Modify**.

4. In the **Category** list, select **Barrier at section** and, in the **Options** list, select **Yes**.

5. Choose **OK** to close each dialog box and return to your document.

▶ **To prevent a floating object from appearing after a designated point**

1. Add the *placeins* package to your document.

2. Position the insertion point where you want accumulated floating objects to appear.

3. Enter an encapsulated TEX field.

4. In the entry area, type `\`**FloatBarrier**.

5. Choose **OK**.

Making Additional Typesetting Changes

Your typesetting tasks may differ from those discussed in this chapter. The table beginning on the next page identifies many additional tasks and suggests packages that can help you accomplish them. Most of these packages work with most *SWP* and *SW* documents; that is, the documents will compile successfully. However, you may not be able to preview the document with TrueTEX. See Chapter 3 "Using LATEX Packages" for more information.

To	Use Package
Acronyms	
- Create a list of acronyms.	Acronym
- Ensure that all acronyms are spelled out at least once.	Acronym
Algorithms	
- Prevent algorithm statements from breaking over page boundaries.	Algorithm
- Create a list of algorithms on the table of contents page.	Algorithm
- Include complex algorithm statements in documents.	Algorithmic
AMS Documents	
- Produce documents for publication in AMS journals.	AMSMath, AMSFonts
APA Documents	
- Format citations according to APA requirements.	Apacite
- Produce documents meeting requirements of APA Publication Manual.	Apalike, Apalike-plus
Arrays	
- Format columns.	Array
- Align numbers on decimal point in tabular or array columns.	Dcolumn
Bibliographies	
- Indicate references in citations and reference lists with labels instead of numbers.	Drftcite
- Find uncited bibliography items.	Drftcite
- Print the key for each bibliography item in the margin of the page on which it occurs.	Showkeys
- Produce bibliography entries acceptable to APA journal style.	Apalike, Apalike-plus
- Improve bibliography spacing in a 2-column document.	Bibmods
- Automatically include the bibliography in the table of contents.	Tocbibind
BIBTeX Bibliographies	
- Produce BIBTeX bibliographies formatted according to *The Chicago Manual of Style, Ed. 13.*	Chicago
- Format documents for astronomy journals.	Astron
- Customize citations for seven BIBTeX bibliography styles.	Harvard
- Required with BIBTeX bibliography style newapa.bst.	Newapa
- Produce BIBTeX bibliographies with four varieties of author-date citations.	Authordate1-4
- Create separate BIBTeX bibliographies for each included file and for the document as a whole.	Chapterbib
Boxes	
- Create a boxed area on the page.	Boxedminipage
- Place boxes around content.	Fancybox
- Create simple bar charts.	Bar

To	Use Package
Captions	
- Rotate a figure or table caption.	Rotating
- Customize width, alignment, style, and font of captions for floating objects, including objects presented in landscape.	Caption
- Place captions to the right or left of floating graphics or tables.	Sidecap
Citations	
- Compress and order inline or superscripted lists of numerical citations to show a range of numbers.	Cite
- Format citations according to APA requirements.	Apacite
- Indicate references in citations and reference lists with labels instead of numbers.	Drftcite
Color	
- When the installed dvi driver supports color, produces boxes or entire pages with colored backgrounds.	Color
Columns	
- Improve bibliography spacing in a 2-column document.	Bibmods
- Format text in up to 10 columns.	Multicol
- In multi-column documents, balance the final columns of text for an attractive appearance.	Multicol
- In 2-column documents, save marks from first column.	Fix2col
- Align text in two columns or on facing pages.	Parallel
Comments	
- Include material that may or may not be typeset.	Version
Cross-references	
- Print the key for each cross-reference in the margin of the page on which it occurs.	Showkeys
- Create cross-references to labels outside the document.	Xr
Double-sided Printing	
- Specify margin offsets for two-sided printing.	Geometry
Double Spacing	
- Specify double spacing.	Setspace
Endnotes	
- Create end notes instead of footnotes.	Endnotes
Equations	
- Enhance the typeset appearance of displayed equations, sub- and superscripts, and other mathematical constructs.	AMSMath
- Change placement of equation numbers and tags.	AMSMath
- Change placement of equations in displayed mathematics.	AMSMath
Exam Questions	
- Print point value of questions in margin.	Newpnts, Points

To	Use Package
Exercises	
- Bind a solution to its exercise.	Answers
Figures and Graphics (see also *Floating Objects*)	
- Rotate a graphic.	Rotating
- Include graphics in documents.	Graphicx
- Produce small graphics in larger floating graphics or tables.	Subfig
- Wrap text around graphics.	Wrapfig, Picins
- Produce simple bar charts.	Bar
Floating Objects	
- Place floating elements on the next page output.	Afterpage
- In 2-column documents, keep floating elements in sequence.	Fix2col
- Ensure that a floating element appears in print only after reference to it.	Flafter
- Produce small graphics and tables within larger floating tables and graphics.	Subfig
- Define floating objects.	Float
- Create a point past which a floating object must not be typeset.	Placeins
Fonts	
- Scale a font up or down.	Scalefnt, Relsize
- Substitute PostScript fonts.	PSNFSS
- Use the Times font for text but leave mathematics in CM fonts.	PSNFSS
- Insert symbol fonts for Blackboard bold, Fraktur.	AMSFonts, AMSSymb
- Change uppercase text to lowercase, or lowercase to uppercase, leaving certain LATEX elements unchanged.	Textcase
- Sample the appearance of a font family.	Fontsmpl
- Read and write verbatim TEX code.	Fancyvrb
Fonts for Mathematics	
- Use the AMS Euler fonts in mathematics.	Euler
- Use Times fonts for text and mathematics and to provide ligatures and improved kerning.	Mathtime
- Insert AMS symbol fonts for Blackboard bold and Fraktur.	AMSFonts
- Use large symbols.	Exscale
- Use 11 symbols not normally available: ℧ ⋈ □ ◇ ⇝ ⊏ ⊐ ◁ ⊴ ▷ ⊵.	Latexsym
- Use Feynman slashed character notation.	Slashed

To	Use Package
Footnotes	
- Place footnotes in tables.	Blkarray
- Customize the appearance of footnotes.	Footmisc
- In 2-column documents, print all footnotes at foot of right-hand column.	Ftnright
- Create end notes instead of footnotes.	Endnotes
- Create independent series of footnotes.	Manyfoot
Headers and Footers	
- Customize content and format of headers and footers.	Fancyhdr
- Specify headers and footers.	Geometry
- In 2-column documents, save marks from first column.	Fix2col
Headings	
- Modify the appearance of division headings.	Sectsty, Titlesec, Fncychap
Hypertext Links	
- Make cross-references into hypertext links for PDF output.	Hyperref
Hyphenation	
- Handle hyphenation, punctuation, and other language-specific issues for non-English documents.	Babel
- Disable hyphenation in selected parts of a document.	Hyphenat
Indention	
- Indent the first line of all sections.	Indentfirst
Indexes	
- Create a document index.	Makeidx
- Print index commands in the margin of the page on which they occur.	Showidx
- Automatically include the index in the table of contents.	Tocbibind
Justification	
- Create less ragged justification.	Ragged2e
Labels	
- Print the key for each label in the margin of the page on which it occurs.	Showkeys
- Print all keys and markers in the margin of the page on which they occur.	Showlabels
LaTeX	
- Format LaTeX counters with a separator every three digits.	Comma
- Prevent counters from being reset.	Remreset
- In 2-column documents, save marks from first column.	Fix2col
Limit Placement	
- Change placement of limits for integrals, operators, summations, and other symbols.	AMSMath

To	Use Package
Line Breaks	
- Break path statements, URLs, and email addresses for better line breaks.	Url
Line Numbers	
- Add line numbers to paragraphs.	Lineno
Line Spacing	
- Produce double, single, or one-and-a-half spacing.	Setspace
List of Figures/List of Tables	
- Automatically include the list of figures and list of tables in the table of contents.	Tocbibind
- Create a table of contents, list of figures, and list of tables for major document divisions.	Minitoc
- Modify the appearance of the table of contents, list of figures, and list of tables.	Titletoc, Tocloft
List of Symbols	
- Create a nomenclature list.	Nomencl
Lists	
- Change spacing for list items.	Paralist
Lowercase Text	
- Change uppercase text to lowercase, leaving certain LaTeX elements unchanged.	Textcase
Margins	
- Customize margins.	Geometry
Mathematics	
- Enhance the typeset appearance of displayed equations, sub- and superscripts, and other mathematical constructs.	AMSMath
- Create non-standard mathematical accents.	Accents
Non-English Documents	
- Manage language-specific issues for non-English documents.	Babel
Numbered Lists	
- Change the style of the counter for numbered lists.	Enumerate
Page Breaks	
- Break tables between pages.	Xtab
Page Layout	
- Customize page layout (margins, orientation, paper size, headers, footers, etc.).	Geometry
- Draw an illustration of the LaTeX layout of the current document.	Layout

To	Use Package
Page Numbers	
- Remove page numbers from opening and other pages.	Nopageno
Page Orientation	
- Rotate content.	Fancybox
- Rotate parts of a page.	Graphicx
- Rotate text 90 degrees.	Lscape
- Change page orientation (portrait, landscape).	Geometry
Page References	
- Print the key for each page reference in the margin of the page on which it occurs.	Showkeys
- Automatically enhance page references with text such as "on the next page" or "on the facing page".	Varioref
- Create page references to labels outside the current document.	Xr
Paper Size	
- Change paper size.	Geometry
Plots and Diagrams	
- Produce simple bar charts.	Bar
- Produce simple commutative diagrams.	AMSCD
Punctuation	
- Manage punctuation and other language-specific issues for non-English documents.	Babel
Scaling	
- Scale parts of a page.	Graphicx
Strikethroughs	
- Strike through text with lines or slashes.	Ulem
Symbols	
- Use large symbols.	Exscale
- Define the lambdabar λ and other symbols.	Revsymb
- Display characters properly in text editors.	Inputenc
- Use 11 symbols not normally available: ℧ ⋈ □ ◇ ⤳ ⊏ ⊐ ◁ ◁ ▷ ▷.	Latexsym
- Use Feynman slashed character notation.	Slashed
Table of Contents	
- Automatically include front and back matter in the table of contents.	Tocbibind
- Create a table of contents, list of figures, and list of tables for major document divisions.	Minitoc
- Modify the appearance of the table of contents, list of figures, and list of tables.	Titletoc, Tocloft

To	Use Package
Tables (see also *Floating Objects*)	
- Rotate a table.	Rotating
- Change table headings on last page.	Xtab
- Control horizontal lines in tables.	Hhline
- Create environments similar to array and tabular.	Blkarray
- Break long tables between pages.	Longtable
- Create footnotes in tables.	Longtable
- Produce colored backgrounds and rules for table columns and rows.	Colortbl
- Align numbers on decimal point in tabular or array columns.	Dcolumn
- Create tables longer than one page.	Ltxtable
- Rotate text 90 degrees.	Lscape
- Produce small tables within larger floating tables or graphics.	Subfigure
- Create tables longer than a page.	Supertabular
- Create a table with a specified width.	Tabularx
- Break tables between pages.	Xtab
- Wrap text around floating tables at the side of the page.	Wrapfig
- Format columns in tabular environments.	Array
Theorems	
- Customize the appearance of theorem and theorem-like environments.	Theorem
Underlining	
- Underline text with single, double, or wavy lines.	Ulem
Uppercase Text	
- Change lowercase text to uppercase, leaving certain LaTeX elements unchanged.	Textcase
Verbatim Representations	
- Include programming and other verbatim statements in documents.	Alltt
- Display information exactly as it is entered at a terminal.	Verbatim
- Read and write verbatim TeX code.	Fancyvrb
Wrapped Text	
- Wrap text around floating elements at the side of the page.	Wrapfig, Picins

2 Working with Typesetting Specifications and Document Shells

Every *SWP* and *SW* document is created from a template called a *document shell.* Each shell carries several sets of specifications that determine its fundamental structure and appearance. Those specifications, and the structure and appearance they define, extend to each new document you create with a given shell.

One set of specifications consist of page setup specifications, print options, and a style file with a .cst extension. These specifications determine the appearance of the shell (and any documents created with the shell) when you preview or print it without typesetting or when you display it in the document window. *These specifications have no effect on the typeset appearance of your document* and they aren't our focus here.

The other set—the typesetting specifications—determines the appearance of the shell (and any documents created with the shell) when you typeset preview or typeset print it. These specifications have no effect on the appearance of your document in the document window or when you preview or print without typesetting. *The typesetting specifications govern all aspects of the typeset appearance of your document,* and they are our primary concern.

In this chapter we discuss several kinds of typesetting specifications and their role in the creation and typesetting of *SWP* and *SW* documents. We explain how to modify the typesetting specifications from within your *SWP* or *SW* document and how to choose an appropriate shell for your work so that extensive modification of typesetting specifications is minimized. The chapter also explains how to open and work with LaTeX documents not created with *SWP* or *SW,* and how to install and use typesetting specifications obtained from an outside source, such as a publisher.

Note Before Version 3.5, we used the word *style* to refer to the typesetting specifications. In newer versions of LaTeX, the *document style* has been renamed the *document class.* We now use the word *style* to refer to the .cst file and not to the typesetting specifications.

Working with Typesetting Specifications

The typesetting specifications establish an essential characteristic of any shell—the LaTeX *document class,* which determines the kind of document the shell will produce. A shell's typesetting specifications may also call LaTeX *packages*—sets of additional typesetting instructions that provide a particular typesetting capability, such as the creation of an index or the production of endnotes. Class and package specifications are contained in separate LaTeX formatting files with extensions of .cls, .clo, and .sty. Individual typesetting instructions may also be contained in TeX and LaTeX commands in your document. Taken together, this collection of specifications governs type face; type size; margins; page size; line spacing; location and appearance of headers, footers, and division headings; title pages; paragraph layout; indention; page breaks; automatic generation of cross-references, tables of contents, and other document elements; and other typographic details too numerous to mention. Regardless of whether you typeset to create a DVI file or, in Version 5, a PDF file, this collection of specifications completely controls the typeset appearance of your document.

LaTeX documents define the typesetting specifications in a mandatory section at the beginning of the document file, called the *preamble*. Beginning with a \documentclass command and, optionally, one or more \usepackage commands, the preamble names the .cls, .clo, and .sty files required by the document. (Note that those files may in turn call other files, which are not named in the preamble.) It may also contain TeX and LaTeX commands that control specific aspects of typesetting behavior. Following the preamble is a \begin{document} command that signals the body of your document. If there is front matter such as a title page or table of contents, it precedes the text of the document; if there is back matter such as an appendix or index, it follows it. The file closes with an \end{document} command.

Most LaTeX document files follow this structure, and files created with *SWP* and *SW* are no exception. Whenever you open a new document, the program automatically creates a preamble, which defines the typesetting specifications for your document by naming the .cls, .clo, and .sty files as specified in the shell. If you save your file as an *SWP/SW* document (using the SWP/SW/SN Document (*.tex) option), the program also inserts at the end of the preamble the command \input{tcilatex}, which calls a special set of macros. The program automatically places \begin{document} and \end{document} commands around the body of your document. You can see the entire structure of an *SWP/SW* document if you open the .tex file for the document using an ASCII editor.

When your document is open in *SWP* or *SW,* you can examine the specified document class and packages as described on pages 63 and 70. You can examine the remainder of the preamble from the Preamble command on the Typeset menu.

▶ **To examine the preamble**

1. From the Typeset menu, choose Preamble.

2. If you're using Version 4.1 or earlier, click the mouse in the entry area.

   Caution If you begin typing without first clicking in the area, you will overwrite any commands already in the preamble. Choose Cancel to leave the preamble unchanged.

3. Choose OK to return to the body of the document.

L#T#X Document Classes

The document class named in the typesetting specifications determines the basic structure of the shell and of any documents you create with it. The class specifies the kind of document to be produced and defines its general structure as a book, report, article, or other kind of document. The class also determines the elements, environments, and constructs allowed in the document. Document class files have an extension of .cls.

About half of the 150 or so shells provided with *SWP* and *SW* have standard L#T#X base classes; they are created with book.cls, report.cls, or article.cls. Although many of the other shells produce similar kinds of documents, they have different, more specialized base classes, as we see with the shells that produce articles formatted for a specific journal or theses formatted to meet the requirements of a particular university.

The rest of the shells have the base class sebase; they were developed with the Style Editor. Using the Style Editor itself to modify Style Editor typesetting specifications is usually more efficient than working from within *SWP* or *SW*. The typesetting techniques we suggest in this manual don't necessarily apply to Style Editor shells or to the documents created with them. You can easily determine the document class for any document.

▶ **To determine the document class for a document**

1. On the Typeset toolbar, choose the Options and Packages button 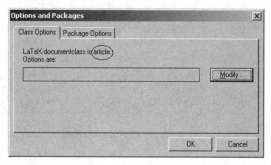 or, from the Typeset menu, choose Options and Packages.

2. Choose the Class Options tab.

   The first line of information indicates the class; in this example, the class is article:

3. Choose OK to return to the document.

Using L#T#X Class Options

Although the document class defines a shell document in broad typesetting terms, L#T#X needs additional typesetting instructions to format a document completely. Some of these instructions come from *document class options,* a collection of formatting instructions that define typesetting in more detail. The options can control body text font size, page orientation, number of text columns, print quality, page size, and many other aspects of document design and typesetting.

Default Class Options

Usually, each class option has several available settings, one of which has been selected as the default, such as *10 point* for the body text font size or *portrait* for the page orientation. The options and their corresponding defaults differ from class to class. The default settings for the three LaTeX base document classes—article, book, and report—appear below. The class option defaults are in effect unless otherwise noted in the shell.

Class Option Defaults for article.cls

Category	Default	Options
Body text point size	10 pt	11 pt, 12 pt
Paper size	8.5x11	a4, a5, b5, Legal size, Executive size
Orientation	Portrait	Landscape
Print side	One side	Both sides
Quality	Final	Draft
Title page	No title page (Title area on page 1)	Title page
Columns	One	Two
Equation numbering	On right	On left
Displayed equations	Centered	Flush left
Bibliography style	Compressed	Open

Class Option Defaults for book.cls

Category	Default	Options
Body text point size	10 pt	11 pt, 12 pt
Paper size	8.5x11	a4, a5, b5, Legal size, Executive size
Orientation	Portrait	Landscape
Print side	Both sides	One side
Quality	Final	Draft
Title page	Title page	No title page
Columns	One	Two
Start chapter on left	No	Yes
Equation numbering	On right	On left
Displayed equations	Centered	Flush left
Open bibliography style	Compressed	Open

Class Option Defaults for report.cls

Category	Default	Options
Body text point size	10 pt	11 pt, 12 pt
Paper size	8.5x11	a4, a5, b5, Legal size, Executive size
Orientation	Portrait	Landscape
Print side	One side	Both sides
Quality	Final	Draft
Title page	Title page	No title page
Columns	One	Two
Start chapter on left	Yes	No
Equation numbering	On right	On left
Displayed equations	Centered	Flush left
Open bibliography style	Compressed	Open

The option settings differ from shell to shell. If you're using a shell based on a customized document class, the default categories and the corresponding options may differ. You can learn which document class options are in effect for a particular shell.

▶ **To examine the class option defaults for a shell**

1. Open a document created with the shell.

2. On the Typeset toolbar, choose the Options and Packages button 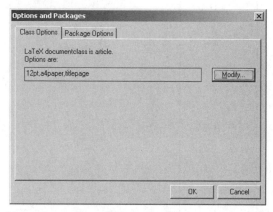 or, from the Typeset menu, choose Options and Packages.

3. Choose the Class Options tab.

   If settings other than the document class defaults are in place, the program displays them in the Options box, like this:

In this example, three options use settings different from the defaults: body text font size (12pt), paper size (a4paper), and title page (titlepage).

4. Choose OK to return to your document.

Default Page Layouts

The following page layout images for the LaTeX article, book, and report document classes reflect the standard defaults for those classes. The keyed notes provide information about the size of the margins, headers, footers, text area, and margin notes, if any. Most measurements are given in points; a point is $\frac{1}{72}$ inch.

If your document uses different class option settings, these page layouts may not apply. For example, if a document uses a4 paper instead of 8.5x11 or two columns instead of one, the margins differ from those shown in these diagrams. You may want to add the *layout* package to your document to generate a page layout diagram (see page 131).

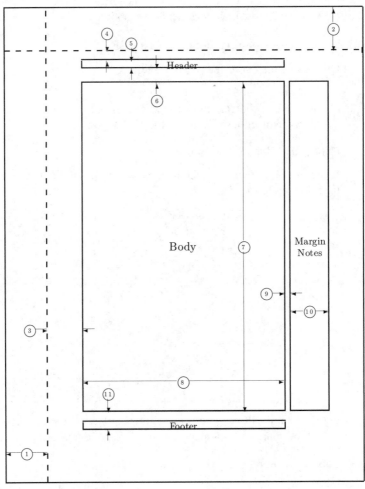

1	one inch + \hoffset	2	one inch + \voffset
3	\oddsidemargin = 62pt	4	\topmargin = 16pt
5	\headheight = 12pt	6	\headsep = 25pt
7	\textheight = 550pt	8	\textwidth = 345pt
9	\marginparsep = 11pt	10	\marginparwidth = 65pt
11	\footskip = 30pt		\marginparpush = 5pt (not shown)
	\hoffset = 0pt		\voffset = 0pt
	\paperwidth = 614pt		\paperheight = 794pt

Default page layout for article.cls

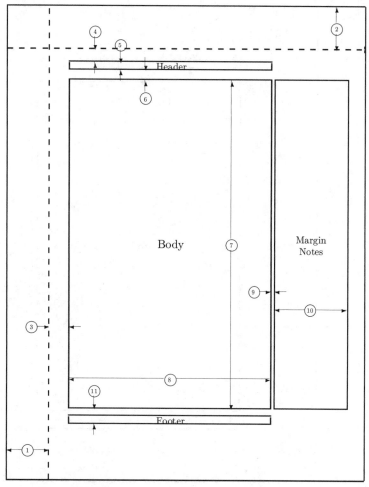

1	one inch + \hoffset	2	one inch + \voffset
3	\oddsidemargin = 35pt	4	\topmargin = 22pt
5	\headheight = 12pt	6	\headsep = 18pt
7	\textheight = 550pt	8	\textwidth = 345pt
9	\marginparsep = 7pt	10	\marginparwidth = 125pt
11	\footskip = 25pt		\marginparpush = 5pt (not shown)
	\hoffset = 0pt		\voffset = 0pt
	\paperwidth = 614pt		\paperheight = 794pt

Default page layout for book.cls

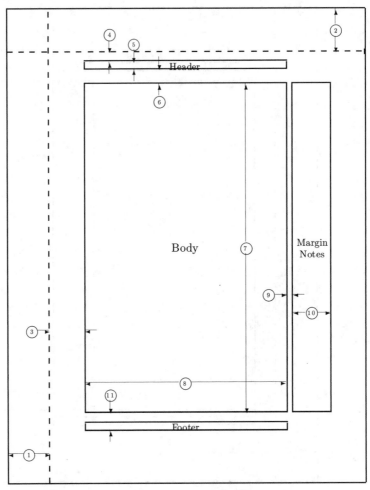

1	one inch + \hoffset	2	one inch + \voffset
3	\oddsidemargin = 62pt	4	\topmargin = 16pt
5	\headheight = 12pt	6	\headsep = 25pt
7	\textheight = 550pt	8	\textwidth = 345pt
9	\marginparsep = 11pt	10	\marginparwidth = 65pt
11	\footskip = 30pt		\marginparpush = 5pt (not shown)
	\hoffset = 0pt		\voffset = 0pt
	\paperwidth = 614pt		\paperheight = 794pt

Default page layout for report.cls

Modifying the Document Class Options

You can override the class option defaults set by the shell. As noted in Chapter 1 "Tailoring Typesetting to Your Needs," modifying the class options may be the easiest way to make the typesetting changes you need. The modification process is fast and easily reversed if it doesn't have the effect you want. If the shell you choose produces the typesetting results you want except, perhaps, for the body text font size or the size of the paper, try modifying the class options before you attempt more complex modifications. We urge you not to modify the shell itself, but rather to save any modifications in a new shell, as explained on page 80.

If no options are listed when you try to modify the document class, you can *go native*, or add LaTeX commands to force the program to use a given option. When you typeset your document, the program passes the information directly to LaTeX or PDFLaTeX. Thus, you must be careful to enter commands using correct syntax to prevent LaTeX errors. If you enter incorrect commands, LaTeX may not be able to typeset your document and you can damage your document beyond repair. We strongly encourage you to save a copy of your document before you attempt any of the modifications suggested here.

Note   Be careful to enter commands correctly. Incorrect commands can cause LaTeX to fail and may damage your document permanently.

▶ **To modify the class options**

1. On the Typeset toolbar, click the Options and Packages button ⊞ or, from the Typeset menu, choose Options and Packages.

2. Choose the Class Options tab.

3. Choose Modify.

4. In the Category box, scroll the list to select the category you want to modify.

5. In the Options box, select the option you want and then choose OK.

6. If you want to add class options that aren't listed, choose Go Native, enter the command for the option you want, and choose OK.

7. Choose OK to return to your document.

8. Save your document and typeset preview it.

LaTeX interprets the class options according to the typesetting instructions in the .cls file for the document class. Some class options can take precedence over other instructions, such as those specified in packages; other class options may be ignored when certain packages are in use. In other words, although you may specify certain class option settings, LaTeX may ignore them. Document classes and packages don't always interact smoothly. If you're making extensive modifications, you may find that you must proceed by trial and error as you experiment with the various sets of specifications and learn how they interact.

LaTeX Packages

The document class specifications establish a basic set of typesetting instructions. LaTeX packages—sets of additional typesetting instructions—extend typesetting instructions by enabling some specific LaTeX behavior or customizing some aspect of the document appearance. When you install *SWP* or *SW*, you automatically install those packages that are included with the standard LaTeX distribution. The packages are installed in the `base`, `required`, and `AMS` subdirectories of the `TCITeX\TeX\LaTeX` directory. Additionally, the `TCITeX\TeX\LaTeX\contrib` directory includes a collection of packages from the Comprehensive TeX Archive Network (CTAN), and the `TCITeX\TeX\LaTeX\SWmisc` directory contains packages from other sources including publishers and universities. Most packages have an `.sty` file extension.

Together, the packages enable a variety of customized typesetting behaviors, such as the creation of an index, the special formatting of footnotes, the content and design of headers and footers, the style of numbered lists, the generation of a list of symbols, and many others. These behaviors are often controlled by options for which you can specify settings, much as you specify class option settings.

When you typeset, LaTeX or PDFLaTeX uses the class and package specifications to determine the typeset appearance of your document. Occasionally, document classes and packages can conflict. If you expect to work frequently with LaTeX packages, we urge you to learn how each package interacts with other packages, with document classes, and with the program. Chapter 3 "Using LaTeX Packages" describes the packages available with *SWP* and *SW*. You can find links to additional and, often, extensive information about the packages in the online Help system.

When you open a document with a particular shell, the program automatically adds to the document any packages that are specified for the shell. You can easily determine which packages are in use for your document.

▶ **To determine the packages in use**

1. On the Typeset toolbar, choose the Options and Packages button ![button] or, from the **Typeset** menu, choose **Options and Packages**.

2. Choose the **Package Options** tab.

   The **Packages in Use** box lists the packages currently in use, as in this example:

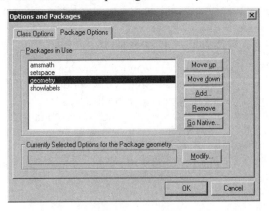

3. Choose **OK**.

When you typeset your document, the program may call additional packages. For example, it adds the *amsmath* package by default to nearly every *SWP* and *SW* document. Also, many packages in turn call other packages when LATEX or PDFLATEX runs; that is, when you typeset the document. The list you see in the **Packages in Use** box includes only those packages that are directly called by the document.

Adding and Removing LATEX Packages

The packages used by *SWP* and *SW* document shells have been carefully chosen to achieve certain typesetting results. However, you may decide that your document needs a package that has not yet been added. Documents created with most shells—that is, documents in most document classes—can accept additional packages. From the **Package Options** tab, you can see the list of packages that are available to be added to your document; the list differs for different versions of the program. You can also remove a package from your document if you don't need the capability it provides.

Note   Unless you're very familiar with LATEX and LATEX packages, we urge you not to remove packages specified by the document shell.

From the **Package Options** tab, you can see the list of packages in effect and those that are available to be added to your document. The list of available packages differs for different versions of the program. The order in which the packages are specified can, on occasion, affect typesetting behavior; see the package documentation.

By default, the program automatically manages LATEX packages, adding certain packages such as *amsmath* to most *SWP* and *SW* documents. If you have Version 5, you can prevent the program from adding packages automatically.

▶ **To add a package to your document**

1. On the Typeset toolbar, click the Options and Packages button 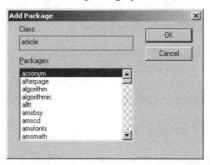 or, from the **Typeset** menu, choose **Options and Packages** and then choose the **Package Options** tab.

2. If the package you want isn't listed in the **Packages in Use** box, choose **Add**.

3. Scroll the **Packages** list to select the package you want and then choose **OK**.

4. If you need to reorder the packages in the **Packages in Use** list, select a package and use the **Move Up** or **Move Down** controls to position the package correctly.

5. Choose **OK** to return to your document.

If the package you want isn't listed as available in your version of *SWP* or *SW*, you can go native to add the LaTeX commands that force the program to use the package. When you typeset your document, the program passes the typesetting information directly to LaTeX for processing. If the commands are in error, LaTeX won't be able to typeset your document or to create a DVI or PDF file. Further, incorrect syntax can damage your document beyond repair.

Note   Be careful to enter commands correctly. Incorrect syntax can cause LaTeX to fail and may damage your document permanently.

▶ **To add a package by going native**

1. On the Typeset toolbar, click the Options and Packages button 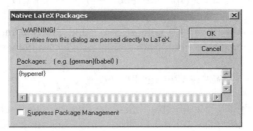 or, from the Typeset menu, choose **Options and Packages**.

2. Choose the **Package Options** tab and choose **Go Native**.

3. Click the mouse in the **Native LaTeX Packages** dialog and scroll to the end of any commands that appear there.

4. On a new line, enter the name of the package you want, enclosed in curly braces.

Remember: The program passes your entries directly to LaTeX and PDFLaTeX. Incorrect syntax will cause typesetting to fail.

5. Choose **OK** twice to return to your document.

You can add package options and arguments for the packages you specify. See "Modifying LaTeX Package Options" on page 75.

▶ **To remove a package from your document**

1. On the Typeset toolbar, click the Options and Packages button 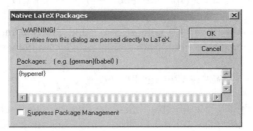 or, from the Typeset menu, choose **Options and Packages**.

2. Choose the **Package Options** tab.

3. From the list of packages in the **Packages in Use** box, select the package you want to remove.

4. Choose **Remove** and then choose **OK**.

▶ **To suppress program management of LaTeX packages**

1. On the Typeset toolbar, click the Options and Packages button ⊞ or, from the Typeset menu, choose Options and Packages.

2. Choose the Package Options tab and then choose Go Native.

3. Check Suppress Package Management and choose OK to close the dialog boxes and return to your document.

Adding LaTeX Packages to the Program Installation

On occasion, you may want to use a package that isn't part of the program installation. Before you can add the package to your document, you must first obtain it from a source such as CTAN and then add it to your installation, placing it in an appropriate program directory so that LaTeX can find it when you typeset your document.

▶ **To add a LaTeX package to the program installation**

- Move the package files to the `TCITeX/TeX` directory or one of its subdirectories in your program installation.
  You may want to create a new subdirectory for packages that aren't part of the original program installation.

  After you have added a package to your installation, you can modify the program interface so that the package and any package options are available via the Options and Packages dialog box. Modifying the interface simplifies working with added packages, but it is optional; alternatively, you can work with an added package by going native to specify options.

  Modifying the interface involves adding information to two files (`classes.pkg` and `packgs.opt`) in the `Typeset` directory of your program installation. The file `classes.pkg` contains a section for each available document class that lists packages that are available to be added to documents of that class. A typical listing begins like this:

```
[article]
acronym
afterpage
algorithm
algorithmic
alltt
amscd
amsfonts
amsmath
amssymb
amstext
answers
apacite
apalike
  ⋮
```

For each package in the program installation, the `packgs.opt` file lists the options available, as shown in this example for the *titletoc* package:

```
[titletoc]
1=Label alignment
1.1=Left - default,leftlabels
1.2=Right,rightlabels
2=Dot after label
2.1=No - default,nodotinlabels
2.2=Yes,dotinlabels
```

The first-level numbers indicate the option category. In this example, the categories are `Label alignment` and `Dot after label`. The second-level numbers indicate the option as it appears in the **Options for package** dialog box, followed by a comma and the name of the option as defined in the package itself. You can determine the available options for an added package by reading the package documentation.

▶ **To modify the program interface for a new LaTeX package**

1. Modify the `classes.pkg` file:

   a. Using an ASCII editor, open the `classes.pkg` file in the `Typeset` directory of your program installation.
   b. For each document class, add a new line and enter the package name.
   c. Save and close the file.

   The package name will appear in the list of available packages the next time you open the **Options and Packages** dialog box.

2. Modify the `packgs.opt` file:

   a. Using an ASCII editor, open the `packgs.opt` file in the `Typeset` directory of your program installation.
   b. On a new line, enter the package name in square brackets and press RETURN.
   c. For each option category, type a first-level entry in the form
      x=categoryname
      where *x* is the number of the category and *categoryname* is the category name as you want it to appear in the **Options for package** dialog box.
   d. For each option category, type a series of second-level entries in the form
      x.y=optionname,option
      where *x* is the number of the category, *y* is the number of the option within the category, *option name* is the description of the option as you want it to appear in the **Options for package** dialog box, and *option* is the name of the option as it is defined in the package. You can leave the *option* field blank.
   e. Save and close the file.
      The categories and their corresponding options will appear in the **Options for package** dialog box the next time you open the **Options and Packages** dialog box.

Modifying LaTeX Package Options

Many packages have a series of options for which you can specify settings; the options differ from package to package. If a package has options available, the program generally lists them on the **Package Options** tab. If an option is marked as *default,* it is in effect. Defaults usually don't appear in the **Currently Selected Options** box. Selecting a default option has no effect other than to display it in the box.

When you select a package option setting that is listed in the **Package Options** tab, the program creates the correct LaTeX syntax for your selection. You can also go native to specify package option settings. However, if you go native, the program passes your commands directly to LaTeX without checking for correct syntax. Be careful to enter the commands correctly.

For information about modifying the options for specific packages, see Chapter 3 "Using LaTeX Packages" and the package documentation provided with the program.

▶ **To modify package options**

1. On the Typeset toolbar, click the Options and Packages button 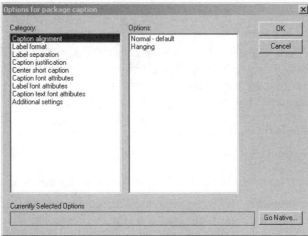 or, from the **Typeset** menu, choose **Options and Packages** and then choose the **Package Options** tab.

2. Select the package you want to modify and choose **Modify**.

3. If the **Options** dialog box lists options for the package,

   a. In the **Category** box, select the option you want.
   b. In the **Options** box, select the setting you want.
   The program displays the selected options in the **Currently Selected Options** area.

   Repeat steps a and b for each option you want to modify.
   c. Choose **OK** to return to the **Package Options** tab.
   Note that if you select the package, the program lists the options you've specified in the **Currently Selected Options** area.

or

4. If the program displays a message indicating that no options are listed for the package,

   a. Choose **Go Native**.

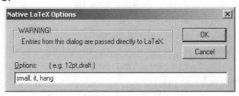

   b. In the **Native LaTeX Options** dialog box, enter the commands for any package options you want to apply.

   The documentation for each package outlines the syntax and arguments of the commands for the available options. Additional information is available in Chapter 3 "Using LaTeX Packages." Remember that incorrect syntax can prevent typesetting and can damage your document.

   c. Choose **OK** twice to return to the **Package Options** tab.

   Note that if you select the package, the program lists the options you've specified.

5. Choose **OK** to return to your document.

T_EX and L^AT_EX Commands

In addition to package options, many packages define a series of commands that you can use to send precise typesetting instructions to LaTeX or PDFLaTeX. The documentation for each package outlines the syntax and arguments of any available commands and explains whether the commands should be placed in the preamble or in T_EX fields in the body of your document. In either case, you must make certain you enter correctly formatted LaTeX to avoid typesetting difficulties and possible damage to your document.

The preamble of your document can contain definitions such as `\newtheorem`, `\renewcommand`, `\def`, and `\newcommand`, but must not contain any commands that generate typeset output. Incorrect commands in the preamble can damage your document irreparably.

▶ **To add a command in the preamble of your document**

1. From the **Typeset** menu, choose **Preamble**.

2. If you're using Version 4.1 or earlier, click the mouse in the entry area.

   Caution If you begin typing without first clicking in the area, you will overwrite what is already in the preamble. Choose **Cancel** to leave the preamble unchanged.

3. Enter the commands and choose **OK**.

Commands in the body of your document appear in T_EX fields, which appear on the screen as small gray boxes containing the words *TeX field,* like this: TeX field . When you save your document, the program interprets the T_EX command and inserts it directly into the document file. If you want to prevent the program from interpreting the command in a T_EX field, you can *encapsulate* and name the field. Then, when you save your document, the program stores the name and the command exactly as you entered them. The program preserves the exact syntax of the field when you save and reload the document. When you open the document again, the program displays the field on the screen as a small gray box with the field name in brackets, like this [create object]. When you typeset, TEX interprets the encapsulated field and inserts the command in the DVI file.

Note   Incorrect code in an *encapsulated* TEX field won't cause the program to fail when you open your document, because the code remains hidden. However, it will prevent LATEX from typesetting the document. Incorrect code in an *unencapsulated* TEX field could damage your document.

▶ **To enter a TeX field**

1. In Version 4.0 or later, click the TEX button 🔳 on the Typeset Object toolbar or, from the Insert menu, choose **Typeset Object** and then choose **TeX Field**.

   or

   In earlier versions, click the TEX button 🔳 on the Typeset Object toolbar or, from the Insert menu, choose **Field** and then choose **TeX**.

2. If you want to encapsulate the field, check **Encapsulated** and name the field.

3. In the entry area, type the TEX command preceded by a backslash (\) and choose **OK**.

Working with Document Shells

When you want to create a new document, you must first choose a shell that will form the basis of the new document. The program then opens a new document and copies the shell into it, along with the shell's typesetting specifications, style, page setup, and print options. Until you change it in some way, the new document is identical to the shell. It has the same class and structure, uses the same LATEX packages, and produces the same appearance in print.

Choosing a Document Shell

The Shells directory of your program installation contains over 150 document shells, which have the extension .shl. In addition to many general-purpose shells, the program includes a collection of shells designed to meet the typesetting requirements of specific universities and scholarly journals. The shells produce documents that fall into these categories, which are reflected in the Shells directory in your program installation:

- **Articles**—short documents intended for publication in scholarly journals or conference proceedings.

- **Author Packages for AMS**—articles intended for publication in journals or conference proceedings published by the American Mathematical Society (AMS).

- **Books**—large documents intended for publication as a separate volume.

- **Exams and Syllabi**—short documents intended for use in the classroom.

- **International**—non-English documents, including German, Russian, Greek, Chinese, and Japanese. You can write and typeset documents in languages that use a non-Roman character set (such as Japanese or Simplified Chinese) with the Omega/Lambda typesetting system included in Versions 4.x and 5.x of *SW* and *SWP*. There is no PDFOmega program, so creating a PDF file from such documents isn't possible from within the program.

- **Other Documents**—miscellaneous document types including faxes, letters, memos, overhead transparencies, slides, and some books and reports, usually developed for earlier releases of *SWP* and *SW*.

- **Scientific Notebook**—documents created with *Scientific Notebook*. Documents created with these shells are intended for printing without the benefit of typesetting.

- **Standard LaTeX**—documents created with the LaTeX base document classes without the addition of any packages.

- **Style Editor**—documents created with shells developed using the Style Editor.

- **Theses**—documents that fulfill thesis formatting requirements at several universities.

In addition to using the shells provided with the program, you can create your own shells; see page 80.

Although many shells are similar, no two are exactly alike. Some shells create documents with a structure and components common to books; other shells create documents with a structure and components common to theses, reports, or articles. Certain shells provide for front matter that includes only a short title section; others provide a title page, table of contents, list of figures, list of tables, acknowledgments, and preface. Some shells create double-spaced, single-column pages; others create single-spaced, double-column pages. Many, but not all, shells provide item tags for theorem environments—such as theorems, lemmas, corollaries, propositions, and conjectures.

As you choose a shell for your new document, keep your typesetting needs in mind, especially if you expect to create a complex document. Make sure the shell you choose produces the type of document you want to create. Don't attempt to write a book using a letter shell or an article using a report shell. Make sure that the shell contains the tags appropriate for your work. If you need theorem environments, for example, choose a shell that has theorem and theorem-like item tags.

If you're unsure of your typesetting requirements, we urge you to choose the Standard LaTeX shell for the type of document you need. These standard shells provide the greatest flexibility and portability. You can achieve almost any typesetting effect by beginning with a standard shell and adding LaTeX packages as necessary.

Important   We strongly recommend that you begin all new documents using one of the standard LaTeX shells, unless you have a compelling reason (such as publisher's instructions) to do otherwise.

A Gallery of Document Shells, provided on your program CD as a PDF file, illustrates the appearance of sample documents that have been typeset with each shell provided with the program. Examine the samples and note the features they illustrate, such as the absence or presence of headers and footers, the placement of page numbers and footnotes, the size of the margins, the appearance and placement of the headings, the extent of the front matter, the use of single or double columns, and the use of single or double spacing. When you find a shell that looks appropriate, open and print a new document with the shell to see if it meets your requirements. The closer the shell fits your requirements, the easier your typesetting tasks will be.

Each time you start *SWP* or *SW*, the program automatically opens a new, untitled start-up document using a default shell. If the shell is appropriate for your work, you can start entering information right away. If you want to create some other kind of document, however, open a new document with a different shell. You can change the default document shell to suit your needs.

▶ **To open a new document with the default shell**

- Start *SWP* or *SW*.
  The program automatically opens a new, empty document.

▶ **To open a new document with a different shell**

1. On the Standard toolbar, click the New button ⬜ or, from the File menu, choose New to open the New dialog box.

2. From the Shell Directories list in the New dialog box, select the kind of document you want.

3. From the Shell Files list, select the shell you want and choose OK.

If most of the documents you create are similar, you can save time by changing the default shell so that the program automatically opens a start-up document that fits your needs.

▶ **To identify the default shell for start-up documents**

1. On the Editing toolbar, click ⬛ or, from the Tools menu, choose User Setup, and then choose the Start-up Document tab.

   The default document shell is highlighted.

2. Choose OK.

▶ **To change the default shell**

1. On the Editing toolbar, click ⬛ or, from the Tools menu, choose User Setup, and then choose the Start-up Document tab.

2. From the Shell Directories list, select the type of document you want.

3. From the Shell Files list, select the shell you want as the default and choose OK.

Tailoring a Document to Your Needs

Once you've opened a new document with a shell that comes close to meeting your typesetting requirements, name and save the new .tex document. Then, you can begin tailoring the document to meet your requirements more precisely. When the document has the typeset appearance you want, save it (or in Version 4.0 and later, export it) as a new shell, as explained on page 80.

Although it is possible to achieve the typesetting results you want by tailoring your document outside *SWP* or *SW,* we focus in this manual on tailoring your document *from within the program* by

- Modifying the document class options (see page 69).

- Adding or removing LaTeX packages (see page 71).

- Modifying the LaTeX package options (see page 75).

- Adding TeX or LaTeX commands to the preamble or body of your document (see page 76).

These techniques often involve adding raw TeX or LaTeX code to your document. That is, they involve adding code that isn't processed by the program but is rather passed directly to LaTeX or PDFLaTeX from *SWP* or *SW* when you typeset your document. Thus, you must be careful to enter commands using correct syntax to prevent LaTeX errors. Incorrect TeX or LaTeX code can cause permanent damage to your document. We strongly encourage you to save a copy of your document before you attempt any modification of the typesetting specifications.

Important Be sure to enter TeX or LaTeX commands correctly. Otherwise, you can damage your document permanently.

Creating a Document Shell

You can create your own shells by saving any document as a shell file in one of the Shells subdirectories in your program installation. If you have carefully tailored a document so that its typeset output meets your needs, we urge you to save your work so that you can use it again. Similarly, if you have obtained typesetting specifications or shells from another source, such as a publisher, you should save them for future use. See Using Typesetting Specifications from Outside Sources on page 82.

Of course, you can use any *SWP* or *SW* document as the shell for a new document—it doesn't have to have an .shl extension—but creating a new shell removes the risk of changing something unintentionally in the original document. Further, if you place a new shell in one of the Shell subdirectories, its name appears in the shell list displayed when you start a new document. If you place the shell in some other directory, the name doesn't appear in the list of available shells and you can't create a new document with the shell using the New command. You can create new shell subdirectories as necessary.

In Version 4.0 and later, you save shells by exporting them as .shl files. Earlier versions use the Save As command.

▶ **To create a shell**

1. Open the document you want to use as a shell.

2. If you're using Version 4.0 or later, from the File menu, choose Export Document.

   or

   If you're using Version 3.5 or earlier, from the File menu, choose Save As.

3. Select a location for the new shell:

   a. In the box labeled Save in, select the `Shells` directory in your program installation.
   b. Select the appropriate subdirectory or create a new subdirectory for the new shell.

4. In the box labeled File name, type a name for the shell.

   The name can include spaces and nonalphabetic characters.

5. In the box labeled Save as type, specify Shell (*.shl).

6. Choose Save.

   The next time you open a new document, the shell name appears on the Shell Files list corresponding to the shell subdirectory you specified.

Working with Documents from Outside Sources

Occasionally you may have to work with LaTeX documents that have been created without the benefit of *SWP* or *SW*. Some existing LaTeX documents can be opened directly by the program with little or no difficulty, but others present more of a challenge. Certain LaTeX constructs need modification with an ASCII editor before they can be opened. In particular, statements of the form `\newcommand` and `\def` often cause problems, and macro definitions that contain unknown environment changes (signaled by `\begin` and `\end` statements) always do. In general, constructs that differ from Plain TeX (such as `array` versus `matrix`) should be modified to use the LaTeX construct.

If you are working with Version 5.0 or earlier of *SWP* and *SW* and the program can't successfully open a non-*SWP/SW* LaTeX document, it displays an error message such as those described on pages 178, 180, or 180. If the program successfully opens a non-*SWP/SW* LaTeX document, you may find that it has not been able to recognize every TeX or LaTeX construct in the file. When it can't recognize a construct, the program attempts to read the code and places the results in gray boxes labeled *unrecognized*. You must try to reconstruct the commands in each unrecognized gray box.

If you are working with Version 5.5 of *SWP* and *SW*, you can take advantage of a new import filter that facilitates your collaborative efforts by successfully reading and interpreting many more TeX and LaTeX constructs than did earlier versions of the program. If you are working with colleagues who use LaTeX directly instead of using *SWP* or *SW*, you may be able to use the filter to import the contents of their documents into *SWP* or *SW* files even if opening them directly in the program is unsuccessful. Similarly, you may be able to import the contents of old LaTeX documents. The new filter can read many macro definitions not created with the program, although some constructs may still result in unrecognized gray boxes.

▶ **To import a non-SWP/SW LaTeX document**

1. Place the file you want to open in a writable directory so that the program can create the necessary temporary files.

2. From the File menu, choose Import Non-SWP/SW LaTeX.

3. Select the file and choose Open.

    The program imports as much of the file as possible into a new document, and gives the document a name using the format *filename*-tmp***000***.tex, where ***000*** is a number. Thus, the first attempt to import a given file will result in a file named filename-tmp0.tex; the second attempt will yield filename-tmp1.tex; and so on.

If you are very familiar with TEX and LaTeX, you can tell the filter how to interpret certain constructs in non-*SWP/SW* LaTeX documents. See the online Help system for more information.

If you successfully read and modify a LaTeX document, then save it as an *SWP/SW* document (using the SWP/SW/SNB Document (*.tex) option), the program inserts the command \input{tcilatex} in the document preamble and uses in the file macros defined in tcilatex, a special set of macros. If instead you save the document as a Portable LaTeX file, the command isn't inserted in the preamble.

Working with Typesetting Specifications from Outside Sources

Although many shells and typesetting specifications are provided with *SWP* and *SW,* you may need to add specifications that you obtain from a publisher or from some other source for TEX and LaTeX files, such as the CTAN. The CTAN directory on your program CD contains the typesetting specifications and files as distributed on CTAN, but only those files needed for typesetting are installed with the program.

We have tested the shells and specifications that we provide with the program to ensure that they work correctly and are compatible with *SWP* and *SW*. However, we can't guarantee that other specifications will work with our products, nor can we guarantee that the documents you create with those specifications will behave as the specifications advertise. Nonetheless, it's important to install specifications correctly, and we offer the instructions below as an aid.

Important   We don't support documents created with typesetting specifications not provided with *SWP* or *SW*.

Adding LaTeX typesetting specifications to your installation involves these steps:

1. Placing the specification files in an appropriate directory.

2. Completing any required installation steps.

3. Testing the specifications by running the associated sample documents through LaTeX.

4. Opening the sample documents in *SWP* or *SW*.

5. Creating or modifying a .cst file, if necessary.

6. Creating a shell for the typesetting specifications.

Note   Don't attempt to add LaTeX typesetting specifications to your installation if you aren't familiar with TeX and LaTeX.

We illustrate these instructions by showing how to install the specifications contained in \CTAN\macros\latex\contrib\uaclasses on your program CD. These files adhere to the typesetting requirements for theses and dissertations at the University of Arizona.

These instructions assume you have installed *SWP* in the directory c:\swp55. If you're using *SW* or your directory is different, remember to substitute the correct directory path in the instructions.

Step One: Place the typesetting specification files in an appropriate directory

A set of LaTeX specifications usually involves a collection of files with extensions including .cls, .clo, and .sty. The specifications may also include installation files with an .ins extension. Most specifications have accompanying sample documents and readme files, which often contain installation instructions.

Whether you download the specifications from a website or receive them by email or on diskette, you must place them in the correct program subdirectory to ensure they are available to TrueTeX. You can place the files anywhere in the TCITeX\TeX directory or its subdirectories. We suggest that for each set of specifications you create a new subdirectory within TCITeX\TeX. If you obtained the files from CTAN, follow the directory structure used there.

Before you move the new specifications to a directory, search *SWP* or *SW* to make certain an older version of the specifications is not installed. If you find an older version, rename it before you add the new files to the installation directory structure.

▶ **To place typesetting specification files in a program directory**

1. Create a new subdirectory for the specifications within TCITeX\TeX.

   For our example, we create a new subdirectory called uaclasses in the existing directory c:\swp50\TCITeX\tex\latex\contrib.

2. Move all the typesetting specification files to the new directory.

Step Two: Complete any required installation steps

Simply moving the files to the new directory may not complete the installation of the specifications. More steps may be required.

▶ **To complete the installation of typesetting specifications**

1. Read the readme file accompanying the specifications and follow any installation instructions it contains.

2. If you must process any files through LaTeX, use the TrueTeX Formatter outside *SWP* or *SW*:

a. From the Windows **Start** menu, select *SWP* or *SW* and then select **TrueTeX Formatter**.

b. In the **Open TeX File** dialog box, specify the directory containing the specification files.

c. In the **File name** box, type *.* to display all files in the directory.

d. Select the file you want to process and choose **OK**.

Processing these files often creates additional files required by the specifications. In our example, the readme file tells us to run LaTeX on two files: ua-classes.ins and ua-classes.dtx.

Step Three: Test the specifications by opening the associated sample documents

Most specifications have associated sample documents that demonstrate the features of the typesetting specifications. Test the sample documents by running them through LaTeX before you try to open them in *SWP* or *SW*.

▶ **To test the sample documents**

1. If a sample document is provided as a .tex file, process it through the TrueTeX Formatter outside *SWP* or *SW* as described in Step Two to create a DVI file.

   In our example, both ua-example.tex and ua-example.dvi are available. To make sure the installation is working, we copy and rename ua-example.tex as newua-example.tex, and then process the renamed file through the TrueTeX Formatter to create a new DVI file.

2. Preview the DVI file with the TrueTeX previewer:

   a. From the Windows **Start** menu, choose **Programs**.

   b. Select the *SWP* or *SW* submenu from the Windows **Programs** list and then select **TrueTeX Previewer**.

   c. From the **File** menu, choose **Open**.

   d. In the **Open DVI File** dialog box, specify the directory containing the specification files.

   e. Select the file you want to process and choose **OK**.

Step Four: Open the sample documents in SWP or SW

Opening sample documents created with native LaTeX can have unpredictable results in *SWP* and *SW*. The program may not handle the documents correctly and might even crash while it tries to load the file. We suggest you make a copy of the .tex files for the sample documents before you attempt to open them.

▶ **To open a sample document in SWP or SW**

1. Make a copy of the .tex file if you have not already done so.

2. Choose 🗁 or, from the **File** menu, choose **Open**.

3. Select the subdirectory you created in Step One.

4. Select the copy of the sample document and choose **OK**.

5. If the program displays a message indicating that an appropriate .cst file was not found, choose **Yes** to load the document using a default .cst file.

   The program chooses a default style from the appropriate Styles directory.

6. Typeset preview the document and compare the results to those obtained when you previewed the DVI file in Step Three.

   Similar results indicate a successful installation. If the document fails to compile, refer to the instructions on page 184 for finding and correcting LaTeX errors.

Step Five: Create and modify a new .cst file

When you open a document, the program uses the associated .cst file to display the document on the screen and to reflect the available environments, objects, and tags. The .cst file has no effect on the document's typeset appearance. Because the new specifications aren't yet associated with a .cst file, you must create a new .cst file.

If the LaTeX specifications you're adding are similar to an existing document class and include no new objects, you can probably create a successful .cst file by copying and modifying the .cst file for a similar document class. The .cst files are installed in the Styles directory of your program installation or in one of its subdirectories. However, if the specifications you're adding implement a new base document class, you need to create a new .cst file that reflects all the environments in the new specifications. If the .cst file doesn't reflect all the environments in the new specifications, *SWP* or *SW* can't open the sample document successfully. After you have created the new .cst file, you must change the sample document to reflect the new .cst file.

In our example, the ua-classes specifications represent a new base document class called ua-thesis, so we must create a new .cst file and save it in a new subdirectory in the Styles directory. Then we have to modify the file so that the screen display reflects any new document elements, objects, and environments implemented by the typesetting specifications.

Modifying the .cst file involves determining which new objects are implemented by the typesetting specifications and then creating corresponding sections in the .cst file. Study the new typesetting specifications and the sample document, if any, to determine which tags the new .cst file must have. Look in the .cls file for new environments, theorem objects, and especially front matter elements. These objects are often signalled with \def or \newcommand statements. You may be able to find another .cst file that reflects the object. If so, you can copy the object to the new .cst file.

In our example, the ua-thesis specifications add an abstract to the standard LaTeX report class, so the .cst file must reflect the new object. We can search other .cst files to find an abstract object, copy it, and add it to ua-thesis.cst. You can find the resulting .cst file, Styles\ua-thesis\ua-thesis.cst, on your program CD.

▶ **To create a new .cst file**

1. Use an ASCII editor to open the .cls file associated with the new typesetting specifications.

2. Search for a statement that indicates the base document class for the new specifications.

   In our example, the .cls file indicates that the ua-thesis document class derives from the standard LaTeX report document class.

3. In the Styles directory of your program installation, find a .cst file that corresponds to the document class basis.

   In our example, we use report.cst in the Styles\report directory.

4. Rename the file using the same name as the document class name and save it in the Styles directory, either in a new subdirectory or in the [Special] subdirectory.

   We copy Styles\report\report.cst and rename the copy as Styles\ua-thesis\ua-thesis.cst.

5. If the new specifications have an environment that isn't contained in the .cst file, search for another .cst file that contains a similar object and copy the object to the new .cst file.

6. When you have added all necessary environments, save the new .cst file in a new subdirectory in the Styles directory.

   Note   If the new subdirectory contains only one .cst file, you don't have to change the name of the .cst file in the sample document.

▶ **To change the sample document so that it will use the new .cst file**

1. Change the name of the .cst file:

   a. Open the file in *SWP* or *SW,* and from the **File** menu, choose **Style**.
   b. Choose **Advanced**.
   c. In the **Style File** box, browse to the directory containing the new .cst file.
   d. Select the file and choose **OK**.

2. Change the appearance of the tag environments in the document window, if necessary:

   • If you're using Version 4.0 or later, use the **Appearance** command on the **Tag** menu to change the tag attributes.
      or
   • If you're using an earlier version, use an ASCII editor to modify the tag attributes.

   Remember   Modifications to the .cst file have no effect on the typeset appearance of your document.

Step Six: Create a new shell document for the typesetting specifications

We suggest you use the sample document as the shell document, modifying it as needed.

▶ **To create a shell document for the typesetting specifications**

1. In *SWP* or *SW*, open the .tex file for the sample document.

2. Make any changes you want to the file.

3. Save the file as a shell:

   a. If you're using Version 4.0 or later, from the File menu, choose Export Document.
   or
   If you're using an earlier version, from the File menu, choose Save As.
   b. In the Save in box, specify the directory for the shell.
   Choose an appropriate subdirectory within the Shells directory of your program installation. In our example, we save the shell as Thesis - University of Arizona Thesis.shl in the Shells\Theses directory.
   c. In the File name box, type the name of the shell.
   d. In the Save as type box, select Shell (*.shl).
   e. Choose Save.

Optional steps: Modify the program interface

Although it isn't necessary, you can modify the program interface to simplify working with added typesetting specifications:

- Modify Typeset/classes.pkg as explained on page 73 to be able to select new packages from the Options and Packages dialog box.

- Modify Typeset/classes.opt in your program installation to be able to select document class options from the Options and Packages dialog box. The classes.opt file contains a section for each available document class. Each section lists the options available for the class, as shown in this partial list for the document class article:

```
[article]
1=Body text point size
1.1=10pt - default,
1.2=11pt,11pt
1.3=12pt,12pt
2=Paper size
2.1=8.5x11 - default,letterpaper
2.2=a4,a4paper
2.3=a5,a5paper
2.4=b5,b5paper
2.5=Legal size,legalpaper
2.6=Executive size,executivepaper
```

▶ **To modify the program interface for a new LaTeX document class**

1. Using an ASCII editor, open the `classes.opt` file in the `Typeset` directory of your program installation.

2. On a new line, enter the document class name in square brackets and press RETURN.

3. For each option category, type a first-level entry in the form

   x=categoryname

   where *x* is the number of the category and ***categoryname*** is the category name as you want it to appear in the Options for documentclass dialog box.

4. For each option category, type a series of second-level entries in the form

   x.y=optionname,option

   where *x* is the number of the category, *y* is the number of the option within the category, ***option name*** is the description of the option as you want it to appear in the Options for package dialog box, and ***option*** is the name of the option as it is defined in the document class You can leave the ***option*** field blank.

5. Save and close the file.

3 Using LaTeX Packages

LaTeX packages extend TeX typesetting capabilities by enabling some specific behavior for your document. The creation of an index, the inclusion of special bibliography lists, the use of color, the formatting of footnotes, and many other typesetting behaviors can be enabled with packages.

When you install *SWP* or *SW*, you automatically install those packages that are included with the standard LaTeX distribution. In addition, the installation includes packages that add specific typesetting capabilities to *SWP* and *SW* documents or that support the shells designed for certain publishers or universities. Certain packages are included in the installation only for purposes of compatibility with earlier versions of the program. Packages have an `.sty` extension and are loaded into the `TCITeX/TeX` directory and its various subdirectories at installation. The directory assignments, which are noted in the discussion below, reflect TeX convention:

Directory	Contents
`TCITeX/TeX/generic`	Input files used by many different formats
`TCITeX/TeX/LaTeX`	Files used with new versions of LaTeX
`TCITeX/TeX/latex209`	Files used only with LaTeX2.09*
`TCITeX/TeX/plain`	Files used only with Plain TeX

*Note that packages that are installed in the `latex209` directory may or may not work for later implementations of LaTeX.

If the package you want doesn't appear in the list of packages available for your document, you can go native to add it, as described on page 72.

Most of the packages included with your installation work successfully with most *SWP* and *SW* documents; that is, you can correctly compile most *SWP* and *SW* documents to which one or more of these packages have been added, whether you are creating a device independent (DVI) file or, in Version 5, a Portable Document Format (PDF) file. However, even though LaTeX correctly compiles a document, you may not be able to preview it. Also, certain packages require the use of different print drivers. You may need to change your driver configuration to use certain packages.

Note, though, that when you change drivers, you tell LaTeX not to use the default driver configuration for the local LaTeX installation. If you subsequently try to compile your document in a different LaTeX installation, LaTeX will ignore the defaults for the new installation. Thus, you may need to make additional changes to your document to accommodate the new LaTeX setting. For the greatest portability, we recommend that you usually leave the driver configurations unchanged.

This chapter focuses on those packages that enhance general typesetting capabilities in most typeset documents. We have omitted a discussion of any packages (such as those whose names begin with `sw20`) that have been designed to support a single document shell rather than provide a capability for LaTeX documents in general. You can learn more about these packages from their `.sty` files and from the corresponding document shell. See also *A Gallery of Document Shells* on your program CD to explore the typeset appearance of documents created with the many shells provided with the program.

Organized alphabetically by package, this chapter explains the function of each package and briefly describes any available package options and commands. The chapter notes any known package conflicts with document classes and with preview and print drivers. Because complete instructions for using each package are outside the scope of this chapter, we encourage you to read the documentation accompanying the packages you want to use. You can find links to additional and, often, extensive package information in the `SWSamples\OptionsPackagesLaTeX.tex` file in your *SWP* or *SW* installation. Also, you may find helpful information in the `.sty` files for certain packages. A basic knowledge of TeX and LaTeX will help you understand some of the more technical information. See Chapter 2 "Working with Typesetting Specifications and Document Shells" for information about basic program tasks related to using packages, such as adding packages, selecting options, and inserting commands in encapsulated TeX fields or in the document preamble.

Important   Modifying the typesetting specifications can damage your document. Do not attempt extensive modifications unless you are familiar with TeX and LaTeX.

Although many packages are available for use with *SWP* and *SW* documents, you may be able to obtain all the typesetting capability you need by learning to use just a few of them. The table beginning on page 54 will help you identify the packages that you need most often. In particular, these packages often prove useful: *breakcites, caption, cite, color, endnotes, fancyhdr, float, geometry, longtable, nomencl, setspace, tocbibind,* and *wrapfig*.

Accents

The *accents* package provides several tools for creating mathematical accents. Using commands in TeX fields in the body of your document, you can create artificial mathematical accents using nonstandard accent symbols such as *. You can also group multiple accents vertically, using standard and nonstandard accent symbols. Accents can appear above or below the accented character; the package modifies the leading between symbols to create a pleasing image. See the package documentation for information about the available commands, generally of the form *\command{accent}{symbol}*.

The package is installed in the `TCITeX/TeX/LaTeX/contrib/bezos` directory.

Acronym

The *acronym* package helps you manage acronyms and acronym lists in your documents. You can define each acronym within a special acronym environment and then use macros in the text to define how each occurrence of the acronym will appear when you typeset the document. If you define the list in the document preamble, it appears before the body of the document. If you define the list in the body of the document, it appears where you place it. You may want to add a heading to designate the list. The *acronym* package requires that you typeset your document with two LATEX passes for proper resolution of any acronyms in use.

The program doesn't understand the package macros, but you can successfully use the macros in your document if you place them inside encapsulated TEX fields.

▶ **To define acronyms in the text**

1. Add the *acronym* package to your document.

2. Begin the acronym environment:

   a. Place the insertion point where you want the list to appear in your document.
   b. Enter a TEX field.
   c. In the entry area, type **begin{acronym}**.
   d. Choose OK.

3. For each acronym,

   a. Enter an encapsulated TEX field.
   b. To define the acronym and include it in the list of acronyms, type **acro{***acronym***}{***definition***}** and choose OK.
      or
      To define the acronym and exclude it from the list of acronyms, type **acrodef{***acronym***}{***definition***}** and choose OK.

4. Following the last definition, end the environment:

   a. Enter an encapsulated TEX field.
   b. In the entry area, type **end{acronym}** and choose OK.

▶ **To define acronyms in the preamble**

1. Add the *acronym* package to your document.

2. From the Typeset menu, choose Preamble.

3. Click the mouse in the entry area.

4. On a new line, type **begin{acronym}** and press ENTER.

5. For each acronym,

   • To define the acronym and include it in the list of acronyms, type **acro{***acronym***}{***definition***}** and press ENTER.
     or
   • To define the acronym and exclude it from the list of acronyms, type **acrodef{***acronym***}{***definition***}** and press ENTER.

6. Type **end{acronym}** and choose OK.

▶ **To use acronyms**

1. Place the insertion point where you want an acronym to appear.

2. Enter an encapsulated TEX field.

3. In the entry area, type the command to insert the acronym formatted according to your preferences:

Command	Effect
\ac{*acronym*}	Expand and identify the acronym the first time; use only the acronym thereafter
\acf{*acronym*}	Use the full name of the acronym
\acs{*acronym*}	Use the acronym, even before the first corresponding \ac command
\acl{*acronym*}	Expand the acronym without using the acronym itself

Suppose you've defined the acronym *SW* as *Scientific Word*. Now you want to use it in the sentence *(acronym) documents are beautifully typeset*.

These examples show the result of using the four available acronym commands, assuming that the acronym has already been used once in the document:

Command	Effect
\ac{SW}	SW documents are beautifully typeset.
\acf{SW}	Scientific Word (SW) documents are beautifully typeset.
\acs{SW}	SW documents are beautifully typeset.
\acl{SW}	Scientific Word documents are beautifully typeset.

4. Choose **OK**.

In addition to using the available commands, you can change the package option to place expanded acronyms in the body of the document or at the foot of the page as footnotes. The option is available through the **Options and Packages** command on the **Typeset** menu.

See an example of the package in use in the PackageSample-acronym.tex file in the SWSamples directory of your program installation. The package is installed in the TCITeX/TeX/LaTeX/contrib/acronym directory.

Afterpage

The package implements the \afterpage command and causes LATEX to expand its argument after the current page is filled and output. Although you can specify any command in the \afterpage argument, using the \clearpage command is a particularly useful way to force the printing of any floating objects (graphics and long tables) that haven't yet been anchored to a position. LATEX fills the page on which the \afterpage command occurs and then prints any unanchored floating objects before continuing with the text. Use the \afterpage command in an encapsulated TEX field. The package has no options.

Algorithm   93

► **To use the *afterpage* package to output floating objects**

1. Add the *afterpage* package to your document.

2. Place the insertion point on the page after which you want accumulated floating objects to appear.

3. Enter an encapsulated TeX field.

4. In the entry area, type **\afterpage{\clearpage}**.

5. Choose OK.

Although you can add the *afterpage* package to documents in most document classes, note that the package doesn't work for two-column layouts. The package is installed in the `TCITeX/TeX/LaTeX/required/tools` directory and is part of the Standard LATEX Tools Bundle.

Algorithm

The *algorithm* package defines a floating environment for algorithm descriptions so they don't break over a page boundary. The package also enables algorithm numbering. If you're using a report or book shell, you can produce a list of numbered algorithms for inclusion after the table of contents. The list appears on a separate page, similar to a list of figures or list of tables. You must process your document through LATEX outside *SWP* or *SW* to generate the list of algorithms and you must run LATEX at least twice.

Options that affect the appearance and numbering of algorithm environments are available through the Options and Packages command on the Typeset menu. The package is designed to be used with the *algorithmic* package, but it can be used separately.

► **To use the algorithm environment**

1. Add the *algorithm* package to your document.

2. If it is present, remove the definition of the algorithm `newtheorem` environment from the document preamble:

   a. From the Typeset menu, choose Preamble.
   b. Click the mouse in the entry area.
   c. Delete the definition, which looks something like this:
      `\newtheorem{algorithm}[theorem]{Algorithm}`
   d. Choose OK.

3. Place the insertion point where you want the algorithm to appear and begin the algorithm environment:

   a. Enter an encapsulated TeX field.
   b. Type **\begin{algorithm}**.
   c. Choose OK.

4. Type the commands for the entire algorithm.

5. End the algorithm environment:

    a. Enter an encapsulated TeX field.
    b. Type **end{algorithm}**.
    c. Choose OK.

▶ **To add a list of algorithms to a document**

1. Place the insertion point at the beginning of the body of your document.

2. Enter an encapsulated TeX field.

3. Type **listofalgorithms**.

4. Choose OK.

5. Save the document.

6. From outside *SWP* or *SW*, typeset compile the document file:

    a. From the *SWP* or *SW* program group, choose the TrueTeX Formatter.
    b. Select the file and choose OK.
      LaTeX generates an `.loa` file for the document.

7. Typeset preview the document.

    The package is installed in the `TCITeX/TeX/LaTeX/contrib/algorithms` directory.

Algorithmic

The *algorithmic* package defines an environment in which you can use a number of commands for typesetting complex algorithmic constructs. Available commands include if-then-else constructs; for, while, until, and infinite loops; pre- and postconditions; and comments. Please see the package documentation for information about the commands. Line numbering is optional. An option to suppress end statements is available for the algorithmic environment. The package is designed to be used with the *algorithm* package, but can be used separately.

▶ **To use the algorithmic environment**

1. Add the *algorithmic* package to your document.

2. Begin the algorithm environment:

    a. Enter an encapsulated TeX field.
    b. Type **begin{algorithmic}** and choose OK.

3. Type the commands for the entire algorithm.

4. End the algorithm environment:

  a. Enter an encapsulated TeX field.

  b. Type \end{algorithmic} and choose OK.

Here is an example of how an algorithm presented in the algorithmic environment:

Require: $n \geq 0$
Ensure: $y = x^n$
  $y \Leftarrow 1$
  $X \Leftarrow x$
  $N \Leftarrow n$
  while $N \neq 0$ **do**
    if N is even **then**
      $X \Leftarrow X \times X$
      $N \Leftarrow N/2$
    else $\{N$ is odd$\}$
      $y \Leftarrow y \times X$
      $N \Leftarrow N - 1$
    end if
  end while

The file `PackageSample-algorithmic.rap` in the `SWSamples` directory of your program installation contains additional examples of the *algorithmic* package in use. The file includes instructions for modifying a style (`.cst`) file to add the algorithmic environment as a Section/Body tag. The packages are installed in the `TCITeX/TeX/LaTeX/contrib/algorithms` directory.

Alltt

The *alltt* package provides a verbatim-like environment in which the meaning of slashes and curly braces is unchanged by LaTeX. Thus, you can embed other TeX commands and environments inside the alltt environment to produce formatted mathematics and mathematics symbols.

Assume you want to include mathematics in a typeset verbatim paragraph. Ordinarily, the mathematics appears as LaTeX code when you typeset the document without the *alltt* package, as shown here:

```
This verbatim paragraph contains both text
and mathematics. Here, the use of the
Pythagorean theorem, $a\sp{2}+b\sp{2}=c\sp{2}$,
demonstrates this feature.
```

With the package, the mathematics appears as correctly formatted mathematics:

```
This verbatim paragraph contains both text
and mathematics. Here, the use of the
Pythagorean theorem, a² + b² = c²;
demonstrates this feature.
```

You must place the entire alltt environment in an encapsulated TeX field.

▶ **To use mathematics in a verbatim-like environment**

1. Add the *alltt* package to your document.

2. Enter an encapsulated TEX field.

3. Type **\begin{alltt}** to begin the alltt environment.

4. Begin entering the content of the verbatim environment.

5. For each mathematical element,

   a. Type **\(** to begin mathematics.
   b. Type the commands for the mathematical statement or symbol you want.
   c. Type **\)** to end mathematics.

6. Complete the content.

7. Type **\end{alltt}** to close the environment.

8. Choose OK.

The package has no options. *Alltt* is provided automatically with LATEX and is installed in the `TCITeX/TeX/LaTeX/base` directory.

AMS Packages

The American Mathematical Society ($\mathcal{A}_{\mathcal{M}}\mathcal{S}$) publishes three main types of publications: articles, proceedings, and books or monographs. Each has detailed publication format specifications, which are reflected in three $\mathcal{A}_{\mathcal{M}}\mathcal{S}$ shell documents: AMS Journal Article; AMS Proceedings Article; and AMS Book or Monograph. The specifications are supported by $\mathcal{A}_{\mathcal{M}}\mathcal{S}$-LATEX, a required component of the standard LATEX distribution, and by a series of $\mathcal{A}_{\mathcal{M}}\mathcal{S}$ packages. Most of the packages are installed in the `amscls` and `ams-math` subdirectories of the `TCITeX/TeX/LaTeX` directory. The *amsfonts* package is installed in the `TCITeX/TeX/plain` directory.

AMSCD

The *amscd* package defines a CD environment to produce simple rectangular commutative diagrams, such as this:

$$
\begin{CD}
A @>>> B @>>> C \\
@VVV @AAA @AAA \\
D @>>> E @>>> F
\end{CD}
$$

The package provides single and double horizontal and vertical arrows, with or without labels; see the package documentation for details. No diagonal arrows are provided. The notation is easier to use than standard LATEX code and the results are more attractive.

After adding the package to your document, create the diagram inside a CD environment defined in a T_EX field in the body of your document.

AMSFonts

The *amsfonts* package is a collection of fonts of symbols and characters that aren't always included in standard distributions of T_EX, but that correspond to those used in $\mathcal{AMS}$ print and online publications and in the MathSci online database. The fonts include Blackboard Bold, Fraktur, the Euler family; certain sizes of Computer Modern mathematics, caps, and small caps fonts; extra mathematical symbols; and Cyrillic. *SWP* and *SW* automatically call the *amsfonts* package when it is required.

Other than adding the package to your document, no action is required. No options are available for the *amsfonts* package. Note that the program adds the package if it is needed by features in use in the document. The Portable LaT_EX filter always adds the *amsfonts* package, along with *amsmath, amssymb,* and *graphicx.*

AMSSymb

The *amssymb* package is a subset of amsfonts that defines the full set of symbol names for two fonts of extra symbols included in the amsfonts collection. The two fonts, msam and msbm, contain symbols, including uppercase Blackboard Bold, needed by the $\mathcal{AMS}$ publishing program and MathSci online database. The package requires no special commands in the document, and no options are available. The program adds the package if it is needed by features in use in the document.

AMSMath

This package, which is provided automatically with LaT_EX, enhances the typeset appearance of mathematical formulas, especially those involving displayed equations, multiline sub- and superscripts, and other mathematical constructs. The *amsmath* package is included automatically in most *SWP* and *SW* shells. The program adds the package if it is needed by features in use in the document.

The package calls several auxiliary packages as needed:

- *amstext*—Allows typesetting of a small amount of text inside mathematics mode and adjusts font sizes for text in sub- and superscript locations.

- *amsopn*—Allows the declaration of new operator names.

- *amsbsy*—Included for backward compatibility only. This package has been superseded by the newer *bm* package that comes with LaT_EX.

You can use two other packages in documents created with $\mathcal{AMS}$ document shells:

- *amscd*—Provides a CD environment for commutative diagrams; doesn't support diagonal arrows.

- *amsxtra*—Provides miscellaneous seldom-used commands that enhance compatibility with documents created using earlier versions of $\mathcal{AMS}$-T_EX.

AMSMath Options

With the Options and Packages command on the Typeset menu, you can set six options for the *amsmath* package. They affect the placement of limits, equation numbers, and equations themselves. The options you set for this package may override options set for the document class.

Answers

The *answers* package provides a way to bind a solution to an exercise in a LaTeX environment. This package was designed for the general LaTeX community and may not be the best choice for *SWP* and *SW* documents. We urge the use of the Exam Builder.

With the *answers* package, you can store the bound solutions in several different files at once, so that you can print them at different times, such as in the appendix of a book as well as a handout for students. Further, you can create and include many different solutions files in a document, such as one for each section or chapter of a book. The package supports any number of solution types, including hints for students.

Available commands associate the exercises with the solutions and define, open, and close the solutions files. See the package documentation for more information about using the commands and for examples of using the package. The option to create solutions files is available through the **Options and Packages** command on the **Typeset** menu.

The package is installed in the `TCITeX/TeX/LaTeX/contrib/answers` directory.

Apacite

The *apacite* package formats citations according to the complex requirements of the American Psychological Association (APA). The package works with the bibliography style file `apacite.bst` to produce citations in a variety of APA formats. It improves on the capabilities of the *apalike, apalike-plus,* and *newapa* packages. In particular, the package provides "no parentheses" citation commands. Except in rare cases, the package will format every reference correctly.

Commands are available to handle various types of citations. See the package documentation for more information. The *apacite* package is installed in `TCITeX/TeX/latex/contrib/bibtex`.

Apalike and Apalike-plus

The *apalike* package formats text according to specifications in the American Psychological Association *Publication Manual (4th edition),* to produce typesetting suitable for APA journals. In particular, the package works in conjunction with `apalike.bst` to produce BibTeX bibliography entries that are formatted alphabetically by author's last name. The package also produces single and multiple author-date citations in the text.

The *apalike-plus* package extends the features of *apalike* with TeX commands that provide optional titles for the list of references and include the selected title in headers and the table of contents. The commands are as follows:

- `\bibtitle`—generates *References* as the default bibliography title.

- `\bibheadtitle`—generates *REFERENCES* as the default text to be used in page headers.

- `\addcontentsline{toc}{...}{\bibtitle}`—generates an appropriately titled entry for the bibliography in the table of contents.

These two packages have no effect on manual bibliographies. To use the packages successfully, you must specify that you want to create a BibTeX bibliography and choose the corresponding BibTeX style.

► **To create a list of references with *apalike* or *apalike-plus***

1. Add the *apalike* or *apalike-plus* package to your document.

2. From the Typeset menu, choose Bibliography Choice.

3. Check BibTeX and choose OK.

4. Insert BIBTEX citations as needed throughout your document.

5. Insert the list of references:

   a. Place the insertion point where you want the bibliography to appear in your document.
   b. If you're using *apalike-plus,* enter package commands in an encapsulated TeX field to specify the bibliography title and page headers and to include the list in the table of contents.
   c. From the Insert menu, choose Typeset Object and then choose Bibliography.
   d. Select the BIBTEX database file you want to use.
   e. Scroll down the Style list to select apalike.bst or apalike2.bst.
   f. Choose OK.

6. Save and compile the document.

No options are available for either package. Both *apalike* and *apalike-plus* are installed in `TCITeX/TeX/latex209/contrib/misc`.

Appendix

The *appendix* package provides for modifying the typesetting of appendix titles. It provides a subappendix environment for use as an appendix to a chapter or section. Although package commands are available, you can use the package more effectively with the options available from the Options and Packages command on the Typeset menu. The options affect the formatting of headers and titles in the appendix.

The subappendices environment creates an appendix section at the end of a chapter or an appendix subsection at the end of a section. It numbers the subappendix in sequence with the other sections or subsections and attaches an uppercase letter to the section number. Subappendices appear in the table of contents.

► **To create a subappendix**

1. Add the *appendix* package to your document.

2. Begin the subappendices environment:

   a. Place the insertion point where you want the subappendix to appear.
   b. Enter an encapsulated TeX field.
   c. In the entry area, type **begin{subappendices}** and choose OK.

3. Type a heading for the subappendix.

4. If the subappendix is in a chapter, apply the section tag to the heading.

or

If the subappendix is in a section, apply the subsection tag to the heading.

5. Enter the content of the subappendix.

6. End the subappendices environment:

a. At the end of the subappendix, enter an encapsulated TeX field.
b. In the entry area, type **\end{subappendices}** and choose **OK**.

The *appendix* package is designed to work only with those document classes that have chapters or sections. The package is known to conflict with the LaTeX kernel \include command. See the package documentation for additional information. The *appendix* package is installed in `TCITeX/TeX/LaTeX/contrib/appendix`.

Array

The *array* package extends the implementation of the LaTeX array and tabular environments by providing options for column formatting, including lines and paragraph indention. You can use the package to achieve alignment within cells, like this:

x x x x x	y y y y y	z z z z
x x x x x	y y y y y	
x x x x x		

x x x x x		
x x x x x	y y y y y	z z z z
x x x x x	y y y y y	

x x x x x		
x x x x x	y y y y y	
x x x x x	y y y y y	z z z z

You can also obtain special effect using vertical rules with variable widths:

z z z z z	y y y y y	x x x x x
9 8 7	6 5 4	3 2 1

and you can format paragraph indention within cells:

x x x x	y y y y y	z z z z z
x x x x x	y y y y y	
x x x x x		
x		

The package provides other column spacing capabilities.

The package has no options, so you must enter commands for the entire tabular environment in an encapsulated TeX field. See the package documentation for instructions and for additional examples of package effects. The package is installed in the `TCITeX/TeX/LaTeX/required/tools` directory and is part of the Standard LaTeX Tools Bundle.

Astron

The *astron* package produces author-year citations in two forms: (Author, year) and (year). It is required by these BibTeX bibliography styles:

- `astron.bst`—produces bibliographies in the format required by the European astronomical journal *Astronomy and Astrophysics*.

- `apa.bst`—produces bibliographies in the American Psychological Association format.

- `bbs.bst`—produces bibliographies approximately in the format of *Behavioral and Brain Sciences*.

- `cbe.bst`—produces bibliographies approximately in the Council of Biology Editors format.

- `humanbio.bst`—produces bibliographies with a format similar to that used in *Human Biology*.

- `humannat.bst`—produces bibliographies with a format of *Human Nature and American Anthropologist*.

- `jtb.bst`—produces bibliographies based loosely on the format used in the *Journal of Theoretical Biology*.

Other than adding the package to your document, no action is required. The *astron* package is installed in the `TCITeX/TeX/LaTeX/contrib/bibtex` directory.

Authordate1-4

The package implements four options for creating author-date citations. The options are required when using the BibTeX styles `authordate1.bst`, `authordate2.bst`, `authordate3.bst`, or `authordate4.bst`. The package has no effect on manual bibliographies. It produces BibTeX bibliographies in four slightly differing formats:

- **authordate1** produces author-date reference lists with the author's name typeset in Roman. Any uppercase letters that occur in the titles of articles, journals, or books are left as given in the BibTeX file.

- **authordate2** produces author-date reference lists with the author's name typeset in Roman and "downstyle" titles. That is, working from the BibTeX file, the package changes to lowercase any uppercase letters except the first that occur in the titles of articles, journals, or books; any letter that follows a colon; and any letters protected by the right and left parenthesis marks.

- **authordate3** produces author-date reference lists with the author's name typeset in small capitals. Otherwise, the lists are as produced by authordate1.

- **authordate4** produces author-date reference lists with the author's name typeset in small capitals and downstyle titles as in authordate2.

The formats are based loosely on the recommendation of *British Standard 1629 (1976 edition)*, Butcher's *Copy-editing* (Cambridge University Press, 1981) and *The Chicago Manual of Style (1982 edition)*.

Be sure to select BIBTEX bibliographies from the **Bibliography Choice** dialog box on the **Typeset** menu. Once you have added the package to your document, you must specify the .bst file you want when you insert the BIBTEX field.

► To create an author-date reference list

1. Add the *authordate1-4* package to your document.

2. From the **Typeset** menu, choose **Bibliography Choice**.

3. Check **BibTeX** and choose **OK**.

4. Insert BIBTEX citations as needed throughout your document.

5. Specify a .bst file for the *authordate* package:

   a. Place the insertion point where you want the bibliography to appear in your document.
   b. From the **Insert** menu, choose **Typeset Object** and then choose **Bibliography**.
   c. Select the BIBTEX database file you want to use.
   d. Scroll down the **Style** list to select the .bst file for authordate1, authordate2, authordate3, or authordate4.
   e. Choose **OK**.

6. Save and compile the document.

The package has no options. The package is installed in the `TCITeX/TeX/LaTeX/ contrib/bibtex` directory. See the *harvard* package on page 127 and the *chicago* package on page 109 for information about other ways to create author-date citations.

Babel

The *babel* package addresses language-specific issues so that TEX works more reliably to typeset documents written in languages other than English. When the appropriate language hyphenation patterns are included in the format file, the package switches the active hyphenation patterns as the base language is switched. The multilingual format file created with a standard *SWP* or *SW* installation includes these hyphenation patterns: English, American English, French, German, and German new orthography.

If you need a different pattern, you must use a different TrueTEX format file. The program CD for Version 3.51 and for Version 4.1 and later (but not for Version 4.0) includes several format files in the `Extras/TrueTeX/TrueTeXFormatFile` directory. If these don't include the hyphenation pattern you need, you must create a format file that does. You can find instructions in the online Help.

The *babel* package also corrects problems with embedded English strings in LaTeX, such as *Chapter* or *Bibliography*. When *babel* is running with a specific language, it uses strings appropriate for that language in place of the embedded English strings.

However, theorem objects must be treated separately. Typically, words that are typeset in the lead-in objects of theorem statements are set in the `\newtheorem` statements in the document preamble. To change the words, modify the statements in the document preamble.

If you're working with a non-English document created with a Style Editor style, you may need to modify the style so that *babel* substitutes the correct strings for automatic division headings. The online Help contains instructions.

With the *babel* package, LaTeX can successfully typeset multiple languages in the same document. The language options shown below are available through the Options and Packages command on the Typeset menu.

Language	Options	Language	Options
Afrikaans	Include, Exclude	Hungarian	Magyar, Hungarian, None of the above
Bahasa	Include, Exclude		
Breton	Include, Exclude	Irish Gaelic	Include, Exclude
Catalan	Include, Exclude	Italian	Include, Exclude
Croatian	Include, Exclude	Lower Sorbian	Include, Exclude
Czech	Include, Exclude	Norwegian	Norsk, Nynorsk, None of the above
Danish	Include, Exclude		
Dutch	Include, Exclude	Polish	Include, Exclude
English	English, U.S. English, American, UK British, British, None of the above	Portuguese	Portuges, Portuguese, Brazilian, Brazil, None of the above
		Romanian	Include, Exclude
Esperanto	Include, Exclude	Russian	Include, Exclude
Estonian	Include, Exclude	Scottish Gaelic	Include, Exclude
Finnish	Include, Exclude	Spanish	Include, Exclude
French	Use French, Use francais, None of the above	Slovakian	Include, Exclude
		Slovenian	Include, Exclude
Galician	Include, Exclude	Swedish	Include, Exclude
German	Austrian, Austrian new orthography, German, German new orthography, GermanB, None of the above	Turkish	Include, Exclude
		Ukrainian	Include, Exclude
		Upper Sorbian	Include, Exclude
		Welsh	Include, Exclude
Greek	Greek, Polutroniko, None of the above		

Once you have added the package to a document, you can switch languages within your document. When you typeset the document, LaTeX uses the appropriate language to typeset embedded strings and hyphenate text.

▶ **To typeset documents using multiple languages**

1. Add the *babel* package to your document.

2. Ensure that the appropriate language hyphenation patterns are included in the format file in use.

3. Modify the package options to select the language or languages you want.

LaTeX uses the last language you specify as the default language for embedded strings and hyphenation. See page 65 for information about viewing package options.

4. If you want to switch to a different language at some point in your document,

   a. Place the insertion point where you want to begin the language.
   b. Enter an encapsulated TeX field.
   c. In the entry area, type **selectlanguage**{*language*}
      where *language* is the language you want to use at this point in the document. Be sure you have selected the language option.
   d. Choose **OK**.
      When you typeset, LaTeX treats the new language correctly.

No standard exists for transporting files that rely on the availability of a certain language. Each file must be handled on an ad hoc basis. In Version 3.5 and earlier, the package requires the Multilingual LaTeX installation option. The *babel* package is installed in the `TCITeX/TeX/LaTeX/required/babel` directory.

Bar

The *bar* package produces simple flat and three-dimensional bar charts. The commands defining the chart are wholly enclosed in a barenv environment housed in a TeX field in the body of the document. Commands in this form

$$\textbf{\textbackslash bar\{ordinate\}\{\textit{hatchmark\_index}\}[optional value]}$$

define each data point. These hatchmarks are available:

hatchmark_index	1	2	3	4	5	6	7	8
Effect								

A series of \set commands defines the chart axes and labels.

The package has no options. See the package documentation for more information about available commands. The package is installed in the `TCITeX/TeX/latex209/contrib/misc` directory.

Bibmods

The *bibmods* package modifies the TeX thebibliography environment to improve spacing, especially for two-column documents. Adding the package to your document provides the package functions; no further action is required. No options or commands are defined for the package. The package is installed in the `TCITeX/TeX/latex209/contrib/misc` directory.

Blkarray

The *blkarray* package defines array and tabular environments not unlike those defined by the *array* package. When the insertion point is in math, the *blkarray* package implements a blockarray environment that functions similarly to the array environment in standard LaTeX. When the insertion point is in text, the package implements an environment that functions similarly to the tabular environment.

However, the *blkarray* package differs in that it defines column types differently, making all column specifiers equal. The package lends itself to detailed formatting of blockarray environments. The package implements different formatting for blocks of cells within a table, such as a header row. Information can span several columns and doesn't have to be aligned with information in other cells. You can add rules to separate rows.

Additionally, the package implements the use of delimiters as column specifiers. That is, you can use a delimiter around blocks of cells within an array, like this:

$$\begin{bmatrix} 1 & 2 \\ 4 & 5 \\ 7 & 8 \\ 1 & 2 \\ 4 & 5 \end{bmatrix} \left.\begin{matrix} 3 \\ 6 \\ 9 \\ 3 \\ 6 \end{matrix}\right\}$$

Blkarray environments can accept footnote commands. Depending on options selected, resulting footnotes may appear at the end of the table or the foot of the page.

Package options aren't available. You must specify them in encapsulated TeX fields, just as you do for the *array* package. The content of the encapsulated field includes and defines the entire tabular environment. See the package documentation for complete instructions and for additional examples of blkarray effects. The standard LaTeX command \hline doesn't work with *blkarray*. While the package produces various kinds of tables, it may not be an appropriate substitution for array and tabular environments.

The *amsmath* package, which is added automatically to documents that you save as SW/SWP/SN (*.tex) or Portable LaTeX (*.tex) documents, has been updated since the *blkarray* package was released and now conflicts with the *blkarray* package. To avoid the conflict, modify the preamble of documents that use the *blkarray* package.

▶ **To modify the preamble of documents that use the *blkarray* package**

1. Save and close the file, then reopen it.

2. From the Typeset menu, choose Preamble and click the mouse in the entry area.

3. On a new line at the end of the preamble, type
   \makeatletter \newbox\BA@first@box \makeatother

4. Choose OK.

The package is in TCITeX/TeX/LaTeX/contrib/carlisle.

Boxedminipage

The package creates a LaTeX minipage environment surrounded by rules, like this:

> This environment is useful for emphasizing information.

You can control the width of the environment. Additionally, you can use the standard TeX commands \fboxrule and \fboxsep to determine the thickness of the rules and the distance between the rules and the inside edge of the box, respectively.

> This environment is useful for emphasizing
> information of a mournful nature.

No package options are defined for the package. Instead, you enter the package commands in encapsulated TeX fields. The package is installed in TCITeX/TeX/ latex209/contrib/misc.

▶ **To use the boxedminipage environment**

1. Add the *boxedminipage* package to your document.

2. Place the insertion point where you want the boxed environment to begin.

3. Enter an encapsulated TeX field and type **begin{boxedminipage}{x}** where *x* is the desired width of the minipage.

   The command for first example on page 105 is

   \begin{boxedminipage}{1.75in}

   The commands for the second are

   \setlength{\fboxrule}{4pt}
   \setlength{\fboxsep}{12pt}
   \begin{boxedminipage}{3in}

4. Choose OK.

5. Move the insertion point to the end of the information you want to box.

6. Enter an encapsulated TeX field.

7. Type **end{boxedminipage}**.

8. Choose OK.

Breakcites

The *breakcites* package allows LaTeX to create line breaks within long citations or citations with remarks, resulting in better line spacing in your typeset document. No action is required beyond adding the package to your document and creating the citations you need. The package has no options. It is installed in the TCITeX/TeX/LaTeX/ contrib/misc directory.

Caption

The *caption* package implements customized captions within floating environments. In particular, the package allows definition of the caption width and alignment, caption label font size and font attributes, and caption font size. The package also supports rotated captions for floating objects that are presented sideways.

Note that the TrueTEX Previewer provided with *SWP* and *SW* doesn't support rotation; you must use a different DVI previewer and print driver if you want to use the *caption* package to rotate captions in a DVI file. However, PDF viewers do support rotation, so you can use the package to create rotated captions in typeset PDF files.

With the Options and Packages command on the Typeset menu, you can set options that affect the alignment, centering, font size, and font attributes of captions. Additional commands are available for changing other caption attributes, such as the margins used for captions and the space around captions. The installation program places the package in the `TCITeX/TeX/LaTeX/contrib/caption` directory.

Chapterbib

With the *chapterbib* package, you can create a BIBTEX bibliography for each file you include in your document. If each included file represents a separate chapter, then each chapter can have its own bibliography. Thus, your document can contain multiple small BIBTEX bibliographies as well as a comprehensive BIBTEX bibliography for the whole. You can also create a bibliography for the whole document, such as a recommended reading list, that is unrelated to cited works. The bibliography items can be cited in more than one bibliography.

Your document requires several changes to use *chapterbib.* Each file that you include must have its own `\bibliographystyle` and `\bibliography` commands. To generate the bibliography, you must run BIBTEX on each included file separately. If you also want a bibliography for the whole document, the master document should have its own `\bibliographystyle` command. Generally, to generate the bibliographies, you must typeset your document (one pass through LATEX), run BIBTEX on each included file, and then typeset your document again (two passes through LATEX). The more complex your document, the more complex the process.

▶ **To generate bibliographies for included files**

1. Add the *chapterbib* package to your master document.

2. Scroll through the document to find each subdocument you have included.

   Subdocuments appear as gray boxes containing the subdocument name.

3. Replace each subdocument with a TEX field:

   a. Enter an encapsulated TEX field.
   b. In the entry area, type **\include{*subdoc*}** where ***subdoc*** is the name of the subdocument to be included. Do not include the .tex file extension; LATEX will provide that automatically.
   c. Choose OK.

4. Save the document.

5. From outside *SWP* or *SW,* typeset compile the document file:

   a. From the *SWP* or *SW* submenu on the Windows **Programs** list, choose the TrueTEX Formatter.
   b. Select the file and choose **OK**.
   LATEX generates .aux files for each subdocument included.

6. Run BIBTEX on the .aux file for each subdocument and for the main document, if it also has a bibliography:

   - In Version 4.0 and later,
     i From the **Typeset** menu, choose **Tools**.
     ii Choose **Run BibTeX**.
     or
   - In earlier versions,
     i From the Windows **Start** menu, choose **Run**.
     ii In the **Open** box, type **swp35\TCITeX\SWTools\bin\bibtex.exe** and choose **OK**.
     Change the name of the program directory as necessary.
     iii Specify the .aux file.
     iv Choose **Create**.
     BIBTEX creates a .bbl file.
     v Choose **OK**.

7. From outside *SWP* or *SW,* typeset compile the document file at least twice more.

8. From inside *SWP* or *SW,* typeset preview the document.

Additional commands provide customized entries in a list of citations and multiple bibliographies without using the \include command. With package options you can repeat or gather all chapter bibliography entries at the end of the document, create a bibliography for the entire document, and format the bibliography title.

This package is compatible with the *cite* package (see page 110) and the *drftcite* package (see page 116). The files are in the TCITeX/TeX/LaTeX/contrib/cite directory.

Chbibref

The LATEX document class article sets a default name of *References* for the bibliography, but the report and book classes set the default name to *Bibliography*. The *chbibref* package sets a standard name for the bibliography for all three LATEX document classes.

▶ **To change the title of the bibliography for all three document classes**

1. If you're using Version 3.5 or earlier, obtain and install the *chbibref* package.

   The package is distributed with later versions.

2. Add the *chbibref* package to your document.

3. From the Typeset menu, choose Preamble, and click the mouse in the entry area.

4. At the end of the preamble, add a new line and type \setbibref{*name*} where *name* is the bibliography title you want.

   Note If you're using *babel,* place the command in the body of the document inside a TEX field.

5. Choose OK.

No package options are available. The package is installed in the TCITeX/TeX/ LaTeX/contrib/misc directory.

Chicago

The *chicago* package is used in combination with chicago.bst to produce BIBTEX bibliographies formatted according to *The Chicago Manual of Style, Edition 13.*

▶ **To create a bibliography formatted according to** *The Chicago Manual of Style*

1. Add the *chicago* package to your document.

2. From the Typeset menu, choose Bibliography Choice.

3. Check BibTeX and choose OK.

4. Specify the chicago.bst file:

   a. Place the insertion point where you want the bibliography to appear.
   b. From the Insert menu, choose Typeset Object and then choose Bibliography.
   c. Select the BIBTEX database files you want to use.
   d. Scroll down the Style list to select chicago.bst and choose OK.

5. Save and compile the document.

The package also supports a variety of citation formats, as shown on the next page. Although the program interface doesn't directly support these modifications, you can achieve the citation format you want by using TEX fields to insert the commands shown in the table.

▶ **To modify the format of bibliography citations**

1. Place the insertion point where you want the citation to appear.

2. Enter an encapsulated TEX field.

3. Type the command for the citation format you want, substituting the key for the BIBTEX reference.

4. Choose OK.

No package options are available. For more information, open a new document with the Standard LATEX Article (Chicago) shell. The package is installed in the TCITeX/TeX/ LaTeX/contrib/bibtex directory.

Command	Citation Format
\cite{key}	Full author list and year: (Pearson 2005; Swanson, MacKendrick, and Medd 2003)
\citeNP{key}	Full author list and year, but without enclosing parentheses: Pearson 2005; Swanson, MacKendrick, and Medd 2003
\citeA{key}	Full author list without year: (Pearson; Swanson, MacKendrick, Medd)
\citeANP{key}	Full author list without parentheses: Pearson; Swanson, MacKendrick, Medd
\citeN{key}	Full author list, no parentheses around authors, parentheses around year: Swanson, MacKendrick, Medd (2003) note that....
\shortcite{key}	Abbreviated author list and year: (Swanson et al. 2003)
\shortciteNP{key}	Abbreviated author list and year, no parentheses: Swanson et al. 2003
\shortciteA{key}	Abbreviated author list: (Swanson et al.)
\shortciteANP{key}	Abbreviated author list, no parentheses: Swanson et al.
\shortciteN{key}	Abbreviated author list and year, parentheses around year: Swanson et al. (2003)
\citeyear{key}	Year information only, with parentheses: (2005)
\citeyearNP{key}	Year information only, without parentheses: 2005

Cite

The *cite* package sorts numerical citations in ascending order and compresses lists of at least three consecutive numerical citations that occur together in the text. The sorted and compressed citations appear inline by default but can be superscripted. The package produces in-line citations that are preceded by a space, enclosed in brackets, and separated by a comma and a small space. For superscripted citations, the package omits surrounding brackets, ignores spaces that occur before a citation, moves most trailing punctuation in front of the superscript, and suppresses doubled punctuation.

For example, when you typeset using the *cite* package, a citation of bibliography items 7, 5, 1, and 4 becomes[1, 4, 5, 7] or [1, 4, 5, 7] and a citation of items 2, 6, 4, 7, and 3 becomes[2-4, 6, 7] or [2-4, 6, 7].

▶ **To order and compress citations created with SWP and SW citations**

1. Add the *cite* package to your document.

2. If you want superscripted citations,

   a. On the Typeset toolbar, click the Options and Packages button ▦ or, from the Typeset menu, choose Options and Packages.

   b. Choose the Packages Options tab.

  c. From the **Packages in Use** list, select the *cite* package and choose **Modify**.

  d. In the **Category** list, select **Superscript citations** and, in the **Options** list, select **Yes**.

  e. Choose **OK** to close each dialog box and return to your document.

3. Create the bibliography list.

4. Place the insertion point where you want a citation to occur.

5. Choose ▌▌▌ or, from the **Insert** menu, choose **Typeset Object** and then choose **Citation**.

6. In the **Key** box,

  • Type the keys for the references you want to cite, in any order and separated by a comma.

 or

  a. Select the key for the first reference from the drop-down list.

  b. Select the contents of the **Key** box and copy the selection to the clipboard.

  c. Select the key for the next reference from the drop-down list.
   Note that because the first key was selected, the new key overwrites the previous one.

  d. Type a comma.

  e. Paste the contents of the clipboard to the **Key** box.

  f. Repeat steps b–e until you have entered all the references you want to cite.

7. Choose **OK**.

 When you typeset the document, LaTeX orders and compresses the list.

In addition to the command to create superscripted citations, many commands are available through the **Options and Packages** command on the **Typeset** menu to vary the spacing within a list of citations and in the text immediately surrounding it. Commands are also available to disable sorting and compression. By adding a command to the preamble, you can omit the brackets surrounding in-line citations.

▶ **To omit the brackets surrounding in-line citations**

1. From the **Typeset** menu, choose **Preamble** and click the mouse in the entry area.

2. On a new line at the end of the preamble entries, type **\let\cite=\citen**.

3. Choose **OK**.

The *cite* package is compatible with two packages also installed in the `TCITeX/TeX/LaTeX/contrib/cite` directory: *drftcite* (see page 116) and *chapterbib* (see page 107). The *cite* package now includes the features previously contained in another related package, *overcite*, which has been superseded.

Color

The *color* package produces boxes or entire pages with colored backgrounds. The package implements LaTeX support for color when the active typeset output driver can produce colored text. Many driver options are available through the **Options and Packages** command on the **Typeset** menu. For flexibility, we recommend that you leave the options unmodified. The local LaTeX installation sets the driver defaults. If you leave the configuration unchanged, you can compile your document without changes in another LaTeX environment. The package works successfully with PDF files.

You can predefine the colors you want to use in the preamble of your document or specify them at the point you need them with commands in encapsulated TeX fields. The commands specify whether you want a box or a page in color. The commands also specify which of four common color models you want to use: rgb (red, green, blue); cmyk (cyan, magenta, yellow, black); gray; or named (names known to the selected driver). The `monochrome` option turns off all colors and is useful if you want to preview your document using a previewer that cannot produce color. Command arguments specify the exact color. See the package documentation for more information about using the package commands.

▶ **To use color in a document**

1. Add the *color* package to your document.

2. If necessary, change the driver configuration:

   a. Modify the package options to select the driver you want to use.
   b. Use the **Expert Settings** command on the **Typeset** menu to modify the format, preview, and print driver settings to reflect the driver.
   For instructions, see the online Help or *Creating Documents with Scientific Work-Place and Scientific Word.* The drivers must have been installed separately. They aren't included with *SWP* or *SW.*
   Important Don't attempt to modify the driver settings if you're not very familiar with TeX and LaTeX.

The *color* package is part of the Standard LaTeX Graphics Bundle along with *graphicx* (see page 126). For more information, see the `PackageSample-color.tex` file in the `SWSamples` directory of your program installation. The package is installed in the `TCITeX/TeX/LaTeX/required/graphics` directory.

Colortbl

The package produces colored background panels and rules for specified columns or rows of a table or array. The package implements LaTeX support for color when the active typeset output driver can produce colored text.

You can add color to a row in a table by inserting a package command in the table. Adding color to a column is more complex: you must enter the *colortbl* package commands, along with commands for the entire tabular environment, in an encapsulated TeX field. You indicate the size of each color panel and the corresponding color you want with commands placed at the start of the tabular environment.

The basic command syntax is as follows:

$$\backslash \texttt{columncolor}[\textit{w}]\{\textit{x}\}[\textit{y}][\textit{z}] \; or \; \backslash \texttt{rowcolor}[\textit{w}]\{\textit{x}\}[\textit{y}][\textit{z}]$$

where

w is the color model: rgb (red, green, blue); cmyk (cyan, magenta, yellow, black); gray; or named (names known to the selected driver),

x is the selected color,

y is the amount of left overhang past the widest entry in the column, and

z is the amount of right overhang past the widest entry in the column.

See the package documentation for instructions and for additional examples of package effects.

▶ To add color to a table row

1. Add the *colortbl* package to your document.

2. Create a table.

3. Place the insertion point in the table at the beginning of the row you want to appear in color.

4. Enter an encapsulated TeX field.

5. In the entry area, type **\rowcolor[*w*]{*x*}[*y*][*z*]**, completing the command as described above.

6. Choose **OK**.

▶ To add color to a table column

1. Place the insertion point where you want the table to appear.

2. Enter an encapsulated TeX field.

3. In the entry area, enter the complete tabular environment.

4. Place the insertion point at the beginning of the column you want to appear in color.

   If your table is defined with the command \begin{tabular}{|l|l|l|}, for example, and you want to add color to the first column, place the insertion point after the first |.

5. Type >{**columncolor[*w*]{*x*}[*y*][*z*]}**, completing the command as defined above.

6. Choose **OK**.

Many driver options are available through the **Options and Packages** command on the **Typeset** menu. The package is installed in the TCITeX/TeX/LaTeX/contrib/ carlisle directory. It should work successfully with other packages that have syntax compatible to that of the *array* package, such as *longtable* and *dcolumn*. The package works successfully with PDF files.

Comma

The *comma* package formats LaTeX counter values so that they print with a separator (such as a comma) every three digits. That is, the package prints a counter value of 1374 as 1,374 when the *comma* package is added to the document. The default separator is a comma, but you can customize it to use a period, thin space, or any other symbol that can be represented by a TeX command. LaTeX uses the same separator for all counters.

To use the package, you must add TeX commands to the document preamble or insert TeX fields containing those commands in the body of your document. To place the separator in all counters of more than three digits, place the command at the start of the body of the document. LaTeX applies the command from that point forward.

▶ **To insert separators in printed LaTeX counters**

1. Add the *comma* package to your document.

2. Add the package commands to the preamble of your document:

   a. From the Typeset menu, choose Preamble.
   b. Click the mouse in the entry area and scroll to the end of the entries.
   c. Type **\renewcommand\the*counter*{\commaform{*counter*}}** where *counter* is the LaTeX counter to be printed with a separator, such as the section number counter.
   d. If you want to change the separator from a comma to some other symbol, add **\renewcommand\commaformtoken{*x*}** where *x* is any TeX command.
   e. Choose OK.

   or

   Add the commands in the body of the document:

   a. Place the insertion point at the start of the text.
   b. Enter an encapsulated TeX field.
   c. Type the package commands you need.
   d. Choose OK.

No package options are available. The package is installed in the `TCITeX/TeX/LaTeX/contrib/carlisle` directory.

Dcolumn

The *dcolumn* package provides decimal point alignment for columns of entries in a tabular or array. You can define the separator (usually a period or comma) on which the columns align. Also, you can define a separator for the DVI output file and the maximum number of decimal places allowed in the column.

You must enter the *dcolumn* command, along with the commands for the entire tabular environment, in an encapsulated TeX field. The basic syntax of the column separator command is

D{*separator for the tex file*} {*separator for LaTeX*} {*decimal places*}

where ***separator for the tex file*** is the punctuation used in the document to indicate the decimal point; ***separator for LaTeX*** is the punctuation you want LaTeX to use when you typeset; and ***decimal places*** is the maximum number of decimal places in the column. A negative number in the ***decimal places*** argument indicates that any number of decimal places is acceptable.

▶ **To align column entries on a decimal point**

1. Place the insertion point where you want the table to appear.

2. Enter an encapsulated TeX field.

3. In the entry area, type

   \newcolumntype{d}[0]{D{*separator for the tex file***}{***separator for LaTeX***}{***decimal places***}}**

   and complete the command as defined above.

4. Enter the complete tabular environment, beginning with a **\begin{tabular}{d....d}** command and ending with an **\end{tabular}** command.

5. Choose OK.

No package options are available. The package is installed in the `TCITeX/TeX/LaTeX/required/tools` directory and is part of the Standard LaTeX Tools Bundle.

Delarray

The package enhances the *array* package by adding a system of large paired delimiters around the array. This feature is built into *SWP* and *SW*.

▶ **To define delimiters for an array**

1. Add the *delarray* package to your document.

2. Place the insertion point where you want the delimited array to appear.

3. Enter an encapsulated TeX field.

4. Type **\[\begin{array}|{*c*}|** where | is the delimiter you want and *c* is repeated for each column in the array.

5. Enter the contents of the array.

6. Type **\end{array}\]** and choose OK.

The package has no options. The package is installed in the `TCITeX/TeX/LaTeX/required/tools` directory and is part of the Standard LaTeX Tools Bundle.

Doublespace

This package has been superseded by the *setspace* package (see page 156) and is included in *SWP* and *SW* for compatibility purposes. The package produces double spacing by redefining the LaTeX parameter \baselinestretch to 2. After you have added *doublespace* to your document, you need no additional commands to create a document that is double spaced throughout, with the exception of footnotes. No package options are available. The *doublespace* package is installed in the TCITeX/TeX/ latex209/contrib/misc directory.

Drftcite

The *drftcite* package is designed to manage citations and bibliography items in document drafts. Remove the package or replace it with the *cite* package when you're ready for final printing. *Drftcite* forces LaTeX to print citations and reference lists using the labels of the bibliography items instead of their numbers. (LaTeX stores the correct citation numbers in the .aux file for subsequent use.) In the reference list, the package uses superscripted numbers to note the order in which bibliography items are cited in the text. Thus, the numbers also indicate the order in which the bibliography items should appear in the reference list. Uncited bibliography items are easy to find because they have no superscripted number. Unlike *cite*, the *drftcite* package doesn't order the items in the citation list. *Drftcite* works with both BibTeX and manual bibliographies. Create citations as usual from the Insert menu or Typeset Field toolbar.

▶ **To print citations and reference lists using item labels**

1. Add the *drftcite* package to your document.

2. Place the insertion point where you want a citation to occur.

3. Click [ ] or, from the Insert menu, choose Typeset Object and then choose Citation.

4. Enter the key of the reference you want to cite.

5. Choose OK.

Several citation formatting options are available through the Options and Packages command on the Typeset menu.

The *drftcite* package is compatible with the *cite* package (see page 110) and the *chapterbib* package (see page 107) It is installed in the TCITeX/TeX/LaTeX/ contrib/cite directory.

Dropping

The *dropping* package creates large dropped letters, as you see at the beginning of this paragraph. The number of lines over which you want the letters to extend determines their size. Experimentation will help you determine the most visually pleasing size for your document.

▶ **To enter a dropped letter**

1. Add the *dropping* package to your document.

2. Place the insertion point at the beginning of a paragraph.

3. Enter an encapsulated TEX field.

4. In the entry area, type **dropping[*x*]**{*y*}{*z*} where *x* indicates how far from the left margin the letter should start (0pt is the default); *y* is the number of lines over which you want the capital letter to extend; and *z* is the letter or letters you want to enlarge.

5. Choose OK.

6. Type the remainder of the sentence.

In addition, many driver options are available through the Options and Packages command on the Typeset menu. We recommend that you leave the driver option unchanged. The package is in the `TCITeX/TeX/LaTeX/contrib/dropping` directory.

Endnotes

The package forces LATEX to produce footnotes in a list of notes set in small type at the end of the document, instead of as footnotes set on the bottom of the page on which they occur. The package stores the endnotes in an extra external file with the file extension `.ent`. LATEX generates a new version of the `.ent` file each time you typeset the document.

▶ **To replace footnotes with endnotes**

1. Add the *endnotes* package to your document.

2. Modify the document preamble:

   a. From the Typeset menu, choose Preamble.
   b. Click the mouse in the entry area.
   c. Scroll to the end of the entries and add a new line.
   d. Type **let****footnote**=**endnote** and choose OK.

3. Create the footnotes:

   a. From the Insert menu, choose Note.
   b. In the Type of Note box, select footnote.
   c. Type the footnote and choose OK.

4. Place the insertion point at the end of the document, where you want the endnotes to appear.

5. Enter an encapsulated TEX field.

6. Enter the commands you need:

   a. If you want the endnotes to begin on a new page, type **newpage** and press ENTER.

   b. Type **begingroup** and press ENTER.

   c. If you want an entry for the endnotes to appear in the table of contents, type **addcontentsline{toc}{section}{Notes}** and press ENTER.

   d. If you want the endnotes to be set in a normal size font instead of a smaller font, type **renewcommand{\enotesize}{\normalsize}** and press ENTER.

   e. Type **theendnotes** and press ENTER.

   f. Type **endgroup** and choose **OK**.

7. Typeset your document.

LaTeX places any footnotes in the document in a list at the location of the encapsulated field.

The package implements additional commands to produce numbered endnotes; produce the endnote mark in the text but no corresponding endnote; or produce an endnote but no corresponding mark in the text. Additional commands change the endnote size and produce endnote numbers or marks. See the package documentation for additional information about using the package and see an example of the package in use in the `PackageSample-endnotes.tex` file in the `SWSamples` directory of your program installation. No package options are available for the *endnotes* package. The package is installed in the `TCITeX/TeX/LaTeX/contrib/misc` directory.

Enumerate

The *enumerate* package provides an optional argument for the enumerate (numbered list) environment so that you can define the style in which LaTeX prints the counter. Argument parameters include designations for upper and lowercase alphabetic characters, upper and lowercase Roman numerals, and arabic numerals. To use the *enumerate* package, you must place the entire list in an encapsulated TeX field. Lists may be nested.

▶ **To define a counter style for numbered lists**

1. Add the *enumerate* package to your document.

2. Place the insertion point where you want the numbered list to appear.

3. Enter an encapsulated TeX field.

4. Type **begin{enumerate}**[*x*] where *x* is the designation of the counter numbering scheme:

Scheme	Example	Produces
A	A, B, C, ...	uppercase letters (as produced by \Alph)
a	a, b, c, ...	lowercase letters (as produced by \alph)
I	I, II, III, ...	uppercase roman numerals (as produced by \Roman)
i	i, ii, iii, ...	lowercase roman numerals (as produced by \roman)
1	1, 2, 3, ...	arabic numbers (as produced by \arabic)

5. Choose **OK**.

6. For each item in the list,

   a. Enter an encapsulated TₑX field.
   b. Type **\item** *text* where *text* is the content of the list item.
   c. Choose **OK**.

7. At the end of the list, enter an encapsulated TₑX field.

8. Type **\end{enumerate}** and choose **OK**.

No package options are available for the *enumerate* package. The package is installed in the `TCITeX/TeX/LaTeX/required/tools` directory as part of the Standard LATEX Tools Bundle.

Euler

The *euler* package produces mathematics in LATEX documents using the $\mathcal{AMS}$ Euler family of fonts (Euler Roman, Euler Fraktur, Euler Script, and Euler Extension). After you add the *euler* package to your document, LATEX produces all mathematics in the document using the Euler font family. Several package options for formatting with Euler fonts are available through the **Options and Packages** command on the **Typeset** menu. The package is in the `TCITeX/TeX/LaTeX/contrib/euler` directory.

Exscale

The *exscale* package provides different sizes of large mathematical symbols in LATEX documents. The symbols are based on certain sizes of the cmex10 font and on cmex 7-point to 9-point variants, which are part of the *amsfonts* package. The *exscale* package is redundant in *SWP* and *SW* documents, in which mathematical operators and delimiters are scaled automatically.

The package has no options. *Exscale* is installed in the `TCITeX/TeX/LaTeX/base` directory.

Fancybox

The *fancybox* package provides several different styles of boxes for framing and rotating content in your document. *Fancybox* provides commands that produce boxes with shadows, square-cornered boxes with single or double lines, and round-cornered boxes with normal or bold lines, such as these:

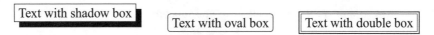

The boxes can contain words, lines, paragraphs, or whole pages, and the boxes can be centered or right- or left-justified.

Note that the TrueTₑX Previewer provided with *SWP* and *SW* doesn't support rotation; you must use a different DVI previewer and print driver if you want to rotate boxed content in a DVI file. However, PDF viewers support rotation, so you can use the package to create rotated boxes in typeset PDF files.

Package options aren't available for the *fancybox* package. Use encapsulated TeX fields to box information in your document.

▶ **To box information in your document**

1. Add the *fancybox* package to your document.

2. Enter an encapsulated TeX field.

3. Type ***command**{*content to be boxed*} where ***command*** is the fancybox command you need:

Command	Effect
fbox	square box
shadowbox	square box with shadow
doublebox	double square box
ovalbox	thin oval box
Ovalbox	thick oval box

4. Choose OK.

Package documentation includes useful information about using LaTeX box macros. The `PackageSample-fancybox.tex` file in the `SWSamples` directory of your program installation contains more examples of fancybox effects. The package is installed in the `TCITeX/TeX/LaTeX/contrib/fancybox` directory.

Fancyhdr

The *fancyhdr* package is a page layout customizing package that replaces the *fancyheadings* package. It handles footers and headers efficiently, but also works with placement of floats. With the package, you can define headers and footers with multiple parts and on multiple lines, place rules in headers and footers, and use a header and footer width different from that of the text. Additionally, you can use different headers and footers for even and odd pages, first pages of chapters, and on pages containing floats, and you can produce dictionary-style headers reflecting the first and last words on a page. *Fancyhdr* also provides control over fonts and upper- and lowercase letters.

No package options are available. However, the package uses a simplified syntax for entering commands.

▶ **To define the content of headers and footers**

1. Add the *fancyhdr* package to your document.

2. Specify a new header and footer setup in the document preamble:

    a. From the Typeset menu, choose Preamble.
    b. Click the mouse in the entry area.
    c. On a new line, type **pagestyle**{**fancy**}.

3. Define the content of the header (note that the text argument in these commands can contain TEX commands):

   a. On a new line, type **\lhead**{*text*} where *text* is the information you want left-justified in the header.

   b. On a new line, type **\chead**{*text*} where *text* is the information you want centered in the header.

   c. On a new line, type **\rhead**{*text*} where *text* is the information you want right-justified in the header.

   d. If you want a rule under the header, type **\renewcommand**{**\headrulewidth**}{*x*} where *x* is the point size of the rule you want.

4. Define the content of the footer (note that the text argument in these commands can contain TEX commands):

   a. On a new line, type **\lfoot**{*text*} where *text* is the information you want left-justified in the footer.

   b. On a new line, type **\cfoot**{*text*} where *text* is the information you want centered in the footer.

   c. On a new line, type **\rfoot**{*text*} where *text* is the information you want right-justified in the footer.

   d. If you want a rule over the footer, type **\renewcommand**{**\footrulewidth**}{*x*} where *x* is the point size of the rule you want.

5. Choose OK.

Defining different headers and footers for double-sided documents increases the definitions, some for even (left) and others for odd (right) pages. You can occasionally combine definitions in the same command by specifying when they should appear. The package uses these settings:

Setting	Prints on
E	Even page
O	Odd page
L	Left
C	Center
R	Right
H	Header
F	Footer

▶ **To define the content of different headers and footers for even and odd pages**

1. Add the *fancyhdr* package to your document.

2. Specify a new header and footer setup in the document preamble:

   a. From the Typeset menu, choose Preamble.

   b. Click the mouse in the entry area.

   c. On a new line, type **\pagestyle**{**fancy**}.

   d. On a new line, type **\fancyhf**{} to clear all fields in the header and footer.

3. Specify the header:

   a. On a new line, type **\fancyhead[*location*]{*text*}** where ***location*** specifies the page and field of the header and ***text*** specifies the information you want to appear. For example, the command `\fancyhead[LE,RO]{\thepage}` puts the page number in the left field of the header on even (left) pages and in the right field of the header on odd (right) pages.

   b. Repeat step a as needed to specify the header fields on both even and odd pages.

4. Specify the footer:

   a. On a new line, type **\fancyfoot[*location*]{*text*}** where ***location*** specifies the page and field of the footer and ***text*** specifies the information you want to appear.

   b. Repeat step a as needed to specify the footer fields on both even and odd pages.

5. Choose OK.

Additional instructions about using the *fancyhdr* package appear earlier in this manual. See page 8 for instructions about adding a rule under a header, page 11 for instructions about moving page numbers, and page 6 for instructions about specifying header and footer information. The package documentation contains complete instructions and useful diagrams of LaTeX page layout elements. The installation program places this package in the `TCITeX/TeX/LaTeX/contrib/fancyhdr` directory.

Fancyvrb

The *fancyvrb* package provides customizable environments and commands for typesetting and manipulating verbatim text. You can change the font family and size, number lines of text, and create frames around code examples with optional arguments to the main package environment, Verbatim. All package commands and the text to be presented in the Verbatim environment must appear in unencapsulated TeX fields, each on a separate line in the body of your document. The package works line by line and creates effects such as this:

```
1   The␣normal␣case␣with␣1-pt␣rules,
2   spaces␣marked,␣and␣line␣numbers␣on␣the␣left.
```

See the package documentation for information about commands and variations on the environment. The *fancyvrb* package is installed in the `TCITeX/TeX/LaTeX/contrib/fancyvrb` directory.

Fix2col

The *fix2col* package modifies the LaTeX two-column output routine by improving the handling of marks. If the first column of a two-column page contains marks, the package tells LaTeX to use `\firstmark` from the first column rather than discarding it. Also, the package improves the handling of floating objects by anchoring both one- and two-column floating objects in a single sequence. Without the package, LaTeX may anchor two-column floating objects after those with a single column.

No action is required beyond adding the package to your two-column document. No package options are available for the *fix2col* package, which is installed in the `TCITeX/TeX/LaTeX/contrib/carlisle` directory.

Flafter

Ordinarily, LaTeX tries to place floating objects at the top of the page, regardless of where the reference to the object occurs. The *flafter* package overrides the ordinary placement to force LaTeX to print the floating object after the reference to it.

No action is required beyond adding the *flafter* package to your document. No package options are available. The package is installed in the `TCITeX/TeX/LaTeX/base` directory as part of the Standard LaTeX Base System.

Float

Instead of being anchored at a specific point in a LaTeX document, floating objects are movable. LaTeX determines their best placement and final position in the typeset document after taking into consideration line and page breaks and division headers. You can suggest a preferred placement to LaTeX by specifying `t` (top of a page), `b` (bottom of a page), `p` (on a page of floating objects), or `h` (where the floating object appears in the document file, if possible).

The *float* package improves the interface for defining and placing floating objects by defining the H (Here) placement option of the superseded *Here* package. The H option tells LaTeX to place a floating object where it appears in the document file, even if the placement is typographically ill advised. If not enough room remains on the page to hold the object, LaTeX moves it to the next page, leaving blank space on the page before.

SWP and *SW* work differently with the *float* package depending on how you save your document. If you save it as an *SWP* or *SW* document, the program automatically uses the H placement option when you select only the Here placement for a floating graphic. If you save the document as a Portable LaTeX document, the program ignores the H option. Using the package reduces the likelihood that LaTeX will accumulate too many floating objects to typeset your document correctly.

▶ **To force the placement of floating objects where they appear in the document file**

1. Add the *float* package to your document.

2. Enter a floating object. (Use the fragment named Table - (4x3, floating) to enter a table that floats.)

3. Edit the properties of the floating object to specify only the Here placement:
   - If the object is a graphic,
     - i Edit the properties of the graphic to open the Graphic Properties dialog box.
     - ii Choose the Layout tab.
     - iii In the Placement area, select Floating, check Here, uncheck the other three placement options, and then choose OK.

       or
   - If the object is a table,
     - i Edit the [B] box in the Table - (4x3, floating) fragment, which contains the command \begin{table}[tbp] \centering.
     - ii Change the [tbp] entry to **[H]** and choose OK.

The *float* package implements two float styles: boxed and ruled floats. Boxed floats are surrounded by a box extending from the right to the left margin, regardless of the size of the floating object. Ruled floats are introduced by a horizontal line; have another line under the caption, if any; and are followed by a third line, all extending from the right to the left margin. You must define the float style and the floating object in an encapsulated TeX field. The package also provides a way to define your own types of floating objects, which can be ruled or boxed. See the documentation for the *float* package for more information.

The *float* package has no options. The installation program places the package in the `TCITeX/TeX/LaTeX/contrib/float` directory.

Fncychap

The *fncychap* package provides six predefined layout styles for chapter headings in books and reports. The styles are provided as options for the package; the option Lenny is shown below. You can modify the styles or use special commands in the preamble to create your own chapter headings, as described in the package documentation.

Chapter 1

Title of the Chapter

To use the package, add it to your document and specify the style option you want. Note that the package doesn't work reliably with numbered chapters that occur before the main matter of the document. The installation program places the package in the `TCITeX/TeX/LaTeX/contrib/fncychap` directory.

Fontsmpl

The *fontsmpl* package produces a test of a font family, such as Computer Modern or Times, showing the font in use in sample text, a table of contents, and a sample of commands. You can use the package to print a sample of the font currently in use in your document or you can open and typeset a sample document that produces a sample of the font family you indicate.

▶ **To print a sample of the font currently in use**

1. Add the *fontsmpl* package to your document.

2. Place the insertion point where you want to sample the font.

3. Enter an encapsulated TeX field.

4. Type **fontsample** and choose OK.

5. Typeset preview the document.

► **To produce a font sample with the sample document**

1. Open the file `fontsmpl.tex` in the `TCITeX/TeX/LaTeX/required/tools` directory.

2. Typeset preview the document.

3. When LaTeX prompts you for a font family, type the font family name, such as **cmr** for Computer Modern or **times** for Times Roman, and press ENTER.

4. Scroll through the document displayed in the TrueTeX Previewer to examine the appearance of the font.

The package has no options. The installation program places the package in the `TCITeX/TeX/LaTeX/required/tools` directory.

Footmisc

The *footmisc* package was designed for customizing footnotes. The package options address the format, positioning, and numbering of single and multiple footnotes. The package provides for using symbols instead of footnote numbers. It also provides some debugging tools.

► **To customize footnotes**

1. Add the *footmisc* package to your document.

2. Modify the package options to select the option you want and choose OK.

The package is installed in the `TCITeX/TeX/LaTeX/contrib/footmisc` directory.

Ftnright

The *ftnright* package formats footnotes for two-column documents. It prints all footnotes that occur on a page at the foot of the right-hand column. Footnotes appear in smaller type than that used for the text. The footnote numbers are set on the baseline rather than as superscripts. The text and the footnotes aren't separated by a line. When you add the *ftnright* package to your document, specify a two-column layout with the document class options instead of the *multicol* package (see page 138). The *ftnright* package doesn't work successfully with *multicol*.

After adding the package to your document, no further action is required. The package has no options. The *ftnright* package is installed in the `TCITeX/TeX/LaTeX/required/tools` directory as part of the Standard LaTeX Tools Bundle.

Geometry

The *geometry* package provides a simple way to customize the page layout of your document. If the shell you're using provides a largely adequate layout, you may be able to use the *geometry* package to customize the shell so that it meets all your typesetting requirements. In particular, the easiest way to change the typeset margins for a document is to add the *geometry* package and then include in the document preamble a command to change the margins.

You can use the package to specify portrait or landscape orientation, margins, margin offsets for two-sided printing, elimination of the space for headers and/or footers, paper size, horizontal and vertical offsets, and many other typesetting details. The package uses automatic completion of layout dimensions; if you don't specify all dimensions, the package supplies the remainder automatically. The *geometry* package also uses auto-centering and auto-balancing mechanisms so that you can use simple, minimal descriptions to define the page layout you want. For example, you can set all the margins to 3 centimeters without any space for headers or footers using this command in the preamble of your document:

```
\usepackage[margin=3cm,noheadfoot]{geometry}
```

The package uses the "key val" (key = value) interface. As seen in the above example, command arguments consist of key val options, separated by commas. Options are usually order-dependent. You can specify commands in multiple lines.

With the Options and Packages command on the Typeset menu, you can set options for the *geometry* package. The options affect page orientation, paper size, print side, margin notes, headers and footers, and magnification. You can make additional specifications with TeX commands in the preamble of your document. See Chapter 1 "Tailoring Typesetting to Your Needs" to learn how to use the *geometry* package to change margins, page orientation, header and footer space, and paper size. The package documentation contains additional instructions and a good illustration of LaTeX page layout concepts. The package is installed in the `TCITeX/TeX/LaTeX/contrib/` `geometry` directory.

Graphicx

The package is one of three packages—with *color* (see page 112) and *graphics*—included as part of the Standard LaTeX Graphics Bundle. Although identical to the *graphics* package in function, the *graphicx* package has an interface that is easier to use and more powerful.

The *graphicx* package implements LaTeX support for including graphics files, rotating parts of a page, and scaling parts of a page. The package depends on having a typeset output driver that can produce these effects. The TrueTeX Previewer provided with *SWP* and *SW* doesn't support rotation; use a different DVI previewer and print driver if you want to use the *graphicx* package to rotate parts of a page in a DVI file. However, PDF viewers support rotation, so you can use the package to rotate parts of a page in typeset PDF files.

You provide additional information to the package with the `\includegraphics` commands placed in TeX fields in the body of your document. The command has optional arguments that define the type of graphic; its desired size, shape, and angle of rotation; and the size and shape of the box surrounding the graphic. See page 49 for instructions about using the *graphicx* package to correct problems with typesetting PostScript graphics. The package is installed in the `TCITeX/TeX/LaTeX/required/` `graphics` directory.

Harvard

The *harvard* package is a family of seven BIBTEX bibliography styles:

Bibliography Style	Meets format requirements of
AGSM	*Australian Government Style Manual*
APSR	*American Political Science Review*
DCU	*Design Computing Unit, Department of Architectural and Design Science, University of Sydney*
JMR	*Journal of Management Research*
J Physics B	*Journal of Physics B*
Kluwer	*Kluwer Academic Publishers*
Nederlands	Dutch conventions

Although the format differs with each style, all seven styles implement standard parenthetical citations:

The definitive work on the subject (Medd 2005)....

Citations can be complete or incomplete. Complete citations can be used as nouns:

Medd (2005) proves that....

or as possessives:

Medd's (2005) definitive work on the subject....

Incomplete citations can contain the author's name without the date:

The definitive work on the subject (Medd)....

or the date without the name:

The definitive work on the subject (2005)....

The options available through the **Options and Packages** command on the **Typeset** menu determine the type of citation (full, abbreviated, or full for the first citation and abbreviated thereafter), type of parentheses, and style of the citations and bibliography. Although the package was designed for use with BIBTEX bibliographies, you can also use it with a manual bibliography. The `PackageSample-harvard-manual.tex` file in the `SWSamples` directory illustrates the use of the package with a manual bibliography. The Standard LATEX Article (Harvard) shell contains more information.

▶ **To use a harvard bibliography style with a** BIBTEX **bibliography**

1. Add the *harvard* package to your document and select any options you want.

2. From the **Typeset** menu, choose **Bibliography Choice**.

3. Check **BibTeX** and choose **OK**.

4. Insert citations as needed in your document.

5. Specify the harvard .bst file you want:

   a. Place the insertion point where you want the bibliography to appear.

   b. From the **Insert** menu, choose **Typeset Object** and then choose **Bibliography**.

   c. Select the BIBTEX database file you want to use.

   d. Scroll down the **Style** list to select one of the harvard .bst files and choose **OK**.

6. Save the document.

7. On the Typeset toolbar, click the Typeset DVI Compile button ![icon] or, from the **Typeset** menu, choose **Compile**.

8. Check **Generate a Bibliography** and choose **OK**.

9. Typeset preview your document.

The *harvard* package is intended to be used with BIBTEX bibliographies. You can also use it with manually created bibliographies by inserting \harvarditem commands in TEX fields to create the bibliography list.

▶ **To use a harvard bibliography style with a manual bibliography**

1. Add the *harvard* package to your document and select any options you want.

2. From the **Typeset** menu, choose **Bibliography Choice**.

3. Check **Manual** and choose **OK**.

4. Create citations as needed in your document.

5. Begin the bibliography list:

   a. Place the insertion point where you want the bibliography to appear in your document.

   b. Enter an encapsulated TEX field.

   c. In the entry area, type **\begin{thebibliography}{*x*}** where *x* is the longest label in the bibliography list and determines the indention of the list items.

   d. Choose **OK**.

6. For each item in the list:

   a. Enter an encapsulated TEX field.

   b. Name the field with the key to provide a visual reminder of the key.

   c. In the entry area, type **\harvarditem{*citation*}{*year*}{*key*}** where ***citation*** is the information to be cited in the text except for the year, ***year*** is the year to be cited, and ***key*** is the key of the reference used in the citation.

   d. Choose **OK**.

   e. Type the reference in full as you want it to appear in the list of references.

7. End the bibliography list:

a. Place the insertion point after the last item.

b. Enter an encapsulated TeX field.

c. In the entry area, type **end{thebibliography}** and choose OK.

8. Save and typeset compile the document.

See an example of the package in use in the `Harvard.tex` file in the `TCITeX/doc/latex/contrib/harvard` directory of your program installation. The package is installed in the `TCITeX/TeX/LaTeX/contrib/harvard` directory.

Helvet

See PSNFSS Packages on page 147.

Hhline

The *hhline* package works with the *array* package (see page 100) to implement fine control of single and double horizontal lines (like \hline and \hline\hline) within typeset tables, as shown here:

a	b	c	d
s	w	p	5.5
1	2	3	4
5	6	7	8

Note that you can achieve similar results in *SWP* and *SW* without the *hhline* package:

a	b	c	d
s	w	p	5.5
1	2	3	4
5	6	7	8

However, when you use double lines around the outside of a table, the *hhline* package may produce a more pleasing appearance at the outside corners.

The lines are governed by the package command \hhline. The command arguments are tokens, or symbols, that indicate the absence, presence, and width of a horizontal line and whether or not it breaks or is broken by an intersecting vertical line. See the package documentation for a discussion of the tokens.

▶ **To create horizontal lines within a tabular environment**

1. Add the *hhline* package to your document.

2. Enter an encapsulated TeX field.

3. In the entry area, type **begin{tabular}** to define a tabular environment.

4. Enter the tabular content.

5. Between rows of content, use \hhline commands with appropriate tokens to define the lines you want.

6. Type **end{tabular}** to end the environment and choose OK.

No package options are available. The *hhline* package is installed in the TCITeX/ TeX/LaTeX/required/tools directory as part of the Standard LaTeX Tools Bundle.

Hyperref

From LaTeX cross-referencing commands, including the table of contents, bibliographies, and page-references, the *hyperref* package creates \special commands that a driver can turn into hypertext links. The package also provides commands with which you can write ad hoc hypertext links, including links to external documents and URLs.

The package extends the hypertext possibilities of .tex documents so that typesetting the document with PDFLaTeX produces a table of contents linked to the body of the document, automatically creating bookmarks, thumbnails, and linked headings.

Note that the TrueTeX Previewer provided with *SWP* and *SW* doesn't support the package, but PDF viewers do, so you can use *hyperref* to maintain active LaTeX cross-references in PDF files that you typeset from your document. When you add the *hyperref* package to your document, move it to the bottom of the Packages in Use list.

The package has macros and options available; see the extensive package documentation for information about the commands. The *hyperref* package is installed in the TCITeX/TeX/LaTeX/contrib directory.

Hyphenat

The *hyphenat* package disables hyphenation in parts of your document or in the document as a whole. Also, it enables hyphenation of words containing nonalphabetic characters, such as underscores, and text that is set in monospaced fonts.

The two available package options turn hyphenation on and off and control hyphenation for monospaced fonts. Note that when you select the None option, which prevents all hyphenation, you may get LaTeX messages about bad line breaks and overfull boxes when you compile your document. For more information, see page 36. The *hyphenat* package is installed in the TCITeX/TeX/LaTeX/contrib/hyphenat directory.

Indentfirst

The *indentfirst* package indents the first line of all sections by the usual paragraph indention. Other than adding the package, no action is required. No package options are available. The package works successfully with all standard document classes. It is installed in the TCITeX/TeX/LaTeX/required/tools directory as part of the Standard LaTeX Tools Bundle.

Inputenc

The *inputenc* package maps non-ASCII characters to their corresponding TEX macros according to the encoding option you select. Available options include ISO Latin-1, ISO Latin-2, and others.

When you use *SWP* or *SW* to open a document with input encoding set, the program correctly interprets the characters. When you use a text editor to open the document, the encoded characters appear correctly rather than as TEX code if the input encoding corresponds to the current code page for the system. For example, when the ISO Latin-1 option is selected as the font encoding scheme, the character Ã appears in a text editor as Ã instead of as \~{A}.

To maintain a consistent interpretation of any non-ASCII characters, you must choose the ASCII (Normal) character set option when you save a document to which you have added the *inputenc* package.

The package may simplify collaboration on documents written in some non-English languages. See the package documentation for additional information. The package is installed in the `TCITeX/TeX/LaTeX/base` directory.

Latexsym

The *latexsym* package provides 11 mathematical symbols that were originally defined in LATEX 2.09 but are no longer defined in the New Font Selection Scheme. The symbols are

$$\Cup \bowtie \Box \Diamond \rightsquigarrow \sqsubset \sqsupset \lhd \unlhd \rhd \unrhd$$

These symbols are also provided by the *amsfonts* and *amssymb* packages (see page 97). Because *SWP* and *SW* call the *amsfonts* package automatically, ordinarily you don't need to add the *latexsym* package to your document to obtain the symbols.

No package options are available. The *latexsym* package is installed in the `TCITeX/ TeX/LaTeX/base` directory.

Layout

The *layout* package illustrates the LATEX layout of the current document with a figure similar to the one on page 132. The circled callouts refer to the accompanying table of standard LATEX page layout values including paperwidth, topmargin, oddsidemargin, textheight, textwidth, headheight, and others. The package is useful for refining the layout of your document.

The options available for the package through the Options and Packages command on the Typeset menu determine the language in which the layout is printed and provide debugging aids.

▶ **To draw the layout of a document**

1. Add the *layout* package to your document.

2. Place the insertion point anywhere in the body of your document, and enter a TEX field.

3. Type **layout** and choose OK.

LaTeX draws the layout in your document immediately after the command.

The *layout* package doesn't work for documents created with Style Editor shells. It is installed in the `TCITeX/TeX/LaTeX/required/tools` directory as part of the Standard LaTeX Tools Bundle.

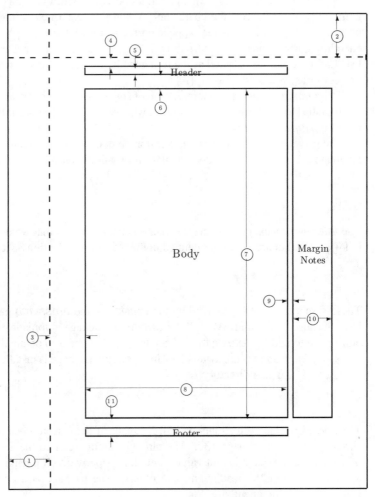

1	one inch + \hoffset	2	one inch + \voffset
3	\oddsidemargin = 62pt	4	\topmargin = 16pt
5	\headheight = 12pt	6	\headsep = 25pt
7	\textheight = 550pt	8	\textwidth = 345pt
9	\marginparsep = 11pt	10	\marginparwidth = 65pt
11	\footskip = 30pt		\marginparpush = 5pt (not shown)
	\hoffset = 0pt		\voffset = 0pt
	\paperwidth = 614pt		\paperheight = 794pt

Lineno

The *lineno* package provides line numbers on typeset paragraphs. By default, the numbers run continuously through the document, but you can reset the line numbers on each page. The package provides a way to create a reference to a particular line number using the cross-reference mechanism.

▶ **To add line numbers to a document**

1. Add the *lineno* package to your document.

2. Modify the package options to select the options you want and choose OK.

3. From the Typeset menu, choose Preamble and click the mouse in the entry area.

4. On a new line, type **linenumbers** and choose OK.

The package is installed in the `TCITeX/TeX/LaTeX/contrib/lineno` directory.

Longtable

The package defines a longtable environment that is a multipage version of tabular. The tables produced by the package can be broken between, but not within, rows by standard TEX page-breaking algorithms. The package maintains consistent column widths from page to page, unlike the *supertabular* package (see page 165). The package provides customized captions on the first and subsequent pages of the table, but you may find the *caption* package more convenient to use for that purpose (see page 107).

The options available through the Options and Packages command on the Typeset menu aid in debugging. The package commands define and customize the longtable environment. Commands are available to split the table into a series of *chunks* for easier management by TEX. Additional commands position the table, define rows, define breaks, and make footnotes available within a table environment. The *longtable* package doesn't require the *array* package, but if *array* is added to the document, the *longtable* package uses extended features. See the package documentation for a discussion of how to use each option, command, and parameter.

To use the *longtable* package in your document, you must define the entire longtable environment in an encapsulated TEX field. Also, you may have to process the document through LATEX three or four times to achieve the correct appearance of columns in a longtable environment. Using the package requires a solid knowledge of LATEX. For more information, see the package documentation and the `PackageSample-longtable.tex` file in the `SWSamples` directory of your program installation. The *longtable* package is installed in the `TCITeX/TeX/LaTeX/required/tools` directory as part of the Standard LATEX Tools Bundle.

Lscape

The *lscape* package creates a landscape environment within which LATEX rotates text 90 degrees. Note that PDF viewers support rotation, so you can use the *lscape* package to create rotated text in typeset PDF files. The TrueTEX Previewer provided with *SWP* and *SW* doesn't support rotation; you must use a different DVI previewer and print driver if you want to use the *lscape* package to rotate text in a DVI file. Although you can use a different driver, we recommend that you leave the driver defaults unchanged. The local LATEX installation sets the driver defaults. If you leave the configuration unchanged for your document, you can compile it without changes in another LATEX environment.

You can define the landscape environment with commands inserted in TEX fields. The *portland* package produces similar results (see page 147).

▶ **To define a landscape environment**

1. Add the *lscape* package to your document.

2. Place the insertion point where you want landscape orientation to begin in your document.

   Place the commands carefully so that LATEX rotates the current page before adding the page header and footer.

3. Enter an encapsulated TEX field.

4. Type **begin{landscape}**.

5. Choose OK.

6. Place the insertion point where you want to return to portrait orientation.

7. Enter an encapsulated TEX field.

8. Type **end{landscape}**.

9. Choose OK.

Many driver options are available for *lscape* through the **Options and Packages** command on the **Typeset** menu. The package is installed in the `TCITeX/TeX/LaTeX/required/graphics` directory as part of the Standard LATEX Graphics Bundle.

Ltxtable

The *ltxtable* package is a combination of two other packages—*longtable* and *tabularx*—that are part of the Standard LATEX Tools Bundle. The package produces multi-page tables with column widths calculated automatically to meet a total specified table width.

Using the package involves placing the longtable environment in a file all its own, then including it in the main document. The command syntax for inputting the file is

```
\Ltxtable{width}{file}
```

No options are available for *ltxtable*. The package is installed in the `TCITeX/TeX/LaTeX/contrib/carlisle` directory.

Makeidx

The *makeidx* package creates an index for your document based on information in \index commands in the text. *SWP* and *SW* automatically add the *makeidx* package to your document when you create the index, but you must add the package yourself if you plan to save your document as a Portable LaTeX file.

▶ **To create an index with *makeidx***

1. Create index entries throughout your document, as needed.

2. Place the insertion point where you want the index to appear.

3. Import the index fragment.

4. Typeset compile your document and choose **Generate an Index** or, from the **Typeset** menu, choose **Tools** and then choose **Run MakeIndex**.

   The program adds the *makeidx* package to your document and the \makeindex command to the document preamble, and generates the index. Note that if you plan to save your document as a Portable LaTeX file, you must add the *makeidx* package to your document.

   No package options are available. The package is installed in the TCITeX/TeX/ LaTeX/base directory.

Manyfoot

The *manyfoot* package provides independent series of footnotes for your document and groups the footnotes by series at the bottom of the page. The package automatically separates groups of footnotes with vertical space; you can also add separating rules. The package provides a customized appearance for footnotes, either in standard footnote form or grouped in run-in paragraphs. You can control enumeration automatically or manually using standard enumeration schemes. Note that using the scheme fnsymbol is not recommended. The package is useful for producing critical editions and for other applications that require multiple independently numbered series of footnotes.

Using the package involves placing \newfootnote or \DeclareNewFootnote commands in the preamble of your document, then placing TeX fields containing the commands\footnotemark and \footnotetext in the body of the document where you want footnotes.

The paragraph format created by the *manyfoot* package conflicts with the *footmisc* package; otherwise, the two packages are compatible. The package is installed in the TCITeX/TeX/LaTeX/contrib/ncctools directory. See the package documentation for more information about implementing the features.

Mathpazo

See PSNFSS Packages on page 147.

Mathptmx

See PSNFSS Packages on page 147.

Mathtime

The package enables the use of PostScript New Font Selection Scheme (PSNFSS) Math-Time fonts, including MathTime Plus fonts, in LaTeX documents. When you typeset your document, MathTime fonts provide ligatures and improved kerning in Times text. The *mathtime* package implements mathematics set in Times and calls the *times* package directly, so that documents containing both mathematics and text can use Times throughout, rather than a combination of font families. The result is a more portable document with a nicer appearance. See also the *times* package, page 149. When you add the *mathtime* package to your document, move it near the bottom of the **Packages in Use** list.

The *mathtime* package has several options for font use available through the **Options and Packages** command on the **Typeset** menu. The No TS1 option must be set for use with the TrueTeX Formatter included with *SWP* and *SW*.

▶ **To use MathTime fonts in a document**

1. On the Typeset toolbar, click the Options and Packages button ▦ or, from the **Typeset** menu, choose **Options and Packages** and then choose the **Package Options** tab.

2. Select the font package currently in use.

3. Choose **Remove**.

4. Add the *mathtime* package to your document.

5. Modify the package to select the **No TS1** option.

   The package won't work correctly without this setting.

6. Choose **OK**.

The package is installed in the TCITeX/TeX/LaTeX/required/mathtime directory. See the online Help and the package documentation for more information about the implementation of the *mathtime* package in a TrueTeX environment. See also the file OptionsPackagesLaTeX.tex in the SWSamples directory.

Minitoc

The *minitoc* package uses commands in the preamble and the body of the document to create a table of contents and, optionally, a list of figures and a list of tables, at the beginning of each major division of a document, as shown in this example:

Chapter 1

Standard LaTeX Books

Contents

If the document class defines \part, you can create a table of contents and figure and tables lists at the beginning of each part. If the document class defines \chapter, you can create a table of contents and figure and tables lists at the beginning of each chapter. You can create the *minitoc* elements for document sections only when the document class doesn't define \chapter. That is, chapter level and section level *minitoc* elements can't be used in the same document.

▶ **To create a table of contents for a document division**

1. Add the *minitoc* package to your document.

2. From the Typeset menu, choose Preamble and click the mouse in the entry area.

3. On a new line, type the commands for the environments you want:

Command	Environment
\doparttoc	Table of contents for parts
\dopartlof	List of figures for parts
\dopartlot	List of tables for parts
\dominitoc	Table of contents for chapters
\dominilof	List of figures for chapters
\dominilot	List of tables for chapters
\dosecttoc	Table of contents for sections
\dosectlof	List of figures for sections
\dosectlot	List of tables for sections

4. Choose OK.

5. For each minitoc environment you want,

    a. Place the insertion point immediately after the heading for the division for which you want a minitoc environment.

    b. Enter a TeX field.

    c. In the entry area, type the appropriate command for the environment:

Command	Environment
\parttoc	Table of contents for parts
\partlof	List of figures for parts
\partlot	List of tables for parts
\minitoc	Table of contents for chapters
\minilof	List of figures for chapters
\minilot	List of tables for chapters
\secttoc	Table of contents for sections
\sectlof	List of figures for sections
\sectlot	List of tables for sections

    d. Choose OK.

More information is available in the program documentation. The package is installed in the `TCITeX/TeX/LaTeX/contrib/minitoc` directory.

Multicol

The *multicol* package implements up to 10 columns of text in the multicols environment and balances the length of the final columns for a nice appearance. The package permits both single- and multicolumn formats on the same page. It places footnotes across the bottom of the page rather than under each column. (Thus, it is incompatible with the *ftnright* package, page 125.) Note that within the multicolumn environment, only page-wide floating elements are permitted and not those in a selected column.

▶ **To create multiple columns of text**

1. Add the *multicol* package to your document.

2. Place the insertion point where you want multiple columns to begin.

3. Enter an encapsulated TeX field.

4. Type **\begin{multicols}{*x*}** where *x* is the number of columns you want.

5. Choose OK.

6. Place the insertion point where you want multiple columns to end.

7. Enter an encapsulated TeX field.

8. Type **\end{multicols}** and choose OK.

The package has a debugging option available through the Options and Packages command on the Typeset menu. The use of the *multicol* package can occasionally cause LaTeX errors related to line spacing and footnote numbering in *SWP* and *SW* documents. The package is installed in the `TCITeX/TeX/LaTeX/required/tools` directory as part of the Standard LaTeX Tools Bundle.

Natbib

The *natbib* package is used in combination with three bibliography styles (`abbrvnat.bst`, `plainnat.bst`, and `unsrtnat.bst`) to produce both author-date and standard numerical citations for BIBTEX bibliographies. The package is compatible with standard BIBTEX style files, such as `plain.bst`, and with those for the *harvard, apalike, chicago, astron,* and *authordate* packages. It serves as a single interface for most available bibliographic styles.

The package also supports a variety of author-date and numerical citation formats, including multiple citations, as shown in the examples in the following table. Most are based on two basic citation commands: \citet for text citations and \citep for parenthetical citations. The commands may take optional arguments to add text before and after the citation. See the package documentation for more extensive information about available commands.

Command	Citation Format
\citet{key}	Abbreviated author list in text, year in parentheses:
	Author-year: Swanson et al. (2004)
	Numerical: Swanson et al. [21]
\citet*{key}	Full author list in text, year in parentheses:
	Author-year: Swanson, Hughes, and Medd (2004)
\citep{key}	Abbreviated author list and year, in parentheses:
	Author-year: (Swanson et al., 2004)
	Numerical: [21]
\citep*{key}	Full author list and year, in parentheses:
	Author-year: (Swanson, Hughes, and Medd, 2004)
\citet[chap~2]{key}	Abbreviated author list in text, year and chapter in parentheses:
	Author-year: Swanson et al. (2004, chap. 2)
	Numerical: Swanson et al. [21, chap. 2]
\citep[chap~2]{key}	Abbreviated author list, year, and chapter, in parentheses:
	Author-year: (Swanson et al., 2004, chap. 2)
	Numerical: [21, chap. 2]
\citep[see][]{key}	Reference to abbreviated author list and year, in parentheses:
	Author-year: (see Swanson et al., 2004)
	Numerical: [see 21]
\citep[see][chap~2]{key}	Reference to abbreviated author list, year, and chapter, in parentheses:
	Author-year: (see Swanson et al., 2004, chap. 2)
	Numerical: [see 21, chap. 2]
\citep{key, key}	Abbreviated author lists and years, in parentheses:
	Author-year: (Medd et al, 2003; Swanson et al., 2004)
	Numerical: [19; 21]

The program interface doesn't directly support these commands, but you can achieve the citation format you want by inserting the commands in TeX fields.

▶ To create a bibliography for *natbib* citations

1. Add the *natbib* package to your document.

2. From the Typeset menu, choose Bibliography Choice.

3. Check BibTeX and choose OK.

4. Specify one of the *natbib* bibliography style files:

   a. Place the insertion point where you want the bibliography to appear.
   b. From the Insert menu, choose Typeset Object and then choose Bibliography.
   c. Select the BIBTeX database files you want to use.
   d. Scroll down the Style list to select abbrvnat.bst, plainnat.bst, or unsrtnat.bst, and choose OK.

5. Save and compile the document.

▶ To create a *natbib* citation

1. Add the *natbib* package to your document.

2. Place the insertion point where you want the citation.

3. Enter an encapsulated TeX field.

4. Type the command for the citation format you want, substituting the key for the BIBTeX reference.

5. Choose OK.

The *natbib* package is compatible with the *chapterbib, hyperref, showkeys* and *babel* packages, and can emulate the sorting and compressing functions of the *cite* package. The package is installed in the TCITeX/TeX/LaTeX/contrib/natbib directory.

Newapa

This package is required when you use the BIBTeX bibliography style newapa.bst. Other than adding the package to your document, no action is required. No options are available for the package, which is installed in the TCITeX/TeX/LaTeX/contrib/bibtex directory.

Newpnts

See Points and Newpnts on page 146.

Nomencl

The *nomencl* package produces a nomenclature list or list of symbols for your document by using TEX instructions inserted throughout the document as input for the makeindex program. You can use the package to create a list of symbols, a glossary, or an index-like list, such as an author index. Your document can have only one list created with the package.

Generating a nomenclature list is a multistep process involving adding the package to your document, identifying each symbol to be included in the list, indicating where the list should appear in the document, and finally running makeindex and compiling your document with LATEX.

▶ **To create a nomenclature list**

1. Add the *nomencl* package to your document.

2. If your document meets these three conditions:
   - you are using the *SWP* or *SW* output filter (not the Portable LaTeX filter)
   - the highest division level in your document is section
   - the chapter division isn't used

   then

   a. Save, close, and reopen the document.
   b. From the **Typeset** menu, choose **Preamble**.
   c. Click the mouse in the entry area and scroll to the bottom.
   d. After the line \input{tcilatex}, add a new line and type
      let**chapter****undefined**.
   e. Choose **OK**.

3. Add the \makeglossary command to the document preamble.

   a. From the **Typeset** menu, choose **Preamble** and click the mouse in the entry area.
   b. Scroll to the end of the preamble commands and begin a new line.
   c. Type **makeglossary** and choose **OK**.

4. Add \nomenclature commands in the text for each symbol to be included in the nomenclature list:

   a. Place the insertion point immediately after the first use of the symbol.
   b. Enter an encapsulated TEX field.
   c. In the entry area, type **nomenclature**{*x*}{*y*} where *x* is the symbol you want to appear in the list and *y* is the corresponding definition.
   d. Choose **OK**.

5. Add the \printglossary command:

   a. Place the insertion point where you want the nomenclature list to appear in your document.
   b. Enter a TEX field.
   c. In the box, type **printglossary** and choose **OK**.

6. Save and compile your document.

The compilation yields a .glo file with the same name as your document and places it in the same directory.

7. Run makeidx.

The *makeidx* package uses the .glo file as an input file. It creates an output file with a .gls extension and the same name and directory as your document. The .gls file contains the correctly ordered nomenclature list.

a. From the Windows **Start** menu, choose **Run**.

b. In the **Open** box, type the command appropriate for your installation and substitute the correct file name for the .glo and .gls files (where line breaks occur in this instruction, enter a space):

- For Version 5.5:
  c:\swp55\TCITeX\web2c\makeindex -o
  c:\swp55\docs*filename*.gls -s
  c:\swp55\TCITeX\TeX\LaTeX\contrib\nomencl\nomencl.ist
  c:\swp55\docs*filename*.glo
- For Version 4.x or 5.0:
  c:\swp50\TCITeX\web2c\makeindex -o
  c:\swp50\docs*filename*.gls -s
  c:\swp50\TCITeX\TeX\LaTeX\contrib\supported\nomencl\nomencl.ist
  c:\swp50\docs*filename*.glo
- For Version 3.5 or earlier:
  c:\swp35\TCITeX\SWTools\bin\makeindx -o
  c:\swp35\docs*filename*.gls -s
  c:\swp35\TCITeX\TeX\LaTeX\contrib\supported\nomencl\nomencl.ist
  c:\swp35\docs*filename*.glo

Correct the path names for your installation, if necessary.

c. Choose **OK**.

8. Typeset compile the document file from outside *SWP* or *SW*.

Note that if you compile using *SWP* or *SW*, the compiler won't find the .gls file and won't include the nomenclature list in the typeset document.

a. From the *SWP* or *SW* program group, choose the TrueTEX Formatter.

b. Select the file and choose **OK**.

If your document contains a table of contents or cross-references, you may need to compile it two or three times.

The available package options include language choices and the use of equation and page references. See more information on page 23 and additional documentation for the *nomencl* package in the `PackageSample-nomencl.tex` file in the SWSamples directory of your program installation. The package is in the `TCITeX/TeX/LaTeX/contrib/nomencl` directory.

Nopageno

The *nopageno* package provides a simple way to remove page numbers from both the opening pages and the normal pages of all classes of LaTeX documents. Other than adding the package to your document, no action is necessary. No package options are available. The package installs in the `TCITeX/TeX/LaTeX/contrib/carlisle` directory.

Numinsec

The *numinsec* package provides numbering of equations, figures, and tables within sections. Part of the SIAM document class distribution, the package is useful for other types of documents. The package adds the section number to the numbers of equations, figures, and tables. Thus, if the first equation in section 2 is the eighth in the document, it carries the number 2.1 instead of 8.

No action is required other than adding the package to your document. The package has no options. The *numinsec* package is installed in the `TCITeX/TeX/LaTeX/contrib/siam` directory.

Overcite

The *overcite* package has been superseded by the *cite* package (see page 110) and is included in *SWP* and *SW* for compatibility purposes only. The *overcite* package produces and superscripts compressed, sorted lists of numerical citations occurring in the text.

Paralist

The *paralist* package provides new list environments for itemized, description, and enumerated lists. With the package, lists can be typeset within paragraphs, as paragraphs in themselves, and in a compressed format. The package allows adjustment of the space between list items in the compressed format. The package also provides arguments for formatting labels in most of the list environments. The package incudes a configuration (`.cfg`) file that makes standard list environments typeset as if they were the compressed list environments defined by the package. Although the `.cfg` file isn't part of the default package, the package allows adding a `.cfg` file. The package may conflict with the *babel* package.

The package is installed in the `TCITeX/TeX/LaTeX/contrib/paralist` directory.

Parallel

The *parallel* package creates an environment that aligns text in two columns or on facing pages. You can adjust the column width and separate the columns with a vertical line, as shown here:

This is text in the English language explaining the \foo command.

Dies ist Text in deutscher Sprache, der das Kommando \foo erläutert.

Options are available to format footnotes that occur in the text within the environment; the footnotes are typeset at the end of the environment. After adding the package, you enter the environment and all the text within it in TEX fields in the body of your document. The package is useful for comparing two texts, as in translation projects.

▶ **To enter aligned text in two columns or on facing pages**

1. Add the *parallel* package to your document.

2. Modify the package options to select the footnote format you want. See the package documentation for details.

3. Place the insertion point where you want the parallel environment to begin.

4. Enter an encapsulated TEX field.

5. In the entry area, type

   begin{Parallel}[*option***]{left-width}{right-width}**

   where *option* is one of these commands:

option	Effect
c (default)	print aligned text in columns
v	print a vertical line between columns
p	print text on two facing pages

   If the width parameters are left empty, the package sets each one to about half the width of the text on the page.

6. Type

   ParallelLText{*text that is to appear on the left***}**

   ParallelRText{*text that is to appear on the right***}**

   end{Parallel}

7. Choose OK.

Note that a blank page can result if LATEX has to skip a page in order to place the parallel text on facing pages. Also, large size differences in the right and left text can result in unattractive output. The package is installed in the `TCITeX/TeX/LaTeX/contrib/parallel` directory.

Picins

The *picins* package provides precise control over the placement of inline graphics. It also provides dashed, solid, and shadow frames around the graphics, and allows space for a caption. Tables aren't supported. The placement of graphics is controlled with commands in TEX fields in the body of your document. The commands are generally of this format:

`\parpic[`*x*`]{\includegraphics[natwidth=`*y*`in,natheight=`*z*`in]{`***graphic***`}}`

where *x* indicates the position on the page; *y* and *z* are the width and height, respectively, of the graphic image; and ***graphic*** is the full path name for the graphics file. Additional command elements are available to specify the position of the caption and the kind and size of frame. See the package documentation for details.

For another way to wrap text around graphics, see the *wrapfig* package on page 175. The package is installed in the `TCITeX/TeX/latex209/contrib/picins` directory.

Pifont

See PSNFSS Packages on page 147.

Placeins

The *placeins* package prevents floating graphics or tables from floating into the next section of the document or past a designated point in the document, signaled by a `\FloatBarrier` command. The package successfully controls the placement of floating objects in DVI files, in PDF files, and in files created with the Portable LaTeX output filter. The package thus has a wider use than the *float* package, which controls the placement of floating objects using the H placement option with the FRAME macro in `tcilatex.tex`. Because PDFLaTeXand the Portable LaTeX output filter bypass the FRAME macro, the *float* package method can't be used to control the placement of floating objects in PDF or Portable LaTeX files.

▶ **To prevent floating objects from appearing in the next section**

1. Add the *placeins* package to your document.

2. On the Typeset toolbar, click the Options and Packages button ▦ or, from the Typeset menu, choose Options and Packages and then choose the Package Options tab.

3. From the Packages in Use list, select the *placeins* package and choose Modify.

4. In the Category list, select Barrier at section and, in the Options list, select Yes.

5. Choose OK to close each dialog box and return to your document.

▶ **To prevent a floating object from appearing after a designated point**

1. Position the insertion point where you want accumulated floating objects to appear.

2. Enter an encapsulated TeX field.

3. In the entry area, type **FloatBarrier** and choose OK.

By default, the `\FloatBarrier` command is very strict. It prevents a floating object from appearing above the start of the current section or below the start of the next section, even though the floating object would appear on the same page as its intended section. Each restriction can be relaxed separately by using the `above` and `below` package options. The package is installed in the `TCITeX/TeX/LaTeX/contrib/ misc` directory.

Points and Newpnts

The *points* and *newpnts* packages were developed to help typeset exams. Both packages place point values for exam questions in the left margin. The *newpnts* package places the values slightly farther into the margin for less confusion with list item numbers. The packages also provide a way to resume list numbering that has been interrupted by text. The two features can be used independently.

No options are available for the packages, but you can enter the necessary macros in TEX fields. The packages are distributed with *SWP* and *SW* but, unlike the other packages included with the program, are not available on CTAN. The packages are installed in the `TCITeX/TeX/LaTeX/SWmisc` directory.

▶ **To place a point value for an exam question in the margin**

1. Add the *points* or the *newpnts* package to your document.

2. Create the list of exam questions.

   Note that you don't have to use a numbered list.

3. For each question,

   a. Place the insertion point at the beginning of the list item, immediately to the right of the lead-in object.
   b. Enter an encapsulated TEX field.
   c. Type **POINTS**{*x*} where **x** is the point value for the question.
   d. Choose **OK**.

▶ **To resume numbering of an interrupted numbered list**

1. Add the *points* or the *newpnts* package to your document.

2. Place the insertion point at the end of the paragraph immediately after which you want the list to begin.

   The paragraph can otherwise be empty.

3. Enter an encapsulated TEX field.

4. In the entry area, type **setcounter**{**enumi**}{*x*}**RESUME** where *x* is a value one less than the starting number for the list.

   If you want your list to start with 1, use **setcounter**{**enumi**}{**0**}**RESUME**. Note that the command is case-sensitive.

5. Choose **OK**.

6. Create a numbered list.

7. Interrupt the list with an unnumbered paragraph.

8. Place the insertion point at the end of the unnumbered paragraph.

9. Enter an encapsulated TEX field.

10. In the entry area, type **RESUME** and choose OK.

11. Enter the remaining numbered list items.

LATEX resumes the list with the next sequential list item number.

Portland

The *portland* package implements changing from portrait to landscape orientation and back within your *SWP* or *SW* document. No special drivers are required, but you may need to change the orientation settings for your printer so that your document prints properly. If you have a single page with an orientation different from that of the rest of the document, you may need to print it separately after changing the printer settings accordingly.

You can define portrait and landscape environments with simple commands inserted in TEX fields. No package options are available.

▶ **To define a landscape or portrait environment**

1. Add the *portland* package to your document.

2. Place the insertion point where you want the orientation to change in your document.

3. Enter a TEX field.

4. Type **landscape** to change the page layout orientation from portrait to landscape or **portrait** to change the page layout orientation from landscape to portrait.

5. Choose OK.

The *portland* package is installed in the `TCITeX/TeX/latex209/contrib/ misc` directory of your Version 3.5 or later installation. The `PackageSample- portland.tex` file in the `SWSamples` directory of your Version 4.0 or later program installation contains additional information. If you have an earlier version you can download both the package and the sample file from our website. See also the *lscape* package on page 133.

PSNFSS Packages

The PostScript NFSS bundle is a required part of LATEX. The bundle provides a complete working setup of the LATEX font selection scheme for use with PostScript fonts. The packages are installed in the `TCITeX/TeX/LaTeX/required/psnfss` directory.

The font packages included in the bundle completely replace one or more of the font families used by LaTeX for roman, sans serif, typewriter, or mathematics fonts. If the PostScript fonts are present on your system, adding the *PSNFSS* packages changes the default font families as shown in the table below. The top row indicates the default (Computer Modern) font family. A blank indicates that the package doesn't change the corresponding default font family. Other than installing the packages, no change is required to make the default replacements noted in the table.

	Font Family			
Package	**roman**	**sans serif**	**typewriter**	**math**
(none)	CM Roman	CM Sans Serif	CM Type-writer	≈ CM Roman
mathptmx	Times			≈ Times
mathpazo	Palatino			≈ Palatino
helvet		Helvetica		
avant		Avant Garde		
courier			Courier	
chancery	Zapf Chancery			
bookman	Bookman	Avant Garde	Courier	
newcent	New Century Schoolbook	Avant Garde	Courier	
utopia	Utopia			
charter	Charter			

Several packages that were included in the PSNFSS bundle in the past have been superseded: *mathptm, mathpple,* and *palatino.* Another superseded package, *times,* is still included with *SWP* and *SW;* see more information below. Another package, *pifont,* is available for use in PDF files.

Mathptmx

The *mathptmx* package changes the default roman font family to Adobe Times. The virtual mathptmx fonts are used for mathematics. The package scales large mathematical symbols to fit the base font size. Bold math fonts are not supported.

Mathpazo

The package changes the default roman font family to Adobe Palatino. The virtual mathpazo fonts are used for mathematics. Package options include slanted uppercase Greek letters, upright Δ and Ω, italic bold mathematical symbols, and large mathematical symbols. Using the *mathpazo* package with $\mathcal{AMS}$ symbols requires special attention; please refer to the package documentation.

Helvet

If you have the Helvetica PostScript font installed on your system, adding the *helvet* package changes the default sans serif font family to Helvetica. (Note that Helvetica is slightly larger that other typefaces. The package documentation explains how to adjust for the difference.) If the font isn't installed on your system, adding the package changes the default sans serif font to the Windows Arial font. The other font packages—*avant, courier, chancery, times, bookman, newcent, utopia, charter*—work the same way.

Adding the package doesn't affect the default serif font. If you want your entire document to print in the Helvetica font, modify the preamble of your document.

▶ **To change the default font**

1. From the Typeset menu, choose Preamble.

2. Click the mouse in the entry area and start a new line after the last entry.

3. Type **\renewcommand{\familydefault}{\sfdefault}** and choose OK.

Times

The *times* package implements the use of the NFSS Times font for text but leaves mathematics in the Computer Modern fonts. The package produces ligatures and improves kerning, and its use creates more portable document files. See also the *mathtime* package on page 136. This example illustrates the results produced by the *times* package:

By the triangle inequality for integrals and the above inequalities, for $n \geq N$;

$$\left| \int_c \left[f(z) - \sum_{k=0}^{n} a_k z^k \right] dz \right| \leq \epsilon \cdot (\text{length of } C)$$

Since ϵ is arbitrary, the limit is zero.

▶ **To use the *times* package**

1. On the Typeset toolbar, click the Options and Packages button ▦ or, from the Typeset menu, choose Options and Packages and then choose the Package Options tab.

2. Select the font package currently in use and choose Remove.

3. Add the *times* package to your document and choose OK.

No options are available. See the online Help and the package documentation for more information about the implementation of the *times* package in a TrueTeX environment.

Pifont

The *pifont* package supports symbol fonts and provides commands for using the Zapf Dingbats font in PDF files; see the package documentation for details. The package also provides an interface to other font families.

Ragged2e

The *ragged2e* package provides less extreme raggedness than the standard LaTeX commands \flushleft and \flushright by overwriting the LaTeX default value for interword space. The package redefines standard LaTeX justification commands and allows their modification by the user. See the package documentation for information about using the large number of parameters that define the new commands and environments.

The package requires the *everysel* package. Both packages are installed in the TCITeX/TeX/LaTeX/contrib/ms directory.

Relsize

In LaTeX, these text font size commands, listed from smallest to largest, are available: \tiny, \scriptsize, \footnotesize, \small, \normalsize, \large, \Large, \LARGE, \huge, and \Huge. The *relsize* package provides a way to change the font size of text by stepping through the font size hierarchy. The \relsize command has as its argument a positive or negative number that specifies the number of steps by which the current size should be changed. Thus, if the command \relsize{3} occurs when the current font size is footnotesize, the next text will be typeset as large. Similarly, if the command \relsize{-4} occurs when the current font size is large, the next text will be typeset as scriptsize. The commands appear in TeX fields in the body of your document.

The package includes several shortcut commands, \larger and \smaller, which change the text font size by one step in the corresponding direction. An additional command specifies the text font size based on a scale factor, not unlike the *scalefnt* package.

Two commands are available for stepping through the mathematics size styles. From smallest to largest, the size styles are \scriptscriptstyle, \scriptstyle, \textstyle, and \displaystyle. However, because mathematical operators and delimiters are scaled automatically in *SWP* and *SW*, this package feature is not particularly useful. If you choose to use the commands, note that they are not always reliable because spacing problems can occur.

▶ **To step the text font size up or down**

1. Add the *relsize* package to your document.

2. Place the insertion point where you want the change in font size to begin.

3. Enter an encapsulated TeX field.

4. In the entry area, type **\relsize{*x*}** where *x* is the number of steps you want to move through the hierarchy.

5. Choose **OK**.

The package is installed in the TCITeX/TeX/LaTeX/contrib/misc directory.

Remreset

The *remreset* package removes a counter from the reset list controlled by a second counter. In other words, the package prevents a designated counter from being reset when LaTeX increments a second counter. For example, most reports normally reset the equation number at the beginning of each chapter. You can use this package to remove the reset so that equations are numbered sequentially throughout the report.

▶ **To prevent a counter from being reset**

1. Add the *remreset* package to your document.

2. From the Typeset menu, choose Preamble and click the mouse in the entry area.

3. Add the commands

   \makeatletter
   \@removefromreset{*x*}{*y*}
   \makeatother

   where *x* is the counter you don't want to reset, such as footnote or theorem, and *y* is the controlling counter, such as chapter or section.

4. Choose OK.

The package command \@removefromreset is the opposite of the standard LaTeX command \@addtoreset.

No package options are available. The package is installed in the TCITeX/TeX/LaTeX/contrib/carlisle directory.

Revsymb

The *revsymb* package defines the lambdabar symbol λ and other symbols unique to REVTeX 4. Other than adding the package to your document, no action is required. The *revsymb* package is part of the REVTeX 4 distribution and is installed in the TCITeX/TeX/LaTeX/contrib/revtex4 directory.

Rotating

The *rotating* package implements three environments within which in-line figures, tables, and captions can be rotated by an arbitrary number of degrees. Two additional environments allow rotation of floating objects, which are typeset alone on separate pages.

Note that the TrueTeX Previewer provided with *SWP* and *SW* doesn't support rotation; you must use a different DVI previewer and print driver if you want to use the *rotating* package to rotate figures, tables, and captions in a DVI file. The package options include many drivers. However, PDF viewers support rotation, so you can use the package to rotate figures, tables, and captions in typeset PDF files.

You must enter rotating environments as TeX commands in encapsulated TeX fields, one to begin and another to end the environment. The information to be rotated sits between the two.

▶ **To rotate in-line figures, tables, or captions**

1. Add the *rotating* package to your document.

2. Place the insertion point where you want the rotation to begin.

3. Begin the rotation environment:

   a. Enter an encapsulated TEX field.
   b. In the entry area, type **begin**{*command*}{*x*} where ***command*** is one of the available environments:

Environment	Effect
sideways	Print the contents of the environment turned 90 degrees
turn	Print the contents of the environment turned an arbitrary number of degrees
rotate	Print the contents of the environment turned an arbitrary number of degrees (space for the rotated results isn't necessarily created)

   and *x* is the number of degrees to be rotated. When *x* is positive, the rotation is counterclockwise; when *x* is negative, clockwise. The **sideways** command doesn't require a degree argument.
   c. Choose OK.

4. Enter the figure, table, or caption to be rotated.

5. End the rotation environment:

   a. Enter an encapsulated TEX field.
   b. In the entry area, type **end**{*command*} where ***command*** is the rotation environment.
   c. Choose OK.

▶ **To rotate floating figures and tables**

1. Add the *rotating* package to your document.

2. Place the insertion point where you want the rotation to begin.

3. Begin the rotation environment:

   a. Enter an encapsulated TEX field.
   b. Type **begin**{**sidewaysfigure**}**centering** or **begin**{**sidewaystable**}**centering**.
   c. Choose OK.

4. Enter an in-line table or an in-line graphic.

5. If you want a caption,

   a. Enter an encapsulated TEX field.
   b. In the entry area, type **caption**{*text*} where ***text*** is the text of the caption.
   c. Choose OK.

6. If you want to add cross-references to the table or figure, enter a marker.

7. End the rotation environment:

   a. Enter an encapsulated TeX field.
   b. In the entry area, type **\end{sidewaysfigure}** or **\end{sidewaystable}**.
   c. Choose **OK**.

The package is installed in the `TCITeX/TeX/LaTeX/contrib/rotating` directory.

Scalefnt

The *scalefnt* package implements a command that scales the current font according to a specified scale factor. A factor of 2 doubles the size of the current font, like this. A factor of .5 reduces it by half, like this. You may specify any scale factor. With scalable fonts, LaTeX uses the requested font size. With bitmap font sizes, LaTeX rounds to the nearest available size.

▶ **To scale the size of the current font**

1. Add the *scalefnt* package to your document.

2. Place the insertion point where you want the font scaling to begin.

3. Enter an encapsulated TeX field.

4. In the entry area, type **\begingroup** and choose **OK**.

5. Enter an encapsulated TeX field.

6. In the entry area, type **\scalefont{*x*}** where *x* is the scale factor.

7. Choose **OK**.

8. Place the insertion point where you want the font scaling to end.

9. Enter an encapsulated TeX field.

10. In the entry area, type **\endgroup** and choose **OK**.

If you don't surround the `\scalefont{x}` command with the encapsulated TeX fields containing the `\begingroup` and `\endgroup` commands, the font scaling will apply to the remainder of the document.

You can reverse the font scaling by using the reciprocal of the first scale factor in a second `scalefont` command. For example, you can begin text that is one and one half times normal size by inserting the TeX command `\scalefont{1.5}`. Later, you can return to the normal font size by inserting .66667, the decimal equivalent of $\frac{1}{1.5}$ (the reciprocal of the scalefont factor) in the TeX command `\scalefont{.66667}`.

No options are available. The package is installed in the `TCITeX/TeX/LaTeX/contrib/carlisle` directory.

Sectsty

The *sectsty* package modifies the typeset appearance of division headings in articles, books, reports, and other standard documents. The package commands combine with standard LaTeX font selection commands to affect the font family, size, justification, use of rules, and numbering of division headers. Thus, you can change the text of the section headings from a sans serif font, as used in this manual, to a serif font, such as Computer Modern Roman. Using the package to change the justification for headings that are automatically indented is possible but not advisable. The *sectsty* package doesn't work with documents created with Style Editor shells.

▶ **To change the typeset appearance of section headings**

1. Add the *sectsty* package to your document.

2. From the Typeset menu, choose **Preamble** and click the mouse in the entry area.

3. On a new line, add the command **\\headingcommand{\\fontcommand}** where ***headingcommand*** is the package command indicating the section heading you want to change and ***fontcommand*** is one or more standard LaTeX font selection commands (see below).

4. Repeat step 3 for each type of section heading you want to modify.

5. Choose OK.

The package has no options. Available package commands include, but aren't limited to, those in the table below. See the package documentation for a complete listing of available commands.

Command	Effect
\\allsectionsfont	Changes the appearance of all section headings
\\partfont	Changes the appearance of all part headings and numbers
\\chapterfont	Changes the appearance of all chapter headings and numbers
\\sectionfont	Changes the appearance of all section headings
\\subsectionfont	Changes the appearance of all subsection headings
\\partnumberfont	Changes the appearance of all part numbers
\\parttitlefont	Changes the appearance of all part titles only
\\chapternumberfont	Changes the appearance of all chapter numbers
\\chaptertitlefont	Changes the appearance of all chapter titles only

Standard LaTeX font selection commands include those to select a font family, such as \\sffamily or \\ttfamily; a font shape, such as \\itshape or \\textsc; a font series (width and weight), such as \\bfseries or \\mdseries; or a font size, such as \\Large or \\huge. Font selection commands also include those related to justification: \\centering, \\raggedright, and \\raggedleft.

Thus, although the basic `\section{\fontcommand}` command syntax is the same, the actual commands can vary considerably depending on the extent of the modifications you want to make. An example shows the possibilities available with the package. The command `\allsectionsfont{\raggedleft}` right-justifies all headings in a standard LaTeX report, changing their appearance from the one shown on page to the one shown on page 155 to the one shown on page 156.

Because *sectsty* redefines LaTeX sectioning commands, any package that requires sectioning commands won't necessarily work with the *sectsty* package. The package works for standard document classes only. The package is installed in the `TCITeX/ TeX/LaTeX/contrib/sectsty` directory.

Chapter 1

This is a Chapter

Some text goes here.

1.1   This is a Section Heading

Some text goes here.

1.1.1   This is a Subsection Heading

Some text goes here.

Chapter 1

This is a Chapter

Some text goes here.

1.1   This is a Section Heading

Some text goes here.

1.1.1   This is a Subsection Heading

Some text goes here.

Setspace

The *setspace* package replaces the *doublespace* package. It produces double and one-and-one-half line spacing based on the point size in use. The default is single spacing. With *setspace,* you can set the overall document spacing and the spacing for portions of the document. Changing spacing in the entire document doesn't affect footnotes, for which you must specify spacing individually.

In addition to the package commands described below, a linespacing option is available through the Options and Packages command on the Typeset menu.

▶ **To change the spacing for the entire document**

1. Add the *setspace* package to your document.

2. Modify the package options to select the spacing you want.

3. Choose OK.

▶ **To change the spacing for a portion of the document**

1. Add the *setspace* package to your document.

2. Place the insertion point where you want the spacing to change.

3. Enter a TEX field.

4. Type **\singlespacing** or **\onehalfspacing** or **\doublespacing** and choose OK.

   or

   Type **\setstretch{*x*}** where *x* is a number indicating the spacing you want, and then choose OK.

   For example, the command `\setstretch{3}` produces triple spacing.

5. Place the insertion point where you want to return to the original spacing.

6. Repeat steps 3–4.

Because the onehalfspace environment increases the spacing, you should avoid using it in a double-spaced document. The *setspace* package is installed in the `TCITeX/ TeX/LaTeX/contrib/setspace` directory.

Showidx

The *showidx* package prints the arguments of all index commands in the margin of the page on which they occur. The package facilitates troubleshooting and checking index entries. If you use the package to develop your index, remember to remove it before you typeset the final copy. Besides adding the package to your document, no action is required to use *showidx*. No package options are available. The package is installed in the `TCITeX/TeX/LaTeX/base` directory.

Showkeys

The *showkeys* package prints the keys for each label, cross-reference, page reference, citation, and bibliography item in your draft document. The package prints keys for labels and bibliography items in small boxes in the margin. Keys for cross-references, page references and citations appear where they occur, in small type elevated above the line. The package simplifies management of keys while documents are in development.

Besides adding the package to your document, no action is required to use *showkeys*. However, the package options include displaying reference and citation labels and showing labels in color. When you're ready to print the final copy of your document, choose the `final` option to suppress the action of the package or remove the package alto-gether. The package works with the `fleqn` option, $\mathcal{A}_{\mathcal{M}}\mathcal{S}$-LaTeX packages, and the *varioref, natbib,* and *harvard* packages. The *showkeys* package is installed in the `TCITeX/TeX/LaTeX/required/tools` directory as part of the Standard LaTeX Tools Bundle.

Showlabels

The *showlabels* package facilitates troubleshooting of keys and markers, including the keys for automatically generated equation numbers. The package prints all keys and markers in the margin of the document at the line on which they are defined. Besides adding the package to your document, no action is required to use *showlabels.* How-ever, you can place the labels in the inside or outside margin with the option, available through the Options and Packages command on the Typeset menu. Remember to remove the package before you typeset the final copy of your document.

The package works in two-column formats but doesn't work well with the *mul-ticol* package. The package is installed in the `TCITeX/TeX/LaTeX/contrib/showlabels` directory.

Sidecap

The *sidecap* package provides typeset captions to the left or right side of floating graph-ics or tables. The package defines two environments, SCfigure and SCtable, that create centered side-by-side minipages of customizable width. The environments, which are entered in TeX fields in your document, create floating objects that can be positioned with standard float parameters. Options allow the placement of the caption on the right or left, always on the outside, or always on the inside. Captions can have justified or ragged edges. A `wide` option allows the caption to extend into the margin. Starred versions of the two environments are available for double-column layouts. Be sure to process the document through TeX at least twice to typeset left- and right-hand pages correctly.

▶ **To create captions to the side of graphics or tables**

1. Add the *sidecap* package to your document.

2. On the Typeset toolbar, click the Options and Packages button ▦ or, from the Typeset menu, choose Options and Packages and then choose the Package Op-tions tab.

3. From the Packages in Use list, select the *sidecap* package and choose Modify.

4. Choose the placement option you want:

Option	Effect
outercaption (default)	Caption appears on left on left pages and on right on right pages.
innercaption	Caption appears on left on right pages and on right on left pages.
leftcaption	Caption always appears on left.
rightcpation	Caption always appears on right.
wide	Caption and figure or table may extend into the margin.
raggedright, raggedleft, ragged*	Caption is better justified.

5. Choose OK.

6. Begin the figure or table environment:

   a. Place the insertion point in your document where you want the graphic or table to appear.

   b. Enter an encapsulated TEX field.

   c. In the entry area, type

      \begin{SCfigure}[*relwidth*][*placement*]

      or

      \begin{SCtable}[*relwidth*][*placement*]

      where **relwidth** is an optional caption width relative to the width of the graphic or table, and **placement** is the floating position you want:

placement	Position of the floating frame
h	As close as possible to the entry point in the text
t	At the top of a page
b	At the bottom of a page
p	On a separate page containing only floating frames

   d. On a new line, type **caption**{*text*} where **text** is the text of the caption.

   e. Choose OK.

7. Enter the graphic or table.

   Do not enter the graphic or table as a floating object.

8. End the environment:

   a. Place the insertion point where you want the environment to end.

   b. Enter an encapsulated TEX field.

   c. In the entry area, type **end**{**SCfigure**} or **end**{**SCtable**}.

   d. Choose OK.

The package uses the *ragged2e* package, which is provided with the program. The package is installed in the `TCITeX/TeX/LaTeX/contrib/sidecap` directory.

Slashed

The *slashed* package provides commands that place a slash through a character to produce the *Feynman slashed character* notation. The package works in mathematics. Some customizing of the placement of the slash is possible. Note that the package doesn't produce attractive results with some italic fonts.

You can use the package to produce Feynman characters in two ways: with TeX fields or with TeX fields in combination with negated characters. The second method modifies the program file `tcilatex.tex` to redefine the way a negated character is typeset. Because `tcilatex.tex` isn't used if you save your document with the Portable LaTeX filter, the method is incompatible with Portable LaTeX files.

▶ **To produce a Feynman slashed character with TeX fields**

1. Add the *slashed* package to your document.

2. Place the insertion point where you want the slashed character to appear.

3. Start mathematics.

4. Enter a TeX field.

5. Type **slashed**{*x*} where *x* is the upper- or lowercase letter you want to slash.

6. Choose OK.

▶ **To produce a Feynman slashed character with negated characters**

1. Add the *slashed* package to your document.

2. Place the insertion point in text in your document before the first use of a slashed character.

3. Enter an encapsulated TeX field.

4. In the entry area, type **def****NEG#1**{**ensuremath**{**slashed**{#1}}}.

5. Choose OK.

6. Place the insertion point where you want the slashed character to appear.

7. Enter the character you want to use.

8. Click [🔍]; from the Edit menu, choose **Properties**; or press CTRL+N.

9. Check the **Negate** box and choose OK.

10. Repeat steps 5–8 for any additional slashed characters you want.

No options are available. The slashed package installs in the `TCITeX/TeX/LaTeX/contrib/carlisle` directory.

Subfig

The *subfig* package supports the use of small figures and tables within a single floating figure or table environment. The package supersedes the *subfigure* package but isn't completely compatible with it.

The package supports the positioning, captioning, and labeling of small figures and tables and, perhaps most significantly, the inclusion of their captions in the list of figures or tables. Package options define the placement and caption formatting for the subfigures and subtables. The options are flexible, allowing such variations as captions both for the entire figure and for each subelement, or a caption for the entire figure and only a label for each subelement.

The options available through the Options and Packages command on the Typeset menu define the placement and caption formatting of all subfigures and subtables in the document. Commands in TEX fields in the document body define specific subfigures and subtables. The package works with the *caption* package and uses its features for customizing caption layout. It also requires the *ragged2e* and *everysel* packages, which it calls automatically. The package should be compatible with other packages that modify or extend float environments.

The following instructions don't apply to Portable LATEX documents, because the FRAME macro that defines graphics is defined in `tcilatex.tex`, which isn't included in Portable LATEX files.

▶ **To create subfigures or subtables with the *subfig* package**

1. Add the *caption* package to your document.

2. Add the *subfig* package to your document and make sure it appears after the *caption* package in the Packages in Use list.

3. Modify the *subfig* package options to format the captions as you want.

4. Create a floating environment for subfigures:

   a. Place the insertion point in the body of your document where you want the subfigures to appear.
   b. Enter an encapsulated TEX field.
   c. Type **begin{figure}** to specify a floating graphics environment.
   d. If you want a caption to apply to all the subfigures in the environment, type **caption{*title*}** where *title* is the caption you want.
      This caption will appear in the list of figures for your document.
   e. If you want to create cross-references to the environment, type **label{*x*}** where *x* is the key for the floating environment.
   f. Choose OK.

5. Prepare each subfigure:

   a. Open a new, completely empty document.
   b. From the File menu, choose Document Info and choose the Save Options tab.

    c. Uncheck **Store Relative Graphics Paths** and choose **OK**.

    d. From the **File** menu, choose **Import Picture** to import the graphic image you want as a subfigure.

    e. Choose **Properties** and then choose the **Layout** tab.

    f. In the **Placement** area, check **In Line**.

    g. Make any other modifications you need and then choose **OK**.

    h. Save the document.

    i. Open the `.tex` file with an ASCII editor.

    j. Find the lines that represent the figure and copy them to the clipboard.
    The lines will have an appearance something like this:

```
\FRAME{dtbpF}{3.2534in}{2.2589in}{0pt}{}{}{newdoc35.wmf}{\special{language
"Scientific Word";type "GRAPHIC";maintain-aspect-ratio TRUE;display
"USEDEF";valid_file "F";width 3.2534in;height 2.2589in;depth
0pt;original-width 5.3748in;original-height 3.7187in;cropleft "0";croptop
"1";cropright "1";cropbottom "0";filename
'../graphics/newdoc35.wmf';file-properties "XNPEU";}}
```

6. Return to your original *SWP* or *SW* document and reopen the encapsulated TₑX field for the floating environment.

7. Create the subfigure:

    a. Place the insertion point on a new line below the existing commands.

    b. Type **subfloat**[*entry*][*caption*] where *entry* is the subfigure caption as you want it to appear in the list of figures and *caption* is the subfigure caption as you want it to appear in the body of your document.

    c. Type { .

    d. If you want to create cross-references to the subfigure, type **label**{*x*} where *x* is the key for the subfigure.

    e. Paste the lines representing the figure from the clipboard to the TₑX field.

    f. Type } and choose **OK**.

8. Repeat steps 4–7 for each subfigure in the floating environment.

9. End the floating environment:

    a. Reopen the encapsulated TₑX field for the floating environment.

    b. At the end of the entries, type **end**{**figure**} and choose **OK**.

10. Create a floating environment for subtables:

    a. Place the insertion point in the body of your document where you want the subtables to appear.

    b. Enter an encapsulated TₑX field.

    c. Type **begin**{**table**} to specify a floating table environment.

    d. If you want a caption to apply to all the subtables in the environment, type **caption**{*title*} where *title* is the caption you want.
    This caption will appear in the list of tables for your document.

e. If you want to create cross-references to the environment, type **label**{*x*} where *x* is the key for the floating environment.

f. Choose **OK**.

11. Prepare each subtable:

a. Open a new, completely empty document.

b. On the Standard toolbar, click the Table button or, from the **Insert** menu, choose **Table**.

c. Specify the table size and alignment you want and choose **OK**.

d. Fill the table with information, formatted as you want.

e. Save the document.

f. Open the .tex file with an ASCII editor.

g. Find the lines that represent the table and copy them to the clipboard.

12. Return to your original *SWP* or *SW* document and reopen the encapsulated TₑX field for the floating environment.

13. Create the subfigure:

a. Place the insertion point on a new line below the existing commands.

b. Type **subfloat**[*entry*][*caption*] where *entry* is the subtable caption as you want it to appear in the list of tables and *caption* is the subtable caption as you want it to appear in the body of your document.

c. Type { .

d. If you want to create cross-references to the subfigure, type **label**{*x*} where *x* is the key for the subfigure.

e. Paste the lines representing the table from the clipboard to the TₑX field.

f. Type } and choose **OK**.

14. Repeat steps 10–13 for each subtable in the floating environment.

15. End the floating environment:

a. Reopen the encapsulated TₑX field for the floating environment.

b. At the end of the entries, type **end**{**table**} and choose **OK**.

16. Save and typeset compile your document.

▶ **To include subfigures and subtables in the lists of figures and tables**

1. On the Typeset toolbar, click the Front Matter button or, from the **Typeset** menu, choose **Front Matter**.

2. Place the insertion point after the **Make TOC** field.

3. Press ENTER and apply the Remove Item Tag.

4. Apply the Make LOF tag and choose **OK**.

5. Apply the Make LOT tag and choose **OK**.

6. From the **Typeset** menu, choose **Preamble**.

7. Click the mouse in the entry area.

8. On a new line at the end of the entries, type **\setcounter{lofdepth} {2}** to include subfigure captions in the list of figures.

   or

   \setcounter{lotdepth} {2} to include subtable captions in the list of tables.

9. Choose **OK**.

In the file `PackageSample-subfig.tex` in the `SWSamples` directory of your program installation, you can find several examples and more information about the *subfig* package. The package is installed in the `TCITeX/TeX/LaTeX/contrib/subfig` directory.

Subfigure

This package has been superseded by the *subfig* package (see page 161) and is included in *SWP* and *SW* for compatibility purposes. The package supports the use of small figures and tables within a single floating figure or table environment. It supports the positioning, captioning, and labeling of small figures and tables, and the inclusion of their captions in the list of figures and tables. The *subfigure* package is installed in the `TCITeX/TeX/LaTeX/contrib/subfigure` directory.

Subfloat

This package enables subnumbering of separate floating objects (both figures and tables) so that the relationship between them might more easily be emphasized. When typeset, the objects, which can be separated by text, have numbers such as *Table 1a, Table 1b, Table 1c, ...* The function of the package is similar to that of the subequations environment of the *amsmath* package. It differs from the function of the *subfig* package, which generates numbered subfigures and subtables within a single floating object.

No action is needed other than adding the package to your document and enclosing the floating objects within a subfigures or subtables environment. The two environments can be intermixed. However, four macros are available to customize numbering; see the package documentation for details.

▶ **To create subnumbers for floating objects**

1. Add the *subfloat* package to your document.

2. Place the insertion point where you want the subnumbering to begin.

3. Enter a TeX field.

4. In the entry area, type **\begin{subfigures}** or **\begin{subtables}**.

5. Choose OK.

6. Enter the floating objects for which you want subnumbering.

    The objects can be separated by text.

7. After the final object, enter a TeX field.

8. In the entry area, type **\end{subfigures}** or **\end{subtables}**.

9. Choose OK.

    All floating objects of the same kind between the `\begin` and `\end` statements will share a main figure or table number.

    The package is installed in the `TCITeX/TeX/LaTeX/contrib/subfloat` directory.

Supertabular

The *supertabular* package defines two environments, supertabular and supertabular*, that support tabular environments longer than a single page. The package creates a separate tabular environment for each page. Therefore, the column widths for a continuing table may vary from page to page. (The *longtable* package described on page 133, avoids varying column widths for extended tables.)

The package supports a series of commands for defining the contents of the column headings, any material to be inserted at the end of each page of the environment, and a table caption. See the package documentation for complete information. The basic `\supertabular` command is similar to the standard LaTeX `\tabular` command; please refer to LaTeX sources for further information about using commands of this type. Additionally, a package option determines the extent of error information that is written to the `.log` file.

▶ **To create a multipage table within a supertabular environment**

1. Add the *supertabular* package to your document.

2. Enter an encapsulated TeX field.

3. Enter the commands for the entire supertabular environment, beginning with **\begin{supertabular}** and ending with **\end{supertabular}**.

4. Choose OK.

If you place a supertabular environment inside or on the same page as a floating element, the results are unpredictable. See also the *xtab* package, page 176. The *supertabular* package is installed in the `TCITeX/TeX/LaTeX/contrib/supertabular` directory.

Tabularx

The *tabularx* package defines a tabular environment that generates a table with a specified width. The package automatically adjusts the widths of certain columns rather than adding space between columns. The basic command is similar to the standard LaTeX \tabular*command; please refer to the package documentation for complete instructions and to LaTeX sources for further information about using commands of this type.

▶ **To create a tabular environment of a specified width**

1. Add the *tabularx* package to your document.

2. Enter an encapsulated TeX field.

3. Type **\begin{tabularx}**{*w*}{|**X**|**X** . . .|} where *w* is the desired width of the table and *X* marks each column for which the width is to be adjusted.

4. Type the commands for the remainder of entire supertabular environment.

5. Type **\end{tabularx}**.

6. Choose OK.

The single package option involves debugging. The package is installed in the `TCITeX/TeX/LaTeX/required/tools` directory as part of the Standard LaTeX Tools Bundle.

Textcase

The *textcase* package implements commands that change the case of material in the command argument. The commands change the case of text but leave unchanged any sections of mathematics and any key names, so that references, citations, and labels still work correctly.

▶ **To change the case of specified text**

1. Add the *textcase* package to your document.

2. Enter an encapsulated TeX field.

3. Type

   \lowercase{text}

   or

   \uppercase{text}

   where *text* is the text you want changed to lowercase or uppercase.

4. Choose OK.

The package option addresses the use of standard text case macros. The package is installed in the `TCITeX/TeX/LaTeX/contrib/carlisle` directory.

Theorem

The *theorem* package customizes theorem environments to meet the layout requirements of different journals. Theorem styles determine the appearance of theorem environments. These styles have been defined:

Style	Effect
plain	Similar to the original LaTeX definition, with the addition of parameters that specify the amount of space to skip before and after the theorem
break	Place a line break after the theorem header
marginbreak	Set the theorem number in the margin and place a line break after the theorem header
changebreak	Interchange the header number and text and place a line break after the theorem header
change	Interchange the header number and text but don't place a line break after the theorem header
margin	Set the theorem number in the margin; don't insert a line break

▶ **To customize the appearance of theorem environments**

1. Add the *theorem* package to your document.

2. From the Typeset menu, choose **Preamble**.

3. Click the mouse in the entry area.

4. Place the insertion point on a new line in the preamble, before the \newtheorem statement for the theorem environment you want to customize.

5. If you want the style to apply to all theorem-like objects in the document, type **\theoremstyle{*style*}** where *style* is the style you want.

   or

   If you want the style to apply to a group of theorem-like objects in the document, type {**\theoremstyle{*style*}**, where *style* is the style you want, and then place the insertion point at the end of the group and type } (closing curly brace).

6. If you want to change the font that LaTeX uses for the header of the theorem environment, type **\theoremheaderfont{*font*}** where *font* is the font family you want LaTeX to use.

   Because \theoremheaderfont is a global setting, it changes the header font for all theorem-like environments in the document. The command should be used only once. Values for font can be combined. Possible values for font are:

Family	Effect	Family	Effect
\mdseries	Medium Series	**\upshape**	Upright Shape
\bfseries	Boldface Series	**\itshape**	Italic Shape
\rmfamily	Roman Family	**\slshape**	Slanted Shape
\sffamily	Sans Serif Family	**\scshape**	Small Caps Shape
\ttfamily	Typewriter Family	**\normalfont**	Normal (document main text font)

Not all combinations make sense and LaTeX compensates by placing a warning in the .log file and substituting a similar font.

7. If you want to change the font that LaTeX uses for the body of the theorem environment, type **\theorembodyfont{*font*}** where *font* is the font family you want LaTeX to use.

   Use the command **\theorembodyfont{\upshape}** to use upright text in the body of a theorem. The font used for the body of a theorem-like environment can be restricted to a single environment or a group of environments by using curly braces to enclose the environments.

8. Choose OK.

No options are available through the Options and Packages command on the Typeset menu. The *theorem* package is installed in the `TCITeX/TeX/LaTeX/required/tools` directory as part of the Standard LaTeX Tools Bundle.

Times

See PSNFSS Packages on page 147.

Titlesec

The *titlesec* package is a complete reimplementation for LaTeX heading commands that provides a way to change the typeset appearance of division headings, such as chapter and section. The package includes two interfaces, one basic and one extended. The basic interface provides modification of various division heading attributes (font size, font shape, text alignment, spacing) with the package options available through the Options and Packages command on the Typeset menu. The modifications are applied to all division headings. The extended interface provides commands that allow separate and more elaborate modification of the appearance and placement of headings, including different formats for right and left pages and numbered and unnumbered headings.

▶ **To use the simple interface to change the formatting for division headings**

1. Add the *titlesec* package to your document.

2. On the Typeset toolbar, click the Options and Packages button or, from the Typeset menu, choose Options and Packages and then choose the Package Options tab.

3. From the **Packages in Use** list, select the *titlesec* package and choose **Modify**.

4. Select items from the **Category** list, and for each item select an item from the **Options** list, to specify the format the division headings.

5. Choose **OK** to close each dialog box and return to your document.

If the options available as predefined formatting settings don't meet your needs, you can use an advanced user interface to create elaborate formats for division headings. To use the advanced interface, you add LaTeX commands to the document preamble. See the *titlesec* package documentation for details.

The *titlesec* package doesn't work for documents created with Style Editor shells. It is installed in the `TCITeX/TeX/LaTeX/contrib/titlesec` directory.

Titletoc

The *titletoc* package provides a method for changing the appearance of the table of contents, list of figures, and list of tables. Package options, available through the **Options and Packages** command on the **Typeset** menu, provide for setting the alignment of division labels and placing a dot after the labels. The package provides for appropriate page breaks in the table of contents and lists of figures and tables.

The following example specifies that chapter headings be typeset as bold italics. Modify these sample instructions to create the format you want.

▶ **To change typeset formatting for the table of contents, list of figures, or list of tables.**

1. Add the *titletoc* package to your document.

2. On the Typeset toolbar, click the Options and Packages button [image] or, from the **Typeset** menu, choose **Options and Packages** and then choose the **Package Options** tab.

3. From the **Typeset** menu, choose **Preamble** and click the mouse in the entry area.

4. Create a new line at the end of the preamble entries.

5. On the new line, type
   \titlecontents{chapter}[0pt]{\addvspace{1pc}\itshape}{\contentsmargin{0pt}
   \bfseries\makebox[0pt][r]{\large\thecontentslabel\enspace}\large}
   {\contentsmargin{0pt}\large}{\hfill\contentspage}[\addvspace{.5pc}]

6. Choose **OK**.

See the *titlesec* package documentation for detailed information about the commands available for use with the *titletoc*. The *titletoc* package doesn't work for documents created with Style Editor shells. The package, which is distributed with the *titlesec* package, is installed in the `TCITeX/TeX/LaTeX/contrib/titlesec` directory.

Tocbibind

The package automatically includes the table of contents, list of figures, list of tables, bibliography, and index in the table of contents of your document. The package is designed for use with the standard LaTeX document classes, but may cause difficulties with other document classes. The *tocbibind* package doesn't work with the version of LaTeX included with Version 3.0.

No action is needed other than adding the package to your document, but options are available from the Options and Packages command on the Typeset menu to exclude front and back matter elements from the table of contents and to use and format section headings in the table of contents. The package is installed in the `TCITeX/TeX/ LaTeX/contrib/tocbibind` directory.

Tocloft

The *tocloft* package provides a method for changing the appearance of entries in the table of contents, list of figures, and list of tables. The package can also be used to create new kinds of *List of...* pages.

The commands available for use with the *tocloft* package control the formatting, including fonts, spacing, and dot leaders, used for part, chapter, section, and subsection entries in the table of contents. Additional commands control the formatting of entries in the list of figures and list of tables, and determine whether the lists begin on new pages. The commands are entered in the preamble of your document. See the *tocloft* package documentation for command details and syntax.

▶ **To change the typeset formatting for the table of contents, list of figures, or list of tables**

1. Add the *tocloft* package to your document.

2. From the Typeset menu, choose Preamble.

3. Type the package commands to change the formatting.

   For example, if you want to list chapters in a report using the normal weight font instead of the bold default, type **\renewcommand{\cftchapfont}{\mdseries}**.

4. Choose OK.

   LaTeX formats the table of contents using the normal weight font.

Several package options are also available. Through the Options and Packages command on the Typeset menu, you can use default LaTeX formatting and also select an option required when the *tocloft* package is used together with the *subfigure* package.

The *tocloft* package is compatible with the *tocbibind* package. It doesn't work for documents created with Style Editor shells. It is installed in the `TCITeX/TeX/ LaTeX/contrib/tocloft` directory.

Ulem

The *ulem* package provides several styles of simple underlines and strikethroughs by temporarily changing the behavior of the \em and \emph commands. The underlining and strikethroughs can extend across line breaks and apply to both text and mathematics.

The options available through the **Options and Packages** command on the **Type-set** menu determine how the emphasize tag is applied. The default, which you can turn off, is a single underline. As illustrated below, the package also supports double under-lining, wavy underlining, a single line drawn through text, and text marked over with slashes. It supports the use of a wavy underline in place of bold text.

This package supports single and double underlining, wavy underlining, a single line drawn through text, and text marked over with slashes.

▶ **To add simple underlines**

1. Add the *ulem* package to your document.

2. Select the information you want to underline.

3. Apply the Emphasize tag.

▶ **To add varied underlines and strikethroughs**

1. Add the *ulem* package to your document.

2. Place the insertion point where you want the underline or strikethrough to begin.

3. Enter an encapsulated TEX field.

4. In the entry area, type ***command**{*text*} where ***command*** is one of the following:

Command	Effect
uline	Single underline
uuline	Double underline
uwave	Wavy underline
sout	Line through text
xout	Text marked over with slashes

and ***text*** is the information you want emphasized.

5. Choose **OK**.

In addition to using the package options, you can add underlines and strikethroughs at specific points in the document. The *ulem* package is for use with LATEX or plain TEX. It is installed in the `TCITeX/TeX/LaTeX/contrib/misc` directory.

Url

The *url* package allows spacing and line breaks that result in intelligent printing of email addresses, hypertext links, and path or directory addresses. You must enter package commands in TeX fields. The address, link, path, or directory address specified in the command must not contain unbalanced braces. If it doesn't contain certain other characters (such as % or #) and doesn't end with a backslash, you can use the command in the argument to another command. Most of the path names appearing in this manual have been formatted with the aid of the *url* package.

▶ **To implement intelligent printing of hypertext links and electronic addresses**

1. Add the *url* package to your document and set the options as necessary.

2. Place the insertion point where you want the link or address to appear.

3. Enter an encapsulated TeX field.

4. In the entry area, type **url{*address*}** where *address* is the address or link to be printed.

5. Choose OK.

In addition to package commands, the package options control spacing and line breaks. The package installs in the `TCITeX/TeX/LaTeX/contrib/misc` directory.

Varioref

The *varioref* package enhances page references with text that varies depending on the relative typeset location of the referenced key. The package uses standard references (using a TeX \ref command) when the command and the key occur on the same page. However, when the command and key vary by a page or more, the package inserts strings such as *on the facing page, on the preceding page, on the following page,* or *on the next page.* When the difference is greater than one page, *varioref* inserts both an enhanced reference and a standard reference. The *varioref* package supports *babel* so that the strings produced are customized for different languages. Also, you can customize the text strings as necessary. A package option is available to aid troubleshooting.

▶ **To enhance page references**

1. Add the *varioref* package to your document.

2. Place the insertion point where you want the reference to appear.

3. Enter an encapsulated TeX field.

4. In the entry area, type one of the *varioref* commands:

Command	Effect
\vref{*key*}	Create an enhanced reference
\vpageref[*text*]{*key*}	Create an enhanced page reference
\vrefrange{*key*}{*key*}	Create an enhanced range of references
\vpagerefrange[*text*]{*key*}{*key*}	Create an enhanced range of page references

where *key* is the key you want to refer to and *text* is the enhancement text you want to use if the keys and references are on the same page.

5. Choose OK.

The package is installed in the `TCITeX/TeX/LaTeX/required/tools` directory as part of the Standard LATEX Tools Bundle.

Verbatim

The verbatim environment allows for the display of information exactly as it is entered at a terminal. The *verbatim* package improves that environment by handling text of arbitrary length, even an entire file, as verbatim input. The package also improves the detection of the verbatim environment's closing delimiter. You can display verbatim text with a font different from the default typewriter font.

▶ **To display verbatim text**

1. Add the *verbatim* package to your document.

2. Place the insertion point where you want the verbatim text to appear.

3. Enter an encapsulated TEX field.

4. In the entry area, type **begin{verbatim}** and choose OK.

5. Type the information as you want it to appear.

6. At the end of the information, enter another encapsulated TEX field.

7. In the entry area, type **end{verbatim}** and choose OK.

▶ **To import a verbatim file**

1. Add the *verbatim* package to your document.

2. Place the insertion point where you want the file to appear.

3. Enter an encapsulated TEX field.

4. In the entry area, type **verbatiminput{*filename*}** where *filename* is the complete path name of the file to be imported, with forward slashes substituted for backslashes.

5. Choose OK.

The package has no options. It installs in the `TCITeX/TeX/LaTeX/required/tools` directory as part of the Standard LATEX Tools Bundle.

Version

The *version* package provides a way to include or exclude material conditionally from the LaTeX typesetting process. You can use the package to include in your document text, mathematics, graphics, and other material that will never be typeset or that may be typeset at certain times but not others. The advantage to using the package instead of the Comments fragment included with *SWP* and *SW* is that the material is always displayed in the document window even though it may be ignored by LaTeX.

Package environments determine whether or not the information within the environments will be typeset. A predefined comment environment always excludes material from typesetting.

To include material that will never be typeset.

1. Add the *version* package to your document.

2. Place the insertion point where you want the material to begin.

3. Enter a TeX field.

4. In the entry area, type **begin{comment}** and choose OK.

5. Create the material you want to exclude from typesetting.

6. At the end of the material, enter a TeX field.

7. In the entry area, type **end{comment}** and choose OK.

To include material that may or may not be typeset

1. Add the *version* package to your document.

2. Place the insertion point where you want the material to begin and enter a TeX field.

3. In the entry area, type **begin{*name*}** where *name* is any value that doesn't conflict with existing TeX values.

   The name is case sensitive.

4. Create the material you occasionally want to exclude from typesetting.

5. At the end of the material, enter a TeX field.

6. In the entry area, type **end{*name*}** and choose OK.

7. From the Typeset menu, choose Preamble and click the mouse in the entry area.

8. On a new line, type **excludeversion{*name*}** if you don't want to typeset the material or **includeversion{*name*}** if you do.

9. Choose OK.

You can define as many version environments as you want. The package is installed in the `TCITeX/TeX/LaTeX/contrib/misc` directory.

Wrapfig

The *wrapfig* package allows text to be wrapped around floating objects at the side of the page, as shown here. The package provides two environments, wraptable and wrapfigure. These environments are not regular floats and may print out of sequence, but accompanying captions are correctly numbered. The package has

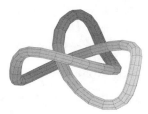

no options available through the Options and Packages command on the Typeset menu. Find additional documentation in the PackageSample-wrapfig.tex file in the SWSamples directory of your program installation.

▶ **To wrap text around a floating figure or table**

1. Add the *wrapfig* package to your document.

2. Enter an encapsulated TEX field.

3. In the entry area, type **begin{wrapfigure}**[*w*]{*x*}[*y*]{*z*} or
begin{wraptable}[*w*]{*x*}[*y*]{*z*}

   where *w* is the number of vertical lines to be narrowed to accommodate the figure or table. We recommend you use this optional argument.

   x is the placement of the figure or table (required). Uppercase indicates *float;* lowercase indicates *exactly here*:

Placement	Effect
r or **R**	Right side of text
l or **L**	Left side of text
i or **I**	Inside edge, near the binding (for two-sided documents)
o or **O**	Outside edge, away from the binding (for two-sided documents)

   y is the amount of overhang—the distance the figure or table should extend into the margin (optional).

   z is the width of the figure or table (required). If you specify a width of zero (0pt), the package uses the actual width of the figure or table to determine the wrapping width.

4. Choose OK.

5. Enter the figure or table as an in-line object.

6. Enter an encapsulated TEX field.

7. In the entry area, type **end{wrapfigure}** or **end{wraptable}** and choose OK.

The package has one option available to print information in the .log file. You can find additional documentation in the SWSamples directory of your program installation. The *wrapfig* package is installed in the TCITeX/TeX/LaTeX/contrib/misc directory.

Xr

The *xr* package uses standard TₑX \ref and \pageref commands to create cross-and page references to labels outside the current document. You can declare as many external documents as you want. You must compile the document outside *SWP* or *SW*.

▶ **To create cross-references and page references to labels in other documents**

1. Add the *xr* package to your document.

2. Declare the external documents:

   a. From the Typeset menu, choose Preamble and click the mouse in the entry area.
   b. On a new line, declare the document for which you want to create a cross-reference by typing **externaldocument{*file*}** where *file* is the name of another document.
   Note   Don't include the file extension.
   c. Repeat step c for as many files as necessary, then choose OK.

3. Place the insertion point where you want the cross-reference to occur.

4. Enter a TₑX field and iIn the entry area, type **ref{*label*}** or **pageref{*label*}** where *label* is the label in the external document.

5. Choose OK.

No options are available. The *xr* package is installed in the TCITeX/TeX/LaTeX/required/tools directory as part of the Standard LATₑX Tools Bundle.

Xtab

The *xtab* package improves page breaking by the *supertabular* package (see page 165). The package allows headings on the last page of a table to differ from those on earlier pages. Be sure to run LATₑX twice when *xtab* is in use. A debugging option is available through the Options and Packages command on the Typeset menu.

▶ **To modify supertabular environments**

1. Add the *xtab* and *supertabular* packages to your document.

2. Enter an encapsulated TₑX field and in the entry area, type the commands for the entire supertabular environment, beginning with **begin{supertabular}** and ending with **end{supertabular}**.

3. Modify the supertabular headings on the last page as necessary by adding *xtab* \tablefirsthead and \tablelasthead commands at appropriate points in the environment. See the package documentation for a list of available commands

4. Choose OK.

Xtab is installed in the TCITeX/TeX/LaTeX/contrib/xtab directory.

4 Troubleshooting

Even the most carefully created documents sometimes contain commands, constructions, or errors that prevent them from being opened, saved, compiled, previewed, or printed. In this chapter we describe common problems that can occur when you're working with *SWP*, *SW*, and LaTeX.

For each problem, we indicate which versions of the program are affected, explain why the problem occurs, and suggest ways to resolve the situation. We also include basic information about isolating and identifying LaTeX errors and, at the end of the chapter, suggestions for repairing damaged documents.

If a problem occurs that you can't resolve with the information provided here, you can obtain additional help from our website at

http://www.mackichan.com/techtalk/knowledgebase.html

or from our Web-based Technical Support forum at

http://www.mackichan.com/techtalk/UserForums.htm

You can also contact our Technical Support staff by email, telephone, or fax. We urge you to submit questions by email whenever possible in case our technical staff needs to obtain your file to diagnose and solve the problem. See page xvi for details.

Resolving Program Errors

Errors can occur when you try to open, save, or typeset documents in *SWP* or *SW*. Although error messages generated by the program are usually self-explanatory, some additional information may help you diagnose and correct errors quickly.

Problems Encountered in Opening and Saving Documents

If you have difficulties when you try to open or save a document, look for information in this section before you attempt the operation a second time. You may be able to avoid damage to your document.

The file (filename) is not valid for the selected filter.

- *SWP/SW* Version 3.5x, 4.x, and 5.x

The file you've tried to open is a non-LaTeX file or is a traditional LaTeX subdocument that doesn't contain `\documentclass` or `\begin{document}` commands. The program can't open the file.

Solution

- If the file isn't a LaTeX file, open it using an ASCII editor or using the application in which the file was created.
- If the file is a LaTeX file, open a new document and use the Import Contents command to read the contents of the LaTeX file into the current document.
- In Version 5.5, try reading the file with the Import Non-*SWP/SW* LaTeX filter. See page 81 for more information.

▶ **To import a non-SWP/SW LaTeX document**

1. Place the file you want to open in a writable directory so that the program can create the necessary temporary files.

2. From the File menu, choose Import Non-SWP/SW LaTeX.

3. Select the file and choose Open.

The document has not been loaded. SW cannot handle certain \def or \newcommand statements in the LaTeX preamble of this document.

- *SWP/SW* Version 3.5x, 4.x, and 5.x

If you've placed complex TeX commands in the preamble of your document or you're attempting to open a LaTeX document not created with *SWP* or *SW*, the program may be unable to load the document into memory. In particular, complex `\def` or `\renewcommand` statements can prevent the document from loading.

Solution

If you have Version 5.5 of *SWP* or *SW*, you may be able to read the document with the Import Non-*SWP/SW* LaTeX filter. See page 81 for more information.

If you have an earlier version of the program, you may be able to read the document by placing the complex statements in an external file and then importing that file from the preamble of your document.

▶ **To place complex TEX statements in an external file**

1. Open your document with an ASCII editor.

2. Select the preamble statements you want to place in the external file and cut them to the clipboard.

3. In place of the lines you deleted, enter **\input{*filename.tex*}**, where *filename.tex* is the name of the ASCII file you will create in steps 5–8.

4. Save the document.

5. Open a new file with the ASCII editor.

6. Paste the statements from the clipboard into the file.

7. Name the file using a `.tex` file extension.

8. Save the file in an appropriate subdirectory in the `TCITeX` directory of your program installation.

   Note   If the file is in a different directory, LATEX won't find it when you attempt to typeset your document, unless you've entered a complete path name in step 3.

9. In *SWP* or *SW,* try to open and typeset the original document.

> **Can't find file (filename). Document may not load correctly. Would you like to continue?**

or

> **Can't find file (filename.cst). File (otherfilename.cst) will be used instead. Would you like to continue?**

- *SWP/SW* Version 3.5x, 4.x, and 5.x

  The program displays the message when the document you're trying to open requires a `.cst` file that the program can't find. The `.cst` file determines the appearance of the document in the document window. The problem can occur when you try to open a document from an outside source, such as a publisher, if that document calls for typesetting specifications that aren't included with *SWP* or *SW*.

Solution

Several options are available:

- Choose **Yes** to ignore the message. The program opens the document using `sci-word.cst`, the default `.cst` file used when a more appropriate `.cst` file can't be found.

- Instead of opening the document directly, start a new document using an appropriate document shell (see page 77) and import the contents of the original document into it.

- Create a new subdirectory in the `Styles` directory of your program installation and name it the same name as the LaTeX class for your document. Then, copy `sci-word.cst` to the directory, rename it with the name of the missing file, and try to open the document again.

- If you're working with typesetting specifications not provided with *SWP* or *SW*, see page 85 for the procedure for creating a `.cst` file for typesetting specifications from outside sources.

Error parsing TeX expression.

- *SWP/SW* Version 3.5x, 4.x, and 5.x

When you attempt to open a file, the program fails to interpret a TeX expression and displays the message. If you choose OK, the program opens the document, but may place the segment containing the problem expression in a TeX field. As you scroll through the open document, you may see TeX fields in place of entire paragraphs.

Solution
Try to isolate and correct the error using the procedure on page 185.

Error while reading paragraph xxx. Document has been truncated.

- *SWP/SW* Version 3.5x, 4.x, and 5.x

The message occurs when the program has tried to read a document and has encountered a LaTeX construction or expression that it doesn't understand. The program truncates the document at the indicated paragraph as it is being loaded into memory, but the file on your hard disk remains whole. The problem can occur particularly with documents obtained from outside sources.

Solution
First, close the document *without saving it.* If you save the file, the program saves the truncated version to your hard disk and you will be unable to recover the truncated information.

Then, examine the file using an ASCII editor to see if you can detect a problem at the indicated paragraph. Remember that paragraph numbers in the `.tex` file don't correspond exactly to the paragraphs in an *SWP* or *SW* document.

If you have Version 5.5 of *SWP* or *SW*, you may be able to open the document with the Import Non-*SWP/SW* LaTeX filter. See page 81 for more information.

If you're unable to isolate and resolve the problem, send the file to our Technical Support staff, as described on page xvi.

Error while writing paragraph xxx. Document was only partially saved.

- *SWP/SW* Version 3.5x, 4.x, and 5.x

The message occurs when the program has tried to save a file, often using the Portable LaTeX option, but has encountered something that it doesn't understand. The program truncates the document at the indicated paragraph as it is being written to the hard disk.

Solution

Although the document has been truncated on the hard disk, the complete file remains in memory, and you may be able to recover it. Don't try to save the file the same way again. Instead, try saving the file to a different document name using a different output filter. That is, if you tried to save the document as Portable LaTeX when the error occurred originally, try saving the file as a standard *SWP* or *SW* document using the SWP/SW/SN Document (*.tex) option. If the program saves the document correctly, no other action is necessary. However, you should examine the document carefully to make sure you haven't lost any information.

If saving with a different output filter fails, you may be able to recover the document using a .bak file if automatic backups were in effect when the problem occurred. The backup copy is the next-to-last saved version of the original file.

▶ **To use the backup file**

1. After the error has occurred, exit the document without saving it.

2. Rename the .bak file and give it a .tex file extension.

3. Make several copies of the renamed file.

4. Open the renamed file and try to save it.

5. If the program saves the file without error, check the document carefully to make certain your most recent changes have been saved.

If these methods fail, contact our Technical Support staff, as described on page xvi.

Problems Encountered During Compilation

Some of the messages that can appear during compilation are issued by *SWP* or *SW* instead of by LaTeX.

Error writing to disk.

- *SWP/SW* Version 3.5x, 4.x, and 5.x

During a LaTeX compilation, the program tries to save the temporary data generated in the course of the process. Some of the required files may be in use by another instance of the TrueTeX Formatter or they may be otherwise inaccessible. If the data can't be saved, the program displays the message.

Solution

- Check to make sure that all files associated with the document are in the correct directories.

- Check that none of the associated files are read-only files.

- Make certain that multiple copies of the TrueTeX Formatter aren't running. Close all instances of the formatter and try the compilation again. If the program still can't save the temporary data, send the file to our Technical Support staff, as described on page xvi.

Error running Tex, DVI file not created.

- *SWP/SW* Version 3.5x, 4.x, and 5.x

When an error prevents the completion of a LaTeX compilation, the LaTeX window closes and *SWP* or *SW* displays the message.

Solution

Follow the instructions on page 185 to identify and isolate the error. Correct the error and typeset your document again.

Failed to find master document (filename). Default document information used. Warning: Print or Preview may fail.

- *SWP/SW* Version 3.5x, 4.x, and 5.x

The message occurs when you try to typeset a subdocument for which the master document is missing. Subdocuments contain no typesetting specifications, document information, or front matter of their own; instead, they use the information in the master document. If the master document is missing, the program must use default information, and the preview or print operation may fail.

If you continue the compilation process with the default information, the program typesets the subdocument as if it were an article. Subdocuments that are intended as book or report chapters won't typeset properly because they contain constructs not normally contained in articles.

The master document may be missing for several reasons. If you received the subdocument from an outside source, the master document may not have been provided with it. Also, if the master document has been renamed, the pointers in the subdocuments may still point to the old name.

Solution

If the master document is unavailable, create a new, independent document from the subdocument. If you've renamed the master document, create a new subdocument for the master document and import the contents of the old subdocument into the new one.

▶ **To create a document from a subdocument**

1. Open a new document.

2. From the File menu, choose Import Contents.

3. Select the subdocument and choose OK.

   The program copies the content of the subdocument into the new document.

4. Create front matter for the new document as necessary.

5. Save and compile the new document.

▶ **To create a new subdocument for a renamed master document**

1. Save the renamed master document.

2. Place the insertion point where you want to include the subdocument.

3. On the Typeset Object toolbar, click the Subdocument button ⊡ or, from the Insert menu, choose **Typeset Object** and then choose **Subdocument**.

4. In the **Subdocument** area, enter a name for the new subdocument.

5. Choose **OK**.

6. Save the master document again.

   The new subdocument now points to the renamed master document.

7. Open the new subdocument.

8. From the **File** menu, choose **Import Contents**.

9. Select the old subdocument and choose **OK**.

   The program copies the content of the old subdocument into the new one.

General Problems

Software programs can, unfortunately, fail from time to time.

A serious program error has occurred.

● *SWP/SW* Version 3.5x, 4.x, and 5.x

   On rare occasions, *SWP* and *SW* can fail. The complete message is as follows:

   ```
   A serious program error has occurred.  All modified documents
   have been saved with the extension .dmp.  The program will now
   exit.
   ```

The program exits and then displays a second message:

   ```
   The program has generated a file describing the state of your
   system at the time of the error:  (filename).  To help us di-
   agnose and fix the problem, please attach this file to an email
   message and send it to support@mackichan.com.
   ```

Solution

If *SWP* or *SW* fails, the program saves all open and modified documents in files of the same name with the extension .dmp, as indicated in the message. After you reopen the program, open the .dmp files and check to make sure they contain your latest changes, then save the files. The program saves the files with the original .tex file extension and you can continue working on them as usual.

   At the time of failure, the program also generates a file containing diagnostic information that our Technical Support staff can use to determine the cause of the failure. As the second message indicates, we urge you to create an email message and attach the file and the document in use when the failure occurred, then send the message to our Technical Support staff, as described on page xvi.

Resolving LaTeX Errors

Routine *SWP* and *SW* documents usually compile without difficulty. However, if your document contains TeX fields or you're working with documents from outside sources, you may see errors when you compile your document with LaTeX or PDFLaTeX.

If LaTeX or PDFLaTeX doesn't properly compile your document, you must find and correct the problem. A thorough knowledge of TeX and LaTeX is invaluable in this process. The information we provide here describes in general how to avoid common LaTeX errors. We also include information about specific errors that stop LaTeX or PDFLaTeX from compiling your document or compromise the compilation in some way, and about errors that can manifest themselves when you preview or print a compiled document.

However, this isn't intended as an exhaustive reference. We encourage you to seek additional enlightenment from the TeX and LaTeX resources listed on page x. These excellent resources contain extensive lists of error messages and careful explanations of possible causes. They also describe in detail how you can attempt to recover from TeX and LaTeX errors as your file is being processed. In addition, you can find helpful information from the Usenet news group at **news:comp.text.tex**.

Techniques for Solving LaTeX Errors

Messages about errors that occur during a compilation are displayed in the LaTeX or PDFLaTeX window as your document is being processed. The messages, which contain information that can help you identify and correct the problem, look something like this:

```
Runaway argument?
! Paragraph ended before \multicols was complete.
<to be read again>
                        \par
l.70

?
```

The exclamation point signals the error and the information on that line describes the nature of the problem. The line number (line 70 in the illustration above) indicates approximately where in your document or in a related typesetting specifications file the error has occurred. Because lines in an *SWP* or *SW* document don't correspond to lines in the .tex file, you may need to use an ASCII editor to locate the error precisely. Often, the message includes a portion of the document text, which may help you find the error.

If all activity ceases, LaTeX may be waiting for you to tell it what to do. You can try to ignore the problem, solve it and keep going, or halt the typesetting process. For example, the question mark in the last line of the message above indicates that LaTeX has a question. If you type **?** and press ENTER, LaTeX responds with this message:

```
Type <return> to proceed, S to scroll future error messages,
R to run without stopping, Q to run quietly,
I to insert something, E to edit your file,
1 or ... or 9 to ignore the next 1 to 9 tokens of input,
H for help, X to quit.
?
```

Now you can choose a course of action.

In addition to being displayed in the LaTeX or pdfLaTeX window during compilation, LaTeX error messages are stored in a file that carries the name of your document and an extension of .log. If you've saved your document before typesetting it, the program saves the .log file in the same directory as the document. Otherwise, the program saves the .log file using a temporary name in the temporary directory associated with your program installation. After processing stops, open the .log file to examine the messages at a more leisurely pace and try to isolate the error.

Using the .log File

The .log file records precisely what happens during the process of compiling your document. Among other information, it includes

- Any warnings and messages related to processing problems, such as unresolved cross-references, improperly matched delimiters, misspelled commands, missing command arguments, or overfull and underfull boxes.

- The document class and any class option files used by the document (see page 63).

- The names of any LaTeX packages used by the document (see page 89).

- The names of any files read and closed.

- The numbers of all pages processed, in square brackets.

- The size of the typeset file.

Open the .log file with an ASCII editor. Pay particular attention to any errors that have occurred in the document preamble. In the .log file, such errors are noted before the indiction of the first page of text, shown as [1].

Isolating a TeX or LaTeX Error

Many error messages point precisely to the cause of the error in your *SWP* or *SW* document, but others are more obscure. If you can't locate and correct the error easily, use the method below to try to isolate the error in your document.

▶ **To isolate a TeX or LaTeX error**

1. Make a copy of the .tex file.

2. Open the .tex file with an ASCII editor and scroll to the area in which the error occurred, as indicated by the page or line number in the .log file.

3. Comment out the portion of the document that you think contains the error by placing a percent sign at the beginning of each line. The formatter ignores these lines.

   Note Be sure not to split a TeX environment when you comment out a portion of your document. That is, if you comment out a \begin statement, be sure to comment out the corresponding \end statement as well.

4. Use the TrueTeX Formatter to compile the document:

   a. From the *SWP* or *SW* program group, choose **TrueTeX Formatter**.
   b. Select the file and choose **OK**.

5. Repeat steps 3 and 4, commenting out larger and larger portions of the document, until LaTeX handles the document correctly.

The area that is commented out contains the error.

6. Beginning from the top of the commented portion of the file, remove the percent signs from several lines of the file.

7. Recompile the document.

8. Repeat steps 6 and 7 until you isolate the lines that seem to cause of the failure.

9. Search for the mistake in that portion of the document.

Common LaTeX Errors

The simplest LaTeX errors to find and fix result from mistyping or omitting commands. In particular, LaTeX reacts negatively when it encounters these conditions:

- Misspelled commands or environment names, as in *beginn{wraptable}*.

- Improperly matched or missing braces or delimiters, as in *begin{multicols]{3}* or *begin{multicols} {3*.

- Improperly using a character with a special meaning in TeX, such as #, %, &, or \.

- Missing \end commands.

- Missing command arguments.

- Incorrect definition statements.

- Statements that hide LaTeX environment changes.

To minimize errors of this type, take the time to proofread when you type TeX commands in TeX fields, in the preamble of your document, or in dialog boxes that pass your commands directly to LaTeX.

Further, LaTeX may not compile your document if it contains certain constructions, even though the constructions are legal in *SWP* and *SW*. As you work with your documents, you can avoid many errors by following these guidelines:

- Avoid placing a display in a chapter or section heading.

- Avoid including in your document a blank line containing only a SHIFT+ENTER.

- Avoid including a graphic in a chapter or section heading if the graphic has a caption.

- Avoid including a hyperlink to a website in a chapter or section heading.

- Avoid including spaces or single quotes in the names of graphics files.

- Avoid putting a \newline command on a line by itself. The command is created by choosing Insert, then Spacing, Break, and Newline.

- Avoid placing a period in a file name, other than the period immediately preceding the file extension.

Errors That Halt LaTeX Compilation

Some errors are severe enough that the document can't be compiled. The compilation errors noted here are the ones that users mention most frequently.

Invalid characters in the file name or path directories.

- *SWP/SW* Version 3.5x, 4.x, and 5.x

When you try to compile a file whose name or directory name contains a space, the program returns this message:

```
Invalid characters in the file name or path directories.  En-
ter alpha-numeric characters, hyphens, and periods only.  No
more than one period in sequence is allowed in the name of a
file or directory.  Do you wish to continue?
```

If you choose **Yes**, TrueTeX will attempt to compile your document, but will halt with a new message:

```
Please type another input file name.
```

File or directory names that contain spaces, such as `new file` or `My Documents`, don't cause problems if you preview or print without typesetting, but do cause problems for LaTeX. As a general rule, avoid using any spaces in directory and file names.

Solution
Cancel the compilation, save the file under a new name that contains no spaces and in a directory whose name contains no spaces. Try the compilation again.

Characters in the file name or directory are invalid on some TeX systems.

- *SWP/SW* Version 3.5x, 4.x, and 5.x

Underscores in file names can cause problems when you try to compile with some versions of TeX. Therefore, we try to be as conservative as possible with file names so that we don't encourage the use of names that aren't portable to all systems. If you try to compile a document has an underscore in its name, the program displays this message and asks whether you want to continue or not:

```
Characters in the file name or directory are invalid on
some TeX systems....
Do you wish to continue?
```

If you choose to continue, everything seems to work as it should, but the names can still cause problems on some systems.

Solution
To make your files as widely portable as possible, use DOS 8.3 file names.

Undefined control sequence.

- *SWP/SW* Version 3.5x, 4.x, and 5.x

This common LaTeX error has many potential causes. It can occur when a package is missing from the document or when the document uses a command name that hasn't been defined. It can also occur when the command name in a TeX field has been mistyped. Also, if you've opened a document from an outside source, the document may include a macro that is undefined on your system.

Solution

Follow the instructions beginning on page 185 to use the .log file to isolate and correct the problem.

Error: Unable to write to .aux file 'swp0000.aux'.

- *SWP/SW* Version 3.5x, 4.x, and 5.0 prior to Build 2606

When you compile your document, the TrueTeX Formatter creates an .aux file and uses the information in the file to resolve cross-references and perform other typesetting functions. If you used a CD-ROM disc to transfer your document and its associated auxiliary files from one computer to another, the files may have been marked as read-only in the process. When you compile the document again, the formatter copies the files to the temporary directory used by the program installation and renames the existing .aux file as swp0000.aux. It retains the read-only attribute, causing the error and preventing the program from opening and writing to the file during the compilation.

This error can also occur if you try to start a new compilation of your document while a previous compilation is still in progress. The formatter locks the files during compilation, so the .aux file is inaccessible.

Solution

- If you have Version 5.0 prior to Build 2606, download and install the latest patch update for Version 5.0 from our website. Then, try to compile the document again. The update addresses the error.

- If you have an earlier version of the software, delete any files associated with your document that don't have a .tex file extension, especially any marked as read-only, in the document directory or the temporary directory of your program installation. Then, try to compile the document again.

- Make sure any previous compilations have completed and no other instances of the TrueTeX Formatter are running before you try to compile your document again.

! Missing $ inserted.

- *SWP/SW* Version affected: 5.x

Graphics files whose names contain spaces cause PDF compilation errors. Files that contain such graphics may compile correctly when you create a DVI file with the **Typeset/Preview** command, but when you try to create a PDF file with the **Typeset/Preview**

PDF command, PDFLATEXdisplays several lines like those below and halts the compilation.

```
!  Missing $ inserted.
<inserted text>
                $
1.54 ...temp/graphics/figure output growth_ _1.pdf}
                                                     %
?
```

Although you can press **R** to continue the compilation, as described in Resolving LATEX Errors on page 184, the graphic identified in the message doesn't appear correctly in the PDF viewer.

In this example, the name of the graphics file includes several spaces followed by a double underscore. The PDFLATEX program assumes the name of the graphic ends with the first space. It processes the rest of the name as if it were ordinary text, interpreting the underscores as a TEX subscript and thus, as requiring mathematics mode. The Missing $ inserted error occurs because the underscore isn't in mathematics. The spaces in the file name cause the original confusion. If the file name contained no spaces, PDFLATEX would interpret the name of the graphics file correctly.

Solution

Avoid using spaces in directory and file names. Also, remember that although *SWP* and *SW* can use many different graphics formats, PDFLATEX understands only a limited number. When you typeset a PDF file from your *SWP* or *SW* document, the program converts any graphics in the document to a format that PDFLATEX can understand (you can select the format you want to use). You can also select the way you want the converted graphics to be named. Choose an appropriate graphics file naming option to avoid the error caused by spaces in the file name.

▶ **To choose a graphics file naming option**

1. From the Typeset menu, select General Settings.

2. Choose the PDF Graphics Settings button to open the PDF Graphics Export Options dialog box.

3. Choose the Graphics File Naming Options button and note the naming options in the dialog box that opens.

   Two options, Original filename and Original filename and graphics sequence number (the default at installation) use the original graphics file name as the basis for the name of the converted graphics file. If the original name contains a space, the error will occur when you try to typeset a PDF file.

4. Select one of the options that doesn't include the original graphics file name in the naming scheme.

5. Choose OK to close each dialog and return to your document.

6. Save the document and try to typeset the PDF file again.

Error: TeX capacity exceeded, sorry [buffer size=5000].

- *SWP/SW* Version 3.5x, 4.x, and 5.x

This error can occur when you typeset a document saved with the Portable LaTeX filter, which uses the *graphicx* package. The package scans for line end characters in the contents of graphics files included in your document. If the graphics files in your document were originally created in a non-Windows environment, they may use either the Macintosh or Unix line end characters, which the package doesn't see. Therefore, when you typeset your document, LaTeX doesn't see the line end and continues to search for it until the buffer size has been exceeded. LaTeX stops at that point, issuing the error message. Because LaTeX stops at the point of the error, the complete document does not appear in the TrueTeX Previewer or in print. The error occurs with .eps graphics in particular.

Solution
Convert the line end characters in the graphics file to Windows line end characters. You may have access to specialized programs for this purpose. If not, use an ASCII editor to search in the graphic for a carriage return and change it to a carriage return with line break.

! LaTeX Error: Command \proof already defined.

- *SWP/SW* Version 3.5x, 4.x, and 5.x

Adding the *amsthm* package to a document and then typesetting the document causes the error message. Although many $\mathcal{AMS}$ packages work well with *SWP* and *SW*, the *amsthm* package does not. *SWP* and *SW* include many \newtheorem statements that define theorem-like environments and a \newenvironment to define the proof environment. However, the *amsthm* package also defines the proof environment, which results in the error when you typeset. Although you can press **R** to continue the compilation, as described in Resolving LaTeX Errors on page 184, any proofs in your document will not be typeset correctly according to the *amsthm* package specifications.

Solution
If you remove the \newenvironment statement from the preamble, the document will compile without errors, but the proof environments in your document will appear as TeX fields. Instead, use a conditional statement around the \newenvironment statement in the preamble. The conditional statement causes the program to see the \newenvironment statement and to display the body of the proof in the document window. However, LaTeX does not see the \newenvironment statement, so it uses the one defined by the *amsthm* package, and typesets the document correctly.

▶ **To add the conditional statement to the preamble**

1. Open your document.

2. From the **Typeset** menu, choose **Preamble** and click the mouse in the entry area.

3. Find the single line that defines the proof environment:

```
\newenvironment{proof}[1][Proof]{\textbf{ #1.}}}{\\rule{0.5em}
{0.5em}}
```

4. Replace the line with these three lines:

   \iffalse
   \newenvironment{proof}[1][Proof]{\noindent\textbf{ #1.} } {\ \rule{0.5em} {0.5em} }
   \fi

5. Choose OK.

Subequation environment ended incorrectly.

- *SWP/SW* Version 3.5x, 4.x, and 5.x

  Using the subequation feature to number equations with both letters and numbers (as in 1a, 1b, 1c, ...) sometimes results in compilation errors similar to this:

  ```
  \begin{subequations} ended by \end{environment}
  ```

  where `environment` is the name of a different environment. The program occasionally places the end of the subequations environment in the wrong position when you set the numbering of a displayed equation by checking the Enable Subequation Numbering box in the advanced Display Properties dialog box.

Solution

Remove the specification in the Display Properties dialog box and place encapsulated TEX commands around the equation.

▶ **To create a subequation environment**

1. Select the equation and choose Properties.

2. In the Display Properties dialog box, check the Auto numbering option for each line of the display for which you want an equation number to appear.

3. Choose Advanced.

4. If you've specified a Key for Whole Display, delete the key.

5. Uncheck Enable Subequation Numbering, and choose OK.

6. Enter an encapsulated TEX field immediately before the display.

7. In the entry area, type **\begin{subequations}** and choose OK.

8. If you want a key for the whole display, from the Insert menu, choose Marker and enter the key you deleted in step 4, above.

9. Enter another encapsulated TEX field immediately after the last equation.

10. In the entry area, type **\end{subequations}** and choose OK.

Problems That Compromise LaTeX Compilation

The problems discussed below are often indicated with messages in the LaTeX or PDFLaTeX window. The errors don't halt the compilation, but may nonetheless result in an incomplete or incorrect DVI or PDF file.

LaTeX Warning: There were undefined references.

- *SWP/SW* Version 3.5x, 4.x, and 5.x

When a cross-reference in your document isn't correctly matched to a marker during compilation, LaTeX posts the warning about undefined references in the LaTeX window and near the end of the .log file. Also, LaTeX inserts two question marks in the typeset text in place of the reference, like this **??**.

Solution

The message occurs if you specify only a single LaTeX pass when you're compiling a document, especially a master document, that contains cross-references. The cross-references may be correctly resolved if you specify two or more LaTeX passes when you compile your document.

Undefined cross-references can also occur because the referenced marker is missing in your document or is incorrectly referenced. Instead of looking through a long document for instances of **??**, examine the .log file for your document to search for the LaTeX warning about undefined references. If the message doesn't appear, all cross-references have been resolved.

▶ **To examine the .log file**

1. Open the .log file with an ASCII editor and scroll to the end of the file.

2. If any cross-references are unresolved, this message will appear near the end of the file.

   LaTeX Warning: There were undefined references.

   If the message doesn't appear, all cross-references have been resolved.

3. If the message does appear, look earlier in the .log file for a more detailed message like this:

   LaTeX Warning: Reference 'markerx' on page xx undefined on input line xx.

4. In your document, insert any missing markers and correct all marker misreferences.

5. Save and compile your document again.

6. Check the new .log file to make certain all cross-references are now resolved.

Too many unprocessed floats.

• *SWP/SW* Version 3.5x, 4.x, and 5.x

Documents that contain many floating objects may occasionally encounter LATEX processing problems. When you typeset your document, LATEX tries to process floating objects as it encounters them, anchoring them throughout the document. However, if it can't place an object because of its size or if float placement options don't fit, LATEX holds the object and all following floating objects until the end of the document. If there are too many such objects for LATEX to handle, it generates the error message.

Solution

You can force LATEX to process floating objects in several ways:

• Place the \clearpage command in a TEX field in the body of your document. The command forces LATEX to output any floating objects that occur in the document before the command.

• If you're not using the Portable LATEX filter or creating a PDF file, add the *float* package to manage the placement of floating objects in your document. See page 52 for detailed instructions, and see page 123 for more information about the *float* package.

• Add the *placeins* package to your document to create barriers in the document beyond which floating objects cannot be placed. See page 52 for detailed instructions, and see page 145 for more information about the *placeins* package.

Overfull \hbox or \vbox.

or

Underfull \hbox or \vbox.

• *SWP/SW* Version 3.5x, 4.x, and 5.x

When you read the compilation messages, you may see frequent references to overfull or underfull boxes, with messages like these:

```
Overfull \hbox (xxpt too wide)  in paragraph at lines 186-187
Underfull \hbox (badness 10000) detected at line 47
Overfull \vbox (xxpt too high) has occurred while \output is
active
Underfull \vbox (badness 10000) has occurred while \output is
active
```

The warnings indicate that LATEX cannot appropriately fit material into the horizontal or vertical space available, creating typeset lines or pages that are too long or too short. The message may indicate where in the document the problem has occurred, as in the first two examples above, or may indicate that the problem occurred during the formatting of running headers and footers, as in the last two examples. The number in parentheses indicates the severity of the problem.

Solution

You can ignore these messages until you've completed work on the content of your document and are ready to make final formatting adjustments. When you examine your typeset document, you may be satisfied with the spacing. In that case, no action is required. However, if the overfull condition is extreme, LATEX may have created awkward word, line, or page breaks: lines may break too soon or extend into the margin, or text may run off the end of the page. If the message indicates a problem with horizontal spacing (\hbox), you may need to adjust the length of one or more lines by introducing hyphenation points, forcing line breaks, or rewording your text so that LATEX can break the line a new way. If the message indicates a problem with vertical spacing (\vbox), you may need to adjust the length of text on the page by including forced page breaks. You may also want to use the enlargethispage command to increase the amount of text on the page slightly.

▶ **To increase the amount of text on the page**

1. Place the insertion point in the text near the top of the page you want to enlarge.

2. Apply the Enlarge Page (TeX Field) fragment.

   The fragment adds the TEX command \enlargethispage*{1000pt}.

3. Place the insertion point where you want the page break to occur.

4. From the Insert menu, choose Spacing, and then choose Break.

5. Select the type of page break you want and choose OK.

6. Compile your document again and examine the typeset file for improved spacing.

Error while attempting to execute BibTeX or MakeIndx.

- *SWP/SW* Version affected: 5.0 prior to Build 2570

Generating a BIBTEX bibliography or an index fails in Version 5.0 of *SWP* and *SW*, and the program displays one of these error messages:

```
Error while attempting to execute C:\swp35\TCITeX\SWTools\bin
\BibTeX.exe
Error while attempting to execute C:\swp35\TCITeX\SWTools\bin
\MakeIndx.exe
```

The error occurs because Version 5.0 has been installed over an existing Version 3.5, changing the configuration of BIBTEX and MakeIndex so that these typesetting tools cannot be started from *SWP*.

Solution

You can resolve the problem by editing the program's initial configuration file. If you're using *SW*, the file and directory names differ slightly.

▶ **To edit the initial configuration file**

1. Close *SWP.*

2. Using an ASCII editor, open the initial configuration file `swp-pro.ins` in the program directory.

   Because Version 5.0 has been installed over Version 3.5, the program directory for *SWP* is `c:\swp35`.

3. Change the BibTeX entries in the file:

   a. Find the group with entries similar to these:
   ```
   [BibTeX]
   BibTeXStyleDir=c:\swp35\TCITeX\bibtex\bst
   BibTeXDataDir=c:\swp35\TCITeX\bibtex\bib
   BibTeXexe=c:\swp35\TCITeX\SWTools\bin\BibTeX.exe
   ```

   b. Change the last line of the group to

   BibTeXexe=BibTeX

4. Change the MakeIndex entries in the file:

   a. Find the group with entries similar to these:
   ```
   [MakeIndex]
   MakeIndxExe=c:\swp35\TCITeX\SWTools\bin\MakeIndx.exe
   ```

   b. Change the last line of the group to

   MakeIndxExe=MakeIndex

5. Find these lines:
   ```
   [Installation]

   MoveToIniDbase=0
   ```

6. Change the lines to

   [Installation]

   MoveToIniDbase=1

7. Save the configuration file.

8. Start *SWP.* The information in the configuration file will be moved to the appropriate location in the Windows registry.

Problems Encountered in LaTeX Previewing and Printing

Although your document may compile without errors or warnings, problems can arise when you preview or print the DVI or PDF file. Examine your previewed document before you print to ensure that all problems have been resolved.

Cross-references do not preview correctly in master documents.

- *SWP/SW* Version 3.5x, 4.x, and 5.x

By default, LaTeX makes only one pass when you preview master documents, so cross-references and other generated document elements may not compile or preview correctly. Unresolved cross-references appear as **??** in the typeset document.

Solution

When the compilation begins, use the LaTeX dialog box to specify the number of passes you want LaTeX to perform. If your document contains cross-references, specify at least two passes. If it has a table of contents, specify three passes.

Previewed mathematics is garbled or appears as blue dots.

- *SWP/SW* Version 4.x and 5.x

When you typeset preview your document, mathematical symbols appear garbled in the TrueTeX preview window. Text and mathematical characters may also display as blue dots. This problem is caused by missing TrueTeX fonts. It occurs when an earlier version of *SWP* or *SW* has been uninstalled following the installation of Version 4.x or 5.x of the program. Because Windows allows only one font of a given name to be installed on the system at any time, it discards old fonts when new fonts of the same name are installed. Thus, when Version 4.x or 5.x and its fonts are installed, Windows discards any fonts from earlier versions whose names are duplicated. If the earlier version of the program is subsequently uninstalled, the fonts that are discarded are those from Version 4.x or 5.x. When you subsequently try to typeset your document, the necessary fonts are missing and the characters appear incorrectly.

Solution

Sometimes, just opening the Windows Fonts applet can restore the TrueTeX fonts. If refreshing doesn't restore the fonts, you must repair or reinstall them.

▶ To refresh the TrueTeX fonts

1. Close *SWP* or *SW*.

2. From the Windows **Control Panel**, choose the **Fonts** applet.

3. When the list of fonts is displayed, check that the various fonts used by *SWP* or *SW* are present.

   Look for the fonts used by the TrueTeX Previewer; they start with *cm, dc, eu,* and other lowercase strings. To see the complete list of fonts used by the TrueTeX Previewer, browse the `TCITeX/TeX/fonts/truetype` directory in your *SWP* or *SW* program installation.

▶ To repair the TrueTeX fonts

1. From the Windows **Start** menu, choose **Run**.

2. Choose **Browse** and select the `setup.exe` file that is on the program CD or that you downloaded.

3. When the installation program prompts you, choose the **Repair** option.

4. Follow the instructions on the screen to complete the process.

▶ **To reinstall the TrueTEX fonts**

1. From the Windows **Control Panel**, choose the **Fonts** applet.

2. Select the TrueTEX Previewer fonts and delete them.

   The font names start with *cm, dc, eu,* and other lowercase strings. To see the complete list of fonts used by the TrueTEX Previewer, browse the `TCITeX/TeX/fonts/truetype` directory in your *SWP* or *SW* program installation.

3. From the **File** menu in the **Fonts** applet, choose **Install new font**.

4. In the **Add fonts** dialog box, navigate to the `TCITeX\TeX\fonts\truetype` directory in your program installation.

5. Wait for the fonts in the directory to be listed.

6. Choose **Select All** and choose **OK**.

7. When all the fonts have been added, exit the applet.

Previewed characters appear as blue dots on systems using localized Windows.

- *SWP/SW* Version 3.5x, 4.x, and 5.x

   When you preview a document that uses one of the Times New Roman fonts, or occasionally some other fonts, characters appear as blue dots. The problem occurs because some localized versions of Windows rename fonts as part of the localization process. The registry may contain the original font name but the font itself may be renamed. For example, in Spanish Windows, the registry refers to "Times New Roman Italic," but the font itself is named "Times New Roman Cursiva." Similarly, "Times New Roman Bold" is named "Times New Roman Negrita." Because TrueTEX doesn't know the localized names, it cannot find the fonts and displays blue dots instead of the correct characters. This problem occurs in Spanish Windows and French Windows, and it may occur in other non-US versions of Windows as well.

Solution
Create a new font substitution file that contains the correct font names, and add it to the list of files used by the TrueTEX Previewer. Font substitution files for these localized versions of Windows are available on the MacKichan Software website: German, French, Spanish, Norwegian, Swedish, Greek, and Russian.

Note   The font substitution files for Greek and Russian can be used only with the TrueTEX Previewer included with Build 2570 and later of Version 5.

If you cannot download an appropriate font substitution file, you must create one. The instructions below illustrate the process. These instructions, which are specific to Spanish Windows, illustrate how to rename the Times New Roman, Arial, and Courier New fonts for Spanish Windows. Modify these instructions as necessary for other localized versions of Windows.

► **To create a font substitution file**

1. For each font that doesn't preview correctly, determine the font name used by the localized version of Windows:

   a. From the Windows Control Panel, choose the Fonts applet.
   b. In the list of fonts, double-click the font to view the font sample.
      For example, double-click Times New Roman Italic.
   c. Note the font name shown at the top of the window.
      This name must be used in the new font substitution file.
   d. Close the font sample.

2. Create a new font substitution file listing the localized names.

   a. Using an ASCII editor, create a new file and type the lines below. Lines that begin with a semicolon are comments and can be omitted.

   ; Additional font substitutions to take care of localized font names (embedded in the font names)
   [fonts]
   ;   Note: the [fonts] section header is mandatory for TrueTeX to recognize a set of font substitution rules.
   ;
   Times New Roman=times
   Times New Roman Negrita=timesbd
   Times New Roman Cursiva=timesi
   Times New Roman Negrita Cursiva=timesbi
   Arial=arial
   Arial Negrita=arialbd
   Arial Cursiva=ariali
   Arial Negrita Cursiva=arialbi
   Courier New=cour
   Courier New Negrita=courbd
   Courier New Cursiva=couri
   Courier New Negrita Cursiva=courbi

3. Save the file to the `TCITeX\TrueTeX` directory of your program installation using an appropriate name, such as SpanishSUBS.ini.

4. Add the new file to the existing list of font substitution files:

   a. From the *SWP* or *SW* program group, choose the TrueTeX Previewer to start the previewer.
   b. From the Options menu, choose Expert.

c. Choose Font Substitution File(s) to open a dialog listing the current font substitution files.

The list usually scrolls past the width of the dialog box.

d. Press the END key to move the insertion point to the end of the existing list.

The new font substitution file must be added to the end of the existing font substitutions.

e. Type a semicolon followed by the complete path name for the new font substitution file. Assuming your program directory is `C:\swp50`, you can add `SpanishSUBS.ini` for this example by typing

C:\swp50\TCITeX\TrueTeX\SpanishSUBS.ini

f. Choose OK and then choose Yes to leave the previewer.

5. Preview the document again.

You should see the correct characters instead of blue dots.

Graphics do not appear in PDF files.

- *SWP/SW* Version affected: 5.x

When you create a typeset PDF file from a master document and its subdocuments, the graphics that are included in the master document appear correctly in the PDF file, but the graphics included in the subdocuments are missing. When you preview the subdocuments, the graphics in the subdocuments appear correctly. This set of circumstances occurs when you've saved the master document, but not the subdocuments, in a form that correctly formats graphics for PDF output.

Solution

Unlike other typesetting specifications, the graphics output settings aren't transferred automatically to the subdocuments unless each subdocument has been opened and saved after the master document has been saved.

▶ **To specify the graphics output format for subdocuments**

1. Open the master document.

2. From the Typeset menu, choose Output Choice.

3. Select PDF output or Both DVI and PDF output, and choose OK.

4. Open the subdocument and make a change to it, such as entering and then deleting a space.

5. Save the subdocument.

6. Repeat steps 4–5 for each subdocument.

7. Create a new PDF file for the master document.

Graphics do not appear in PDF files when documents use graphicx.

- *SWP/SW* Version affected: 5.x

The *graphicx* package implements LATEX support for graphics files (see page 126). Because it depends on the availability of an output driver that can manage the files, the package has options for various drivers. If a driver hasn't been specified, PDFLATEXselects a default driver and automatically uses the correct graphics instructions for creating a PDF file. But if the dvips driver has been selected, PDFLATEXcan't use the correct graphics instructions when it creates a PDF file, and the graphics don't appear.

Solution

▶ **To change the output driver**

1. Open your document.

2. On the Typeset toolbar, click the Options and Packages button ![button] or, from the Typeset menu, choose **Options and Packages**.

3. Choose the **Package Options** tab.

4. In the **Packages in Use** section, select **graphicx**.

5. Choose **Modify**.

6. In the **Options** box, click the currently selected driver to turn off the driver selection.

7. Choose **OK** to close the dialog boxes and return to your document.

8. Save the document.

9. From the **Typeset** menu, choose **Compile PDF** to create a new typeset PDF file.

Poor quality of graphics and plots in PDF files.

- *SWP/SW* Version affected: 5.x

PDFLATEX supports only a few types of graphics formats: .png, .jpg, .tif, and .pdf. When you create a PDF file, any graphics or plots in other formats are converted to .png, .jpg, or .pdf format for inclusion in the PDF file. (The program doesn't export .tif files.) The settings you make in the **PDF Graphics Export Options** dialog box determine which format is used. Generally, the .png and .jpg graphics created for PDF files are of good quality. However, .pdf graphics may be problematic.

Solution
Try the strategies below to improve the quality of graphics in your typeset PDF files.

- Use the latest available version of *SWP* or *SW*.

The conversion program used to create .pdf graphics was updated with Build 2606 of Version 5.0 of the program. If you're using an earlier build of Version 5.0, download a patch update for the later build from the MacKichan Software website. The update solves most of the graphics conversion problems. If problems persist after you've installed the new build, try one of the other strategies below.

- Change the PDF graphics export format for raster graphics to a raster export format.

▶ **To change the PDF graphics export format**

1. From the Typeset menu, choose General Settings.

2. Choose PDF Graphics Settings.

3. For both graphics and plots, set the format you want.

   The program is shipped with these defaults:

Graphic Type	Default Export Format	Recommended Export Format
vector graphic	.pdf	.pdf
raster graphic	.pdf	.png
the set of .jpg, .png, and .tif files	leave unchanged	leave unchanged
plot	.pdf	.pdf

4. Choose OK to close the dialog boxes.

- Change the value in the registry subkey.

   This strategy applies only to the conversion of graphics to .pdf format. The graphics filter behaves differently depending on the graphics conversion method used by PDFLATEX to create .pdf graphics. PDFLATEX can either use a temporary file for the conversion or use the internal Windows graphics format directly. When PDFLATEX uses a temporary file, the conversion process first creates a temporary .wmf file of the graphic and then creates a .pdf image from the temporary file. Any text in the resulting graphic is positioned correctly, but the graphic and the text may be grainy, more like a bitmap image. This is the default setting for Build 2552 of Version 5.0 of *SWP* and *SW*. When PDFLATEX uses the internal Windows graphics format, the resulting .pdf graphic has better resolution, but any text inside the graphic may be positioned incorrectly in the graphic or missing altogether. Images embedded in the graphic may be distorted. This is the default setting for Builds 2557 and later of Version 5.0.

   The conversion method, and thus the behavior of the graphics filter, depends on a setting in the UserGraphicsExport registry key. Inside each key is a subkey whose value determines the conversion method. When the subkey value is set to 1, PDFLATEX uses the temporary file. When the subkey value is set to 0, PDFLATEX uses the internal graphics format directly. You can change the value in the registry subkey using the registry editor.

Note   Directly changing the registry is recommended only for advanced users. Incorrect modifications of the registry can result in a system that will not start.

Remember that this change affects only those graphics exported as .pdf files. It has no effect on the exporting of .png or .jpg files. Changing the registry setting can result in improved graphics, but note that graphics conversions can be affected by other factors, such as the particular graphics in your document and by the version of Windows you're using. In particular, results may differ between Windows XP/2000/NT and Windows Me/98/95. You may also notice problems with colors or incomplete conversion.

▶ **To change the value in the registry subkey**

1. Open the registry editor:

   a. From the Windows Start menu, choose Run.
   b. In the Run dialog box, enter **regedit** and choose OK.

2. Navigate to the registry key for PDF graphics conversions:
   - In *SWP* the registry key is
     `HKEY_CURRENT_USER\Software\MacKichan Software\Scientific Workplace\5.00\UserGraphicsExport`
   - In *SW* the registry key is
     `HKEY_CURRENT_USER\Software\MacKichan Software\Scientific Word\5.00\UserGraphicsExport`

   Note   The version number in the key (5.00 in these examples) may be different for your installation.

3. Double-click the `GfxPDFExportFromFile` entry.

4. Change the value for the entry:
   - To convert graphics by creating temporary graphics files, set `GfxPDFExportFromFile` to **1**.
   - To convert graphics by using the internal graphics format directly, set `GfxPDFExportFromFile` to **0**.

5. Choose OK.

6. Open your document, modify it in some way, then save it.

   If you don't modify and save the document after changing the registry setting, the program won't create any new graphics when you create a new PDF file. Instead, it will use the existing graphics.

Characters appear incorrectly when previewing or printing with PCTₑX.

- *SWP/SW* Version 3.5x, 4.x, and 5.x

Computer Modern fonts are included both with *SWP* and *SW* and with PCTₑX. Although the two sets of fonts use the same font names, the fonts are different and use different encoding. Because Windows doesn't allow two fonts of the same name to be on the system at the same time, the two font sets can't be on the system simultaneously. Incompatibilities result if one product tries to use the fonts intended for the other. If the fonts for the alternate product are installed, your previewed or printed document will have missing or incorrect characters.

Solution

If you expect to use PCTEX all the time, follow the instructions below to install the PCTEX fonts into the Windows Fonts folder. If you plan to switch frequently between programs, consider creating and saving font installation batch files to handle the process. Note that one side effect of making this change is that the kappa character no longer displays in the previewer for *SWP* and *SW,* but it will be displayed in PCTEX.

▶ **To install PCTEX fonts**

1. Remove most of the Computer Modern fonts already installed:

   a. From the Windows **Control Panel,** choose the **Fonts** applet.

   b. Remove all fonts that begin with *CM* except the CMSY fonts. This table lists the fonts to remove:

CMB10.TTF	CMFIB8.TTF	CMR9.TTF	CMSSQ8.TTF
CMBSY10.TTF	CMINCH.TTF	CMSL10.TTF	CMSSQI8.TTF
CMBX10.TTF	CMITT10.TTF	CMSL12.TTF	CMTCSC10.TTF
CMBX12.TTF	CMMI10.ttf	CMSL8.TTF	CMTEX10.TTF
CMBX5.TTF	CMMI12.ttf	CMSL9.TTF	CMTEX8.TTF
CMBX6.TTF	CMMI5.ttf	CMSLTT10.TTF	CMTEX9.TTF
CMBX7.TTF	CMMI6.ttf	CMSS10.TTF	CMTI10.TTF
CMBX8.TTF	CMMI7.ttf	CMSS12.TTF	CMTI12.TTF
CMBX9.TTF	CMMI8.ttf	CMSS17.TTF	CMTI7.TTF
CMBXSL10.TTF	CMMI9.ttf	CMSS8.TTF	CMTI8.TTF
CMBXTI10.TTF	CMMIB10.TTF	CMSS9.TTF	CMTI9.TTF
CMCSC10.TTF	CMR10.TTF	CMSSBX10.TTF	CMTT10.TTF
CMCSC8.TTF	CMR12.TTF	CMSSDC10.TTF	CMTT12.TTF
CMCSC9.TTF	CMR17.TTF	CMSSI10.TTF	CMTT8.TTF
CMDUNH10.TTF	CMR5.TTF	CMSSI12.TTF	CMTT9.TTF
CMEX10.TTF	CMR6.TTF	CMSSI17.TTF	CMU10.TTF
CMFF10.TTF	CMR7.TTF	CMSSI8.TTF	CMVTT10.TTF
CMFI10.TTF	CMR8.TTF	CMSSI9.TTF	

2. Still in the **Fonts** window, install the new fonts:

   a. From the **File** menu, choose **Install New Font** to display a new window.

   b. Display the fonts by browsing to the FONTS\AMS\TTF folder in the directory in which PCTEX is installed.

   c. Choose the **Select All** button and then choose **OK** to begin installing the fonts. If you receive messages that the fonts are already there, choose **OK** to ignore the message.

   d. Choose the FONTS\TEX\TTF folder in the PCTEX directory to display a list of fonts.

   e. Choose the **Select All** button and then choose **OK**. If you receive messages that the fonts are already there, choose **OK** to ignore the message.

   f. Choose **Close.**

Warning: DVI file has too few (less than 4) trailer bytes.

- *SWP/SW* Version 3.5x, 4.x, and 5.x

The error can occur when *SWP* or *SW* runs under Virtual PC on a Macintosh. Virtual PC allows directories to be shared between the Windows and Macintosh file systems, but locating DVI files in a shared directory can cause problems. Although LATEX compiles the document without error, the TrueTEX Previewer cannot open the DVI file and displays the error message.

Solution

Save your *SWP* and *SW* documents in an unshared directory.

JPG graphics preview with a green background.

- *SWP/SW* Version 3.5x, 4.x, and 5.x

Because *SWP* and *SW* graphics import filters aren't compatible with all Adobe Illustrator formats, JPG graphics that have been created with Adobe Illustrator don't always import properly into *SWP* or *SW* documents. The graphics don't typeset correctly and they appear with a green background in the TrueTEX Previewer.

Solution

Open and save the JPG graphics in a program other than Adobe Illustrator, then reimport them into your document.

AI and EPS graphics typeset incorrectly.

- *SWP/SW* Version 3.5x, 4.x, and 5.x

Because *SWP* and *SW* aren't compatible with all Adobe Illustrator formats, AI and EPS graphics that have been created with Adobe Illustrator don't always import properly into *SWP* or *SW* documents. The graphics don't typeset correctly and they appear with a green background in the TrueTEX Previewer.

Solution

Open the AI or EPS graphics in Adobe Illustrator and save them using the format for Version 6.0 or earlier, then reimport the graphics into your document.

Graphics are missing from preview and print.

- *SWP/SW* Version 4.x and 5.x

When you typeset preview or typeset print your document, graphics in the document are missing. Either the names of the graphics or the names of the directories containing the graphics contain a space. Because TEX assigns a special meaning to the space, the document doesn't typeset properly. See also Invalid characters in the file name or path directories, page 187.

Solution

Remove any spaces in the graphics file or directory names.

▶ **To remove spaces in graphics path names**

1. Remove any spaces in the graphics file names or the names of the directories containing the graphics.

2. Reimport the graphics into your document.

3. Typeset preview the document again.

! Package mathtime Error: Bold math is not supported.

- *SWP/SW* Version 3.5x, 4.x, and 5.x

    you've tried to typeset a document that uses the *mathtime* package and also contains bold Greek characters. The bold versions of the Times fonts are missing from the package. The Mathtime Plus fonts provide bold and heavy bold versions of characters using the Times fonts, but these don't work with the version of TrueT#X included in *SWP* and *SW*.

Solution

You can achieve bold Greek characters by mapping the bold Greek letters to the Computer Modern bold Greek font, as described below. Note, however, that you should use this method with care. It can occasionally result in incorrect characters, because the Mathtime fonts and the Computer Modern fonts have incompatible encodings. The TrueT#X Formatter doesn't issue specific warnings about incorrect characters.

▶ **To map bold Greek letters to the Computer Modern bold Greek font**

1. On the Typeset toolbar, click the Options and Packages button 🔳 or, from the Typeset menu, choose Options and Packages and then choose the Package Options tab.

2. If the *mathtime* package isn't listed in the Packages in Use area, add the package.

3. In the Packages in Use area, select the *mathtime* package and choose Modify.

4. From the Category list box, choose Encoding Options, then from the Options list box, choose No TS1.

5. From the Category list box, choose Bold, then from the Options list box, choose Computer Modern.

    Note that if you don't set this option and you save the document as a Portable L#T#X file, the document will compile and print correctly on a system that has the Mathtime Plus fonts.

6. Choose OK to close the dialog boxes and return to your document.

7. Save the document and typeset it again.

EPS graphics in DVI files preview and print incorrectly.

- *SWP/SW* Version 3.5x and 4.x

Occasionally, the PostScript filter supplied with *SWP* and *SW* misrenders EPS graphics. The appearance of the graphic may be incorrect or letters that appear in the graphic may be displaced. The problem arises because LaTeX typesets using the default DVI driver for the current LaTeX installation. The default driver for *SWP* and *SW* installations is `tcidvi`, which uses the supplied PostScript graphics filter. In other words, the graphics can be misrendered if the default driver is used.

Solution

If you're creating a DVI file, you can bypass the problem by adding the *graphicx* package to your document (see page 126), choosing the `dvips` driver, and then saving your document as a Portable LaTeX file, according to the instructions that follow. If your document is a Style Editor document or a LaTeX 2.09 document, it can't be saved as a Portable LaTeX file. However, you can successfully bypass the EPS difficulty if you import the contents of your document into a new document and modify it according to the instructions.

The `dvips` driver is the default for most LaTeX installations. Note that if you actively choose the `dvips` driver option, LaTeX previews using the native PostScript capabilities for the current display device. Therefore, an EPS graphic in your document appears in the TrueTeX Previewer as a box containing the path name of the graphics file. When you print, the graphic appears correctly using the PostScript interpreter in the printer.

▶ **To use the *graphicx* package to avoid EPS graphics difficulties**

1. Add the *graphicx* package to your document.

2. Save the document as a Portable LaTeX file:

   a. From the File menu, choose Save As.
   b. In the Save as type box, select Portable LaTeX (*.tex).
   c. Change the directory and file name as necessary.
   d. Choose Save.

3. On the Typeset toolbar, click the Options and Packages button ⊞ or, from the Typeset menu, choose Options and Packages.

4. Choose the Package Options tab.

5. In the Packages in Use box, select graphicx, and then choose Modify.

6. In the Options box, select dvips.

7. Choose OK.

8. Choose OK to return to your document.

PostScript fonts in DVI files don't print correctly.

- *SWP/SW* Version 3.5x and 4.x

Although PostScript graphics import successfully into your *SWP* or *SW* document, the fonts may not always print. The *SWP* and *SW* graphics filters can handle a maximum of 32 fonts. If the .ini file for the PostScript graphics filter doesn't specify the font you want, the font will not print.

Solution

Edit the .ini file for the PostScript graphics filter to add the font you need or to substitute it for one of the 32 fonts already listed in the file.

▶ **To edit the .ini file for the PostScript graphics filter**

1. Using an ASCII editor, open the file impsi2.ini in your *SWP* or *SW* program directory.

    The Standard Options section of the file is organized in two columns. The column on the left lists the Windows font names, and the column on the right lists the PostScript font names, like this:

    ```
    Font[001]="Helvetica",            "Swiss:Helvetica"
    Font[002]="Helvetica-Bold",       "Swiss:Helvetica Bold"
    Font[003]="Helvetica-Oblique",    "Swiss:Helvetica Oblique"
    Font[004]="Helvetica-BoldOblique", "Swiss:Helvetica Bold
                                       Oblique"
    Font[005]="Times-Roman",          "Roman:Times"
    Font[006]="Times-Bold",           "Roman:Times Bold"
    Font[007]="Times-Italic",         "Roman:Times Italic"
    Font[008]="Times-BoldItalic",     "Roman:Times Bold Italic"
       ⋮
    Font[032]="TECHMath-Mix",         "TECHMath"
    ```

2. Search the file for the name of the font you need.

3. If the name isn't listed, add a new Font line or replace one of the existing Font lines with the information about the font you want, using the syntax shown in the example above.

    If the font doesn't have a separate PostScript name, enter the Windows name in both columns.

4. Save and close the .ini file.

Graphics in DVI files preview but print incorrectly.

- *SWP/SW* Version 3.5x and 4.x

If graphics appear correctly when you typeset preview your document but don't appear at all when you print, processing the graphics may require more memory than is available to the graphics handler provided with *SWP* and *SW*. Another explanation is that your computer may be using so much virtual memory that it cannot process the graphics.

Solution

You may be able to make the graphics print correctly by increasing the memory available to the graphics handler, managing your virtual memory, or managing the size of your graphics files.

▶ **To increase the memory available to the graphics handler (SWP/SW Version 3.5 only)**

The amount of memory available to the graphics handler was increased with Version 3.51. If you have Build 1990 of Version 3.5, follow these instructions to increase the available memory:

1. Using an ASCII editor, open the file `tcispech.ini` in the program directory.

2. Near the beginning of the file, find this line:

   `MaxGraphicsMemoryUsage=4000 kbytes`

3. Replace `4000` with a larger value, such as 8000, 16000, or 32000.

4. Save and close the file.

▶ **To release some of the virtual memory in use**

1. Make sure the DVI file for your document is current, then exit *SWP* or *SW*.

2. Reboot your computer.

3. From the Windows Start menu, start the TrueTEX Previewer.

4. Open the DVI file for your document.

5. From the File menu, choose Print.

6. Close the TrueTEX Previewer.

▶ **To reduce the size of the graphics files**

Smaller graphics files require less memory. If you don't need sophisticated color graphics, use your graphics program to save the images with fewer colors or as black and white images.

Preview and print appearance of $ \check{L} $ doesn't match screen appearance.

● *SWP/SW* Version affected: 3.5x

The TEX command $ \check{L} $ displays as L' on the screen, but it previews and prints as $\check{L}$. This happens because there are two possible representations for this particular Unicode character. Microsoft has chosen to use the first version shown in the preceding sentence in its screen fonts. When you typeset your document, LaTeX interprets the character using the other representation.

Solution

You can create a fragment that contains a TeX command containing several characters, the accent and the character itself. Because there are several characters in the group, the software displays both characters instead of using a single Unicode character. You can use this method to obtain a character that has the same appearance both on the screen and when you typeset.

▶ **To create a fragment**

1. From the Insert menu in Version 3.5, choose Field and then choose TeX.

2. In the input area, type **$ \check{L{ } } $** and choose OK.

3. Save, close, and reopen your document.

   The TeX field should now appear as $\check{L}$.

4. Select the character.

5. On the Fragments toolbar, click the Save Fragments button or, from the File menu, choose Save Fragment.

6. Type a name to be used to recall the fragment.

   Avoid using the name of an existing TeX command.

7. Choose Save.

   The fragment now appears on the fragment list.

Plots don't preview or print.

- *SWP/SW* Version 3.5x, 4.x, and 5.x

   If a plot doesn't appear when you typeset preview or print the document, but does appear when you preview or print without typesetting, no snapshot has been generated for the plot.

Solution

Make sure that automatic snapshot generation is turned on and actively generate a snapshot for the plot.

▶ **To turn on automatic snapshot generation**

1. From the Tools menu, choose Computation Setup.

2. Choose the Plot Behavior tab.

3. Check Generate Plot Snapshots Automatically and choose OK.

▶ **To generate a snapshot**

1. Select the plot.

2. Choose **Properties** and choose the **View** tab.

3. Note the filename of the snapshot.

   If the dialog box indicates **No snapshot file**, a snapshot of the plot hasn't been generated.

4. Click the **Generate Snapshot** button.

5. Choose **OK**.

6. Typeset the document again to make certain all plots appear.

TrueTEX Previewer window is minimized.

- *SWP/SW* Version 3.5x and 4.0

   When the TrueTEX Previewer is started from *SWP* or *SW*, the main window appears maximized. Clicking the Restore button minimizes the previewer's main window, hiding all but the title bar.

Solution
If you're familiar with TEX and LATEX, you can change the command line options that determine the size and location of the TrueTEX Previewer window when it is launched from *SWP* or *SW*. Instructions appear in the TrueTEX readme file that is installed with the program.

Caution   Don't attempt to modify the settings unless you know TEX and LATEX very well.

▶ **To view the readme file**

1. Open the document OptionsPackagesLaTeX.tex in the SWSamples directory of your program directory.

2. Move to the TrueTeX Documentation section and click the first link to open the readme file in the TrueTEX Previewer.

3. Move to the section entitled Initial Window Sizing to find a description of the command line parameter that controls the initial window size of the TrueTEX Previewer.

▶ **To change the command line options**

1. From the **Typeset** menu in *SWP* or *SW*, choose **Expert Settings**.

2. Choose the **Preview Settings** tab.

3. Choose **Add/Modify** and note the entries in the **Command** line to invoke preview driver box. You may see an entry like this:

```
%x "%f" -i% %I -d 0 0 -1 -1
```

The portion of the line beginning with -d changes the window size.

4. Change the setting:

- To specify that the previewer open as a maximized window and to yield a maximized window when Restore is clicked and prevent the problem with a minimized window thereafter, set the final portion of the line to **-d 0 0 -1 -1**. Don't change any other settings on the line.

- To specify that the previewer open as a maximized window and to create a 640x480 window after clicking Restore, set the final portion of the line to **-d -1 -1 640 480**.

You can experiment to find a setting that works best for you. For example, if you have a 1280 x 1024 high-resolution screen, use **-d 0 0 850 -1** to open a window that starts at the top left corner of your screen, with a width of 850 and a maximum height.

5. Choose **OK** to close each dialog box and return to your document.

Repairing Damaged Documents

If your document has been damaged or become corrupted in some way, you may be able to repair it if you can isolate the problem. However, not all documents can be repaired and read successfully. The program does not handle every possible construct that might occur in a native LATEX document.

If your document was originally written in native LATEX and then imported to *SWP* or *SW*, some problems may persist. In general, if a LATEX document contains a construct that differs from Plain TEX (such as `array` versus `matrix`), you may be able to open the document in *SWP* or *SW* if you modify it to use the LATEX construct. Alternatively, you may be able to read the document using the Import Non-*SWP/SW* LATEX filter available in Version 5.5; see page 81.

▶ **To repair a damaged document**

1. Make a copy of the `.tex` file.

2. Use the TrueTEX Formatter to compile the document.

3. Isolate and correct any LATEX errors, and then recompile the document.

4. When the document compiles successfully, try to open the document in *SWP* or *SW*.

5. As the program loads the document, carefully watch the display of paragraph numbers on the Status bar.

6. If the document loads successfully, you've repaired the document successfully. If not, note the paragraph number where the error occurred.

7. Open the document with an ASCII editor.

8. Isolate the error, as described in Resolving LaTeX Errors on page 184.

Because errors that occur at this level are usually document-specific, they don't lend themselves to the kinds of general suggestions we offer in this manual. However, you may be able to make the document work in *SWP* or *SW* by enclosing the lines that cause the error in an encapsulated TEX field. If so, consider it only a temporary solution and pursue a more robust solution to the problem.

Important   Encapsulating erroneous code is a temporary solution.

▶ **To encapsulate information in a TEX field**

1. Open the document with an ASCII editor.

2. If much of the document is still commented out, remove the percent signs from all but the few lines surrounding and containing the error.

3. Copy the commented lines to the clipboard.

4. Save and close the file.

5. Open the document in *SWP* or *SW*.

6. Place the insertion point where the commented lines should appear.

7. Copy the lines to an encapsulated TEX field:

   a. Enter an encapsulated TEX field.
   b. Paste the lines from the clipboard.
   c. Remove the percent sign at the beginning of each line.
   d. Choose **OK**.

8. Typeset compile the document.

9. If the document compiles correctly, you've successfully repaired the document.

   If the document still doesn't compile correctly, remove the TEX field from the document.

Complex \def and \renewcommand statements in the document preamble can prevent the program from loading the document. If your document preamble contains such commands, you may be able to read the file if you place the statements in an external file and then input the file from the preamble.

▶ **To place statements in an external file**

1. Open the document with an ASCII editor.

2. Select the statements you want to place in another file, and cut them to the clipboard.

3. In place of the deleted lines, type **input{*filename.tex*}** where *filename* is the name of the ASCII file you will create in steps 4–6.

4. Open a new file with an ASCII editor.

5. Paste the statements from the clipboard into the file.

6. Name the file with a `.tex` extension and save it in an appropriate subdirectory of the `TCITeX/TeX` directory of your program installation.

   The file must be in a `TCITeX/TeX` subdirectory or LATEX won't find it when you try to compile the document.

7. Try to open and compile the original document in *SWP* or *SW*.

Index

MacKichan
SOFTWARE, INC.

Software

 Scientific WorkPlace®

Scientific WorkPlace makes writing, sharing, and doing mathematics easier than you ever imagined possible. This scientific word processor increases your productivity because it is easy to learn and use. You can compose and edit your documents directly on the screen, without being forced to think in a programming language. With a simple click of a button, you can typeset your document in LaTeX. You can also compute and plot solutions with the included computer algebra system. With *Scientific WorkPlace*, both professional and support staff can produce stunning results quickly and easily, without knowing TeX™, LaTeX, or computer algebra syntax. ***Contact us for a free 30-day trial version.***

 Scientific Word®

The Gold Standard for mathematical publishing since 1992, *Scientific Word* makes writing and sharing scientific documents straightforward and easy. With over 150 LaTeX styles included, *Scientific Word* ensures your documents will be beautiful. This means you can concentrate on the content, not the appearance. It has been estimated that support staff using *Scientific Word* experiences a doubling or tripling of productivity over the use of straight LaTeX. Also, MacKichan Software provides free, prompt, and knowledgeable technical support. ***Contact us for a free 30-day trial version.***

 Scientific Notebook®

Scientific Notebook makes word processing and doing mathematics easy. With this complete word processor, you can enter text and mathematics quickly, without having to use an inefficient equation editor. The built-in computer algebra system lets you solve and plot equations without having to learn a special syntax. After creating your scientific documents and exams in *Scientific Notebook*, you can publish them in print and on the World Wide Web. ***Contact us for a free 30-day trial version.***

 MuPAD® **Pro**

MuPAD Pro is a modern, full-featured computer algebra system in an integrated and open environment for symbolic and numeric computing. Its domains and categories are like object-oriented classes that allow overriding and overloading methods and operators, inheritance, and generic algorithms. The *MuPAD* language has a Pascal-like syntax and allows imperative, functional, and object-oriented programming. A comfortable notebook interface includes a graphics tool for visualization, an integrated source-level debugger, a profiler, and hypertext help. ***Contact us for a free 30-day trial version.***

TO ORDER: Visit our webstore, fax, email, or phone us.
Website: www.mackichan.com ◆ Fax: 360-394-6039 ◆ Email: info@mackichan.com ◆ Toll-free: 877-724-9673
19307 8th Avenue NE ◆ Suite C ◆ Poulsbo, WA 98370

MacKichan
SOFTWARE, INC.

Additional Software

MathTalk™/Scientific Notebook®

MathTalk/Scientific Notebook, created by Metroplex Voice Computing, provides voice input for *Scientific Notebook*. With this program, you can enter even the most complex mathematics using voice commands. You can use it in conjunction with the keyboard and mouse to speed the entry of text and mathematics, or to completely replace the keyboard and mouse. *MathTalk/Scientific Notebook* requires *Dragon NaturallySpeaking*®, which is not included.
Visit *www.mathtalk.com* for more information.

Duxbury Braille Translator

Duxbury Systems leads the world in software for braille. Their *Duxbury Braille Translator* converts *Scientific Notebook* files into braille. Create your print or large print math, save, then open your *Scientific Notebook* file and go to braille. Used with *MathTalk/Scientific Notebook*, the *Duxbury Braille Translator* provides dramatic new power to visually impaired students and professionals.
Visit *www.duxburysystems.com* for more information.

Books

Doing Mathematics with Scientific WorkPlace® and Scientific Notebook®, Version 5

By Darel W. Hardy and Carol L. Walker

Doing Mathematics with Scientific WorkPlace and Scientific Notebook describes how to use the built-in computer algebra system to do a wide range of mathematics, without having to deal directly with the computer algebra syntax.

Creating Documents with Scientific WorkPlace® and Scientific Word®, Version 5

By Susan Bagby

Creating Documents with Scientific WorkPlace and Scientific Word gives you an overview of the process of creating beautiful documents using these two powerful software programs. It covers basic editing and entering of mathematical expressions as well as tables, graphics, lists, indexes, cross-references, tables of contents, and large document management. If you are using *Scientific WorkPlace* or *Scientific Word* to prepare documents for publication, this book is highly recommended.

(Continued)

TO ORDER: Visit our webstore, fax, email, or phone us.
Website: www.mackichan.com ◆ Fax: 360-394-6039 ◆ Email: info@mackichan.com ◆ Toll-free: 877-724-9673
19307 8th Avenue NE ◆ Suite C ◆ Poulsbo, WA 98370

MathTalk™ is a trademark of Metroplex Voice Computing.
Dragon NaturallySpeaking® is a registered trademark of Dragon Systems, Inc.

Books (cont.)

Typesetting Documents in Scientific WorkPlace® and Scientific Word®, Third Edition
By Susan Bagby and George Pearson

Typesetting Documents in ScientificWorkPlace and Scientific Word is an aid to choosing and customizing the typeset appearance of your documents. The manual explains how to work from within these two programs to tailor the typeset appearance of a document; how to choose and add document shells; and how document shells use LaTeX document classes, class options, and packages. The manual also documents many of the LaTeX packages that accomplish specific formatting tasks.

A Gallery of Document Shells for Scientific WorkPlace® and Scientific Word®, Version 5
By Susan Bagby and George Pearson (In PDF format on the program CD-ROM)

A Gallery of Document Shells for Scientific WorkPlace and Scientific Word helps you choose document shells that are appropriate for your typesetting purposes. It illustrates and briefly describes the characteristics of almost 200 shells provided with these two programs.

Doing Calculus with Scientific Notebook®
By Darel W. Hardy and Carol L. Walker

Take the mystery out of doing calculus with this must-have companion to the *Scientific Notebook* software. This book provides activities to complete with *Scientific Notebook* that will help develop a clearer understanding of calculus. Think of *Scientific Notebook* as a laboratory for mathematical experimentation and *Doing Calculus with Scientific Notebook* as a lab manual of experiments to perform.

An Interactive Introduction to Mathematical Analysis
By Jonathan Lewin (Cambridge University Press)

This book is a sequel to *An Introduction to Mathematical Analysis*. It includes an on-screen hypertext version that you can read with *Scientific Notebook*. This on-screen version contains alternative approaches to material, more fully explained forms of proofs of theorems, sound movie versions of proofs of theorems, interactive exploration of mathematical concepts using the computing features of *Scientific Notebook*, automatic links to the author's website for solutions to exercises, and more. It can be ordered at any bookstore.

(Continued)

TO ORDER: Visit our webstore, fax, email, or phone us.
Website: www.mackichan.com ♦ Fax: 360-394-6039 ♦ Email: info@mackichan.com ♦ Toll-free: 877-724-9673
19307 8th Avenue NE ♦ Suite C ♦ Poulsbo, WA 98370

Books (cont.)

Precalculus with Scientific Notebook®
By Jonathan Lewin (Kendall Hunt Publishing Company)

This book contains a standard printed version and an on-screen hypertext version designed for interactive reading with *Scientific Notebook*. The on-screen version includes links to solutions to exercises that reside on the author's website. It can be ordered at any bookstore.

Exploring Mathematics with Scientific Notebook®
By Wei-Chi Yang and Jonathan Lewin (Springer-Verlag)

This book is supplied both in printed form and in an on-screen hypertext version for interactive reading with *Scientific Notebook*. It contains a sequence of modules from a variety of mathematical areas and, in each, demonstrates how the editing, Internet, and computing features of *Scientific Notebook* can be combined to deepen the reader's understanding of mathematical concepts. It can be ordered at any bookstore.

MuPAD® Pro Computing Essentials, Second Edition
By Miroslav Majewski (Springer-Verlag)

Intended for teachers of mathematics and their students, *MuPAD Pro Computing Essentials* presents basic information about doing mathematics with *MuPAD Pro*. It includes basic instructions useful in various areas of mathematics that are facilitated by *MuPAD Pro*. Chapters 1 through 7 focus on the basics of using *MuPAD Pro*: Syntax, programming control structures, procedures, libraries, and graphics. Chapters 8 through 13 focus on applications in geometry, algebra, logic, set theory, calculus, and linear algebra. Each chapter includes examples and programming exercises.

TO ORDER: Visit our webstore, fax, email, or phone us.
Website: www.mackichan.com ♦ Fax: 360-394-6039 ♦ Email: info@mackichan.com ♦ Toll-free: 877-724-9673
19307 8th Avenue NE ♦ Suite C ♦ Poulsbo, WA 98370

Workshops

Scientific WorkPlace®, Scientific Word®, and Scientific Notebook®
By Professor Jonathan Lewin, Ph.D.

Seminars, workshops, and training sessions by Jonathan Lewin are available at professional conferences and, by arrangement, at individual campuses of high schools, colleges, and universities.

Scientific Notebook: This presentation introduces the editing, Internet and computing features of *Scientific Notebook* documents. It also covers the publication of mathematical material on websites and how *Scientific Notebook* can be used as an electronic whiteboard in the classroom.

Scientific WorkPlace and Scientific Word: This presentation introduces the editing and typesetting features of *Scientific WorkPlace* and *Scientific Word*. Participants will be trained in the production of documents that will be printed as professional quality hard copy or submitted to an editor for publication.

Each participant will be given a CD containing sound movies that review the material covered in the workshops. Contact Jonathan Lewin for details at *lewins@mindspring.com* or 770-973-5931.

Scientific WorkPlace® and Scientific Notebook®
By Professor Bill Pletsch, Ph.D.

Bill Pletsch has been using computer algebra systems since the early 1980s. He is available for workshops and training sessions on the use of *Scientific WorkPlace* and *Scientific Notebook* as a research and teaching aid.

The workshops and training sessions begin with a demonstration of the capabilities of *Scientific WorkPlace/Notebook*. The introductory demonstration is followed by a thorough nuts and bolts hands-on session on the basics. Participants learn how to compute numerically and symbolically, graph, and manipulate data. Also included are word-processing, Internet techniques, and utilizing other resources. More advanced topics include the use of *Scientific WorkPlace/Notebook* in the classroom and in the preparation of computer classroom lectures and demonstrations.

An overview of computer algebra systems and why every teacher of mathematics should own a copy of *Scientific Notebook* will accompany the presentation. Included in the workshops will be a CD on the electronic delivery of mathematics instruction. No prior computer experience is required. Contact Bill Pletsch for details at *bpletsch@tvi.edu* or 505-224-3672.

(Continued)

TO ORDER: Visit our webstore, fax, email, or phone us.
Website: www.mackichan.com ◆ Fax: 360-394-6039 ◆ Email: info@mackichan.com ◆ Toll-free: 877-724-9673
19307 8th Avenue NE ◆ Suite C ◆ Poulsbo, WA 98370

Workshops (cont.)

Scientific Notebook®
By Professor John H. Gresham, Ph.D.

John Gresham has been using *Scientific Notebook* since 1997 to prepare materials for classroom instruction. He is available for workshops and training sessions on *Scientific Notebook*, including the use of *Scientific Notebook*'s Exam Builder to generate both objective and free-response test forms. Workshop participants will receive hands-on step-by-step instruction in using *Scientific Notebook* as a mathematics word processor to prepare class notes, overhead transparencies, and exams. *Scientific Notebook* will also be used to view and prepare web materials, including HTML files. Participants will become familiar with the capability of *Scientific Notebook*'s computer algebra system to perform numeric and symbolic computations, solve equations, and generate graphs and tables. Participants will receive printed materials and a floppy disk with sample files. No prior experience with *Scientific Notebook* is required, but familiarity with basic Windows commands will be helpful. For details, contact John Gresham at jgresham@ranger.cc.tx.us or 254-647-3234.

TO ORDER: Visit our webstore, fax, email, or phone us.
Website: www.mackichan.com ◆ Fax: 360-394-6039 ◆ Email: info@mackichan.com ◆ Toll-free: 877-724-9673
19307 8th Avenue NE ◆ Suite C ◆ Poulsbo, WA 98370